# PSYCHOLOGICAL COMMENTARIES
## on the Teaching of
# GURDJIEFF
# & OUSPENSKY

*Volume Five*

## *by Maurice Nicoll*

SHAMBHALA
*Boulder & London 1984*

SHAMBHALA PUBLICATIONS, INC.
Boulder, Colorado 80306-0271

9 8 7 6 5 4 3 2
*First Shambhala edition*
Distributed in the United States by Random House and in Canada by Random House of Canada Ltd.
Distributed in the United Kingdom by Routledge & Kegan Paul Ltd, London and Henley-on-Thames
Printed in the United States of America

*Library of Congress Cataloging in Publication Data*
Nicoll, Maurice, 1884-1953.
    Psychological commentaries on the teaching of
Gurdjieff and Ouspensky.
    Reprint. Originally published: Psychological
commentaries on the teaching of G.I. Gurdjieff and P.D.
Ouspensky. London: Vincent Stuart (Publishers) Ltd: 1956
        1.Gurdjieff, George Ivanovitch, 1872-1949.
2. Uspenskiĭ, P. D. (Petr Demïãnovich), 1878-1947.
I. Title.
B4249.G84.N55    1984        197'.2        83-25194
ISBN 0-87773-288-4    (pbk.: vol. 5)
ISBN 0-394-72694-4    (Random House: pbk.)

# CONTENTS

## Great Amwell House, 1951

## Great Amwell House, 1952

*Great Amwell House, 1953*

## APPENDIX

## THE RECEPTION OF NEW IDEAS
## ABOUT ONESELF AND THE WORLD

Why is it that people find new ideas so difficult to receive? The mind closes early on a few conventional ideas. The mind was once likened to a bird-cage, and ideas to birds. Some quite beautiful birds may come and go. If you value them they may stay. But if in a vision you were to see your own mind represented as a bird-cage, what kind of birds would you perceive in it? A few parrots might be there, and some decaying or dead birds. The bottom of the cage would be filthy. What does this filth represent psychologically? What is its psychological meaning? Wrong ideas, ideas that check the development of the mind, traditional ideas that have become lifeless, or conventional ideas obsequiously imitated are so much filth in the mind. In short, the obsequious mind stinks as much as does the mind swarming with little nasty petty schemes, like mice. Now to receive new ideas and think from them begins to cleanse the mind, and also the countenance. The Work is packed with new and powerful ideas, and if we can bestir and humiliate ourselves just enough to receive them and think from them, our minds will begin to smell less badly in the nostrils of heaven, and our faces will become more distinct, seeing that the mind and the face are connected. One would certainly expect the face to alter after a time as an outward sign of an alteration in the mind, but if it does not, one knows that the new and powerful ideas have not been received.

Now to receive, the mind must be like a bowl or cup. I mean simply that a bowl or cup could represent the receptive mind. Something can be poured in and retained. The bowl or cup upside down—that is, pointing downwards, would then represent the non-receptive mind. Again, the bowl or cup might be filled with dirt so that, until it was cleaned out, nothing could be put in, or put in without contamination. The new and powerful ideas of the Work, therefore, could not be received if the bowl or cup were upside down or filled with filth and we have already seen what filth can represent psychologically. These matters can only be represented by ordinary visual images, because no one can draw a mind or a wrong idea. But using the seen objects of the senses as *representing* things not seen, it is possible to express the invisible in terms of the visible. This is possible provided it is realized that the visible things, made use of, represent invisible things and so are not to be taken literally, but psychologically. So a bowl can mean the mind. Empty and turned up it can mean the mind receptive to ideas; full of filth it can represent the mind as full of false and wrong or dead ideas; and full of clean water, full of true and living ideas. It is, however, quite true to say that this transforming of the literal sense into the psychological sense is repugnant to many and strongly resented by them, to their very great loss. "A bowl is a bowl, Sir, and can only mean a bowl. A man should say what he means, Sir. How in heaven's name can a bowl mean the mind?" Well, that is exactly its meaning in heaven. And if you say that it only represents the mind the retort will no doubt be "Then why the devil don't they say 'mind' straight out instead of messing with bowls, and filth and bird-cages and parrots?" Or you may encounter the polite and slightly amused person who murmurs that it is interesting but rather far fetched, and so on.

So let me hasten on to something else and avoid this valuable but despised little crossing-bridge that leads to that level called Psychological Thinking, and introduces us to a new world of meaning. Let us keep to what is sensible and logical and stand with our feet firmly planted on the solid earth of sensory facts. Unfortunately, if we only do this we may well remain at too low a level of understanding for the Work. We will, indeed, remain mechanical or natural and have nothing of the conscious or spiritual. Also, the bowl will be upside down. If we cannot transform the literal into the psychological, if we cannot transform the sense of the letter into the sense of the spirit—and we are told somewhere that the letter killeth—then we cannot give ourselves the First Conscious Shock. And unless the First Conscious Shock is given a man remains a natural or mechanical man to whom the world is as it appears. Everything is what it seems to him. Such a matter-of-fact man crystallizes out early. His world soon fixes him. He cannot develop. Yes, he soon becomes a fixture in it because he takes the world like that as fixed facts. Do you understand? Can you see that what you are depends on what the world is for you? Now, if you have always had a certain feeling of unreality about the world or if you have felt it as a mystery, or yourself as a mystery, you will not crystallize out like the matter-of-fact people who seem to get on better than you and have no difficulties. However, I would far rather be you, for probably you will be able to receive ideas of a certain quality that the matter-of-fact folk take as nonsense. But certain ideas may be nonsense in one mind and not nonsense in another's mind. To change the metaphor—you may have a landing-ground for certain ideas which can only crash in others. Now the reception of new ideas is necessary for change of being. I can only think in a new way by means of new ideas, and I must really think *for myself* from these ideas to change my mind. You cannot in the Work leave your thinking to others; you must crave for new ideas which transmit new truth, as for water in the desert. No one is going to help you if you do nothing yourself. This seems to surprise some and offend others. I can never understand why. Now if I think in a new way I can see things in a new way. If I change, my view of the world will change. If my view of the world changes, I will change. That is why the Work has two sides to its teaching—one Psychological and one Cosmological. Unless I change, my world will not change. I cannot undergo change in myself and remain in the same world. If I begin to have a new feeling of myself I will also begin to have a new feeling of the world, and I and the world will change together. My new feeling of the world will give again a new feeling of myself. The two feelings will help each other to grow, for the world is my feeling of it and my feeling of the world is me. If I feel there is something higher than myself in myself, I will feel there is something higher than the world behind it. But all this, and many other things beyond expression, can only begin with the reception of new ideas and thinking from them for yourself.

*Amwell, 27.10.51*

## BRIEF NOTE ON WORK ON ONESELF

There are three lines of work. The first line is work on oneself. Although one may have heard this many times and although it may be firmly rooted in the memory, it will not be of any use unless it is done. As you know, the Work must not be only in the memory, but in the life. A few lines along which everyone must observe himself to begin with are laid down. Later on you must observe what particular hindrance prevents you from getting on.

Now in answer to the question: "In what way are you working on yourself now?" what can you reply? It can happen sometimes that people have no idea what they are working on, nor indeed what work on oneself can possibly mean. This is a grave handicap. They may help others in a hearty way, conceiving this to be the second line of work, and do their best to speak enthusiastically to strangers of the system so as to help it along, conceiving this to be the third line, but the difficulty will remain that they do not understand the Work at all, owing to this initial handicap. However, you may tell me that if a person does the second and third lines of the Work in a sincere way, he or she may be useful to it, and I will not disagree. But if by any chance you instance the opposite—namely, a person who only attempts the first line and says the other two lines are not necessary and do not concern him, and if you add that he may all the same be useful—I will not agree with you at all. Such a man serves his own interests only, and so can never get beyond himself. He is a will-worshipper, a worshipper of his own will, a worshipper of self (as Paul said of such people: "which things have indeed a shew of wisdom in will-worship, and humility, and severity to the body . . ." Col. ii.23). The more he works, the more will he inevitably imprison himself in himself—that is, in his self-love and his self-worship. Now, to return: let us suppose that you have reached that stage of work in which you can clearly observe that you are negative. This is just where you can work on yourself. (By doing so you may also, without knowing it, work on the second line.) The point is that you are now observing a definite thing. You have, so to speak, caught it in the

1515

very act, and this is due to your discipline in self-observation, without which work on oneself is impossible. For if you do not observe what is going on in you, if you do not let a ray of light into your inner darkness by the practice of self-observing, you will never have anything real on which to work. Only through the discipline of *uncritical* self-observation will you catch sight of something definite to work upon. Everything else will be so much pseudo-work, invented work, imaginary work. But this question of *uncritical* self-observation requires long self-observation. Only gradually will you notice how instantaneously the demon of self-justifying does everything in its power to prevent it. In this case it will do all it can to protect not you, but the definite negative emotion that you have caught sight of. But this will be no longer good enough for you—that is, if your desire to work on yourself has at last become a felt aim. In all three lines of work, each has an aim which eventually can be felt in the Emotional Centre since they correspond with its right development, and greatly assist one in the battles that have to take place in it at intervals over the years. What, then, are you going to do next with this definite clearly-observed negative emotion if you are no longer eager to fly into self-justifying (such as: "Of course, I'm not to blame. It's always been like this. I don't deserve to be treated in that way. AM I *nothing*? Don't I count? Wouldn't you under the circumstances feel just as I do? You don't understand all I've had to put up with. Of course, you have everything you want. You wouldn't understand. No one ever does", and so on). What, I say, are you going to do if you refuse these aids of self-justifying? If you do nothing, the negative emotion will call to itself other negative emotions. The energies they steal will then begin to regress and to form symptoms. That is, they will go backwards in you and because you cannot unmask their lying guise—for all negative emotions lie—the energies they have filched from you will not be available for ordinary life. They will animate a new sickness or re-animate old typical illnesses—just as a river when obstructed will not only flood backwaters behind it but will stop the water-wheels from working in front of it. If you understand me, this represents very well the wrong distribution of energy that takes place in a person who is negative. Psychic energy in the wrong place acts as a poison. When we are negative we poison ourselves and we poison our bodies—and indeed, we poison other people. But of course through self-justifying we cannot see that this is so. Nothing is ever one's own fault.

To return: what can be done when we clearly see a negative emotion and will not yield weakly to self-justification? I will mention only one thing, among many others, that can be done. Realizing that to permit a negative state to exist unchecked and unarrested is to give it tacit permission to do its worst, and realizing also, as one Eastern system says, that negative emotion, identified with, is similar to a wound in the body, and as serious, one can resolve to hold a court and find out what it is all about. I advise you to hold this court in your mind—not in public.

Let the various sides of you take part. Let the Work, as Deputy-Steward, listen to each speaker. Let each speaker speak clearly. All this requires an atmosphere of inner attention. You will find that indignant, furious, bitter or blaming 'I's begin to leave the court-room one by one, like the accusers of the woman taken in adultery, beginning with the oldest. But there is one important point. In this court there is no judge. In the temple-scene there was no judge. The figure who was expected to judge did not. He merely said: "Neither do I judge thee." After a time you will notice that the whole affair has cleared up and vanished. Then it may happen that the other person connected with your negative state sends you a message, or seems released. I mentioned earlier that if you really do the first line of work, you also do something of the second. Why is the other person released? Because you in your negative state bound that person in prison—then, later, you released the person by your change of state.

I will add one more significant thing. This court held in the mind with its various speakers is to be conducted with a certain grace and seasoned with a little salt. If undertaken heavily, gloomily and literally, it will probably make you more negative. If so, all I can say is that I am glad to hear it and that it serves you right. For nothing useful in this Work can be done without grace and a daily seasoning of salt.

*Amwell, 3.11.51*

## OUTER AND INNER STOP

In the exercises connected with the Work is one called the *Stop-exercise*. At the moment that the command *Stop* is shouted one has to remain motionless in the position one is in. Not only must the body and the limbs become as it were frozen, but the expression of the face and the direction of the eyes must not change. The whole attention must centre on maintaining the same motionless position, until a second command releases you. It was said to us that in some Eastern schools, if you were stopped, say, in a stream rapidly rising in flood, the position had to be kept even when the waters threatened to submerge you. Not until the order to release was given were you allowed to move. This indicated that the body had to be under full control and the teacher fully to be trusted. For some reason this story has become connected with two others in my mind. One is the story of the teacher who plunged the head of a newcomer seeking instruction into a bucket of water. When the astonished man, almost suffocated, was released, he was asked what he had wanted most. He replied that he had wanted above all things to breathe. He was told that when he wanted the teacher's instruction as much as he had wanted air, he would be given it. I imagine he was offended and took himself off. The other story is of a political prisoner who was exercised daily by marching round a courtyard. The barred windows of a room high up opened on this courtyard and the prisoner knew that another prisoner, to whom he urgently desired to send a message, lived in it. He wrapped the message round a stone and every day, while exercising, visualized the movement necessary to throw it up aright, just as a cat does before leaping up a high wall. He also had concealed about him a razor blade for he determined increasingly to cut his throat if he failed. When the opportunity came the stone went straight through the window. These stories seem to me to be connected because they come into my mind together, but I do not quite see the reason. Perhaps you may see.

Now, apart from the exercise where the body is made motionless, which can be called *Outer Stop*, there is another exercise similar but different, where the mind is made motionless. This is called *Inner Stop*. Both have to do with bringing about a state of motionlessness. But the two exercises are not performed in the same sphere. In the case of the first, the body in space is stopped. People may pass you, speak to you, tell you how silly you look, and so on. But your body and your eyes remain motionless in space. In the case of the second, the practice of *Inner Stop*, you stand motionless in your mind. Thoughts pass you, speak to you, ask you what you are up to and so on, but you pay no attention to them. You will see at once that Inner Stop is connected with a form of Self-Remembering. Now you must note that the Inner Stop exercise is not the same as trying to stop your thoughts. Try to stop your thoughts; and if you are sincere about your experiences of yourself—and you cannot work unless you are—you will admit it cannot be done. But to stand motionless *in your mind* is another matter. You can stand internally motionless in the mind, just as your body can externally stand motionless in the world. Now what does motionlessness do? What virtue does it possess? In Nature motionlessness is widely made use of for a definite purpose. Movement is the first thing noticed. The eye perceives movement before it sees colour or shape. The stopping of all movement is a common device in the animal world to escape notice. The object is not to feign death, but to become invisible. Slowing down of movement also makes detection more difficult, as when a cat is stalking a bird. To practise Inner Stop in the mind is like making oneself motionless in space. You are not noticed. Yes—but not noticed by whom? In your mind you are surrounded by different 'I's. Each wants you to believe that you are it. Each wants to speak in your name. Suddenly they cannot find where you are. They look everywhere for you. I assure you that you can experience their searching for you and not finding you. Then you remember that you have not rung up the doctor. The effect is similar to a sudden movement in the jungle. All the animals and birds and reptiles instantly see where you are. The customary worries, irritations, unpleasant thoughts, conceits and anxieties seize upon you once more. The animals and birds roar and scream and the 'I's shout: "We've got him." And that is the end of what is really you for the time being. You are dismembered again. Another person watching you from outside will be aware of a sudden look of anxiety, a quick movement, hurried steps and an urgent voice at the telephone. He may perhaps guess that you will be "out" for the rest of the day. You will be out of yourself. I am not exaggerating when I say that it is like throwing oneself to the lions or casting oneself under the Juggernaut or drowning in the sea. I mean that it is suicide and that we all commit suicide over and over again and no one in the life of the world points this out. Only the Work which comes from sources outside the life of the world points this out. It not only points out that we are daily and continually committing suicide, but it shews us with great patience how not to. Does it not sound strange when put in that way? The trouble is that we prefer to commit spiritual suicide at every moment rather than give ourselves the First Conscious Shock. We find it easier than to remember ourselves. And in connection with this we are told that we are like people who prefer to live in the basements of their houses, although all the rooms belong to them and they can live on what floor they like. Can you conceive anything more weird than a city of fine houses whose inhabitants insist on living only in their basements? The psychological interpretation of basement is the lowest parts of centres where the most mechanical 'I's live. No man can remember himself at that level. To remember himself he must distinguish himself from the inhabitants of the basement in him. To do so he must feel concerning these inhabitants that they are not him. He must say with a conviction that grows over the years: "This is not I", to these inhabitants, one by one, especially to some. An 'I' approaches you by means of thoughts. You can practise Inner Stop towards those thoughts, once you have observed them enough to know for certain that they herald the approach of an evil 'I'. This is practising Inner Stop specifically towards one thing. But Inner Stop in its full sense is to make yourself motionless in your mind, so that you take no notice of any thoughts and thereby become unnoticed. You are then remembering yourself.

*Amwell, 10.11.51*

## INCREASING CONSCIOUSNESS OF ONESELF

The Work teaches us that we are not properly conscious and that our general aim is to increase consciousness. With regard to the side of increasing consciousness that belongs to increase of consciousness of *oneself,* when you go back in your mind into your past, do not try to see others in your life, but yourself. Try to see what kind of a person you were at different stages. It is easier to see other people in our memories, because our senses record them. Our senses do not record ourselves, save perhaps that we had a velvet suit in childhood and a woolly lamb, and hated clean stockings which scratched so. All that is sensational and is stored in the sensory memory. But it does not shew you that you were a very bad-tempered little child who used to lie on the floor and scream if you could not have your own way. You may remember screaming and lying on the floor, for these are sensations, but you will not remember that you were bad-tempered, because that is not a matter of the senses but of self-observation. And if you have never observed yourself, you are possibly still bad-tempered and have not realized it. And similarly if you were once smacked for putting out your tongue at your elders, you may not notice you still do so mentally. So these naughty children continue to live in us and we are not aware of it.

Now you will say: How can we see what we were like in the past if we never observed it? How can we remember what is not in the memory? It comes about in the following way. If I observe something in myself now and remember what I observe, I will become slowly aware of its having existed before I observed it. The observation begins to travel backwards in time, usually very gradually. But it may happen that one experiences a flash of consciousness extending far back into the past of what one has just begun to be conscious of now in the present. One sees one has always been like that. I do not think that a sudden revelation of this kind will ever come without considerable preparation. It is prevented from coming unless one is able to accept it without justifying or criticizing or being negative. It is not pleasant but how can anybody expect to gain an increase of consciousness without being prepared to stand it? We resent every sort of reproof. We are so easily hurt that we are offended at the least thing that touches our self-love. Of course, we do not see all this. We imagine quite otherwise. But can you not see that this is the crux of the whole business of change of being? As we cannot bear being told anything adverse to our imagination of ourselves, we are called upon to observe ourselves uncritically and sincerely and, leaving aside imagination, to begin to *assimilate* what we notice about ourselves. This is indeed to begin to work on oneself. But please notice that I said "assimilate". We must assimilate what we observe about ourselves to ourselves.

Let us take the question of an increase of consciousness of oneself from another angle. We have spoken before of what was called the intractable thing in ourselves. However we try to define it, it is due to a limited consciousness. This intractable thing blocks the fuller and deeper entry of the Work. It admits it only up to a point, but enough to start on. Something will not give way further; something will not do what is required; something will not look where it should look. Something sulks; or something smiles coldly and says nothing. Or something shouts: "I won't, I won't." What can modify this intractable thing that blocks the entry of the Work? Now the more a man works with what he has of the Work and becomes more conscious of what he is and what he has been like, the more can the Work enter him. But if one is beginning to become more conscious of what one is and has been like, something must be beginning to give way to permit it. I ask you all, if you have followed me up to now, to tell me what is beginning to give way. Is it pride and its resulting hardness of heart? or love of power that will not yield? Or is it obstinacy, is it contrariness, is it pigheadedness, or sulkiness, or downright naughtiness, or mere stupidity, or ignorance, or what? Since increasing knowledge of oneself modifies it, its existence must be connected with ignorance—that is, with lack of consciousness, and therefore with lack of knowledge of the nature of oneself. It must, in short, belong to an unredeemed psychology —that is, to a man asleep to himself and the meaning of life, a man who simply takes himself for granted, a mechanical man, who imagines that he is fully conscious and possesses a real unchanging I and has all the rest of the illusions that prevent him from seeing his danger and struggling to wake up.

But to look at the question from another angle, as I mentioned, there is another way of increasing consciousness of oneself that seems especially to weaken the intractable thing in ourselves that we so grandly call strong will, individuality, determination, the power of knowing our own mind, and so on. To begin this way, try sometimes to see the opposite point of view to that which you hold. I do not mean that you are to discard your point of view but to include the opposite as well. This exercise demands first that you can clearly observe your own point of view: and second that you quite sincerely build up its opposite. Energy blocked up by the one-sidedness of our habitual consciousness is not allowed to flow into the opposite, which is kept out of consciousness. The sphere of our usual consciousness is thereby limited. It is narrowed, often ridiculously, and with this narrowness of consciousness I would specially connect the intractable thing in ourselves. If the opposite is genuinely and with effort included in consciousness the sphere of consciousness is greatly increased and a number of unpleasant features in us disappear. Our one-sidedness, which causes our over-sensitive reactions and also our totally wrong ways of self-valuation, is replaced by a broader, fuller consciousness. We can no longer insist we are right nor be cast down when proved to be wrong. We find it more difficult to be petty. In fact, we begin to escape from the prison of ourselves whose bars and gates result from our one-sidedness.

## FURTHER NOTE ON INCREASING
## CONSCIOUSNESS OF ONESELF

We have in recent papers made some commentaries on the fundamental teaching of this Work that it is necessary to increase consciousness. We are not yet properly conscious. We talk and behave, think, feel and judge on the assumption that not only we but others are fully conscious beings. In assembling the different parts of the Work to form an instrument in the mind for the reception of the finer vibrations continually coming from the two Higher Centres that are present in Man, the idea that we are not properly conscious is one of the main supporting parts of the framework of this instrument. In other words, it has to be more and more realized by experience that one is not by any means properly conscious and that other people are not. This changes one considerably. But unless it becomes a truth of experience it cannot take its necessary place in the instrument. It will merely lie unused in the memory. The truth of every part of the teaching must be experienced before it can take its place in the construction of this instrument in the inner world of oneself. Fortunately for us, the ideas of this teaching have an affinity for one another, and once the preliminary underlying barriers of denial give way and re-form at a deeper level, they tend to begin to fit themselves where they belong as best they can in the small space thus made vacant. This seems a long process according to a slow standard of time in which a day can seem a life-time, and a short one according to another standard of time that sees one's lifetime as a day.

Now there are three directions in which an increase of consciousness can be made by means of untensed, unhurried efforts. The first leads to an increase of consciousness of oneself; the second leads to an increase of consciousness of others; the third leads to an increase of consciousness of life. In the recent commentaries we have spoken chiefly about an increase of consciousness of oneself, through which another sense of oneself is imperceptibly brought about, with great relief—for no-one can gain any inner peace and escape from incessant nervous agitations as long as his feeling of himself, or her feeling of herself, remains what it is. Now an increase of consciousness of oneself means more room in the inner world of oneself. But this broadening, this expansion of consciousness, can take place only *at the expense* of the usual feeling of oneself, which is connected with Personality: and this usual feeling of oneself will fight to retain its power, just as any tyrant fights to retain his power. The trouble is that one does not see it in this way. We think that myself is I and even say "I myself", so we cling to the source of our discomforts and distress and resent being separated from it. Yes, we even cling to all the bitterness, anger, and hate in ourselves, never becoming conscious enough to see that we must work on ourselves, while we are "in the way"; or else, whether in recurrence or whatever other after-life one comes into, things will become worse. Now, increasing the consciousness of oneself is, I believe, the only form of work on oneself that can eventually take away this bitterness, anger, or hate—and many other things. Why? Because it will change the feeling of oneself. But why should that take away bitterness, anger, or hate? Because they are caused and kept alive exactly by your present feeling of yourself. In the last paper we touched on one method of increasing consciousness of oneself by trying to see the kind of person one was at different periods of the past, and so all through one's life, instead of merely trying to remember distant scenes or people. We spoke of using a present observation of oneself as a peep-hole into the past, which sometimes leads to seeing how one has *always* been like what one has just observed now. This gives great depth to self-observation. It need not be depressing as some seem to think. I would rather say it is liberating. Everything that one makes conscious results in a sense of freedom. It is actually freeing one in part from the tyranny of oneself. It seems a paradox to say that to become conscious of an unattractive feature operating all through one's life of which one was formerly ignorant gives a sense of liberation; but you can find the reason for yourself. And, of course, we come up here against those tedious self-hypnotists and fatheads who say that they know themselves inside out. Let us leave them to their fond illusions and the heavy odours of their airless minds.

Now the other method that was mentioned was becoming conscious in the opposite. We are one-sided. We admit into consciousness one side of things and not the opposite. One-sidedness can make us, for example, hyper-sensitive, easily upset, over-reactive, and so on: or it makes us the reverse—too insensitive, too complacent, too thick-skinned, and so on. Our opinions and ingrained habits of mind and feeling are one-sided. As was said, to see the opposite side genuinely, demands and constitutes an expansion of consciousness. But such an expansion causes amazement or horror to the fixed mind. Do you not see it would mean losing the customary feeling of oneself? Why, one would feel the ground was being knocked away from under one's feet, wouldn't one? Yes, sir, one would—and that would be a jolly good thing. You would not get in such rages or be so bigoted and humourless, or repeat the same things every day: and you, madam, would also benefit greatly. A widening of consciousness would be a blessing to us all. It can be obtained—provided one sees intelligently what prevents it. Now what do we do with the other sides—the opposite sides—that our consciousness does not embrace? We see them in other people. We do not see them in ourselves, but project them on to others. Other people are at fault, other people are mean, other people are intolerable, other people are unjust, other people have unpleasant minds, other people are bad-tempered—but not us. The result of this non-acceptance causes a most extraordinary world. Only by living in it can you believe how extraordinary. But we prefer to live in imagination and the various hells it creates. Now where you are very identified, there projection is at work: and where projection is at work, there is a one-sided consciousness at work: and no one can become Balanced Man if he remains one-sided. The table of the seven degrees of Man shews clearly that in the movement towards consciousness one must gain the state of Balanced Man— that is, No. 4 Man. We can now see that this necessitates for one thing a greatly increased consciousness of oneself. One way, and the most important way, to this is being more and more conscious of, and then in, the opposites in oneself, so that eventually one projects nothing on to others. Thus one liberates oneself from bitterness, anger, suspicion, hate, and much else characteristic of the customary feeling of oneself— which is derived from one-sidedness and is destroyed by two-sidedness. In short, No. 4 Man or Balanced Man, *cannot* be one-sided. He must be conscious of everything in himself and so will project nothing. If he projects nothing on to others, he will not become identified with others. He will thus attain a great freedom. He will be on the way to No. 5, 6 and 7 Man—that is, he will be on the way to Fully Conscious Man. Reflect, then, all of you, on the fact that Conscious Man is built on Balanced Man—not on mechanical Man—and on the necessity of becoming conscious in the opposites before one can reach the state of Balanced Man.

*Amwell, 24.11.51*

## WHAT IS CONSCIOUSNESS?

In this paper let us consider what consciousness is. We are studying increase of consciousness upon which the Work lays such great stress and in which some cannot see any meaning. Let us first remind ourselves that nothing is learned aright without affection. One manifestation of affection is interest. Anyone can see that no one will learn anything of a subject unless he is interested in it. We cannot therefore expect to see any meaning in all that is taught about increase of consciousness in the Work if we are not interested in the subject. In this case we probably believe in secret that we are fully conscious already. If so, I can only say it constitutes an admirable example of the adoration of oneself and demands a private chapel and an altar with a large coloured photograph of oneself on it.

However, the trouble may not lie in self-adoration. It may be that a person simply does not understand what an increase of consciousness can possibly be like. I mean, that a person may not smugly or blindly assume he is fully conscious and may be willing to admit that he is not, but cannot see what it means to increase his consciousness and feels quite helpless through sheer ignorance. We all know this state. Now to get out of this state we must fall back on valuation of the Work and the reasons why we are seeking the Work. I will say merely that unless we do this we will stick. All efforts will cease, so it is necessary to return inwardly to valuation—and revalue the Work. This releases energy. In terms of the Work-Octave we have to return to the note *Do* and sound it more strongly. Many 'I's attack this note and seek to drain its energy of vibration—mocking 'I's, clownish 'I's, ugly 'I's, cruel 'I's, hard 'I's, arguing 'I's, denying 'I's, mob 'I's. All unpleasant things in you seek to attack this opening note of the Work. They do so because they know, although you do not, that their power over you is eventually threatened by the Work, which brings strange and new values. For valuation of the Work, which is *Do*, is a valuing of new values, and a constant re-newal of them by revaluing is needed and not a constant revaluing of old values. The inward man must be renewed day by day, as St. Paul says. You will be startled to find how faint, how weak, this *Do* can be-come. This is because you do not renew it day by day and have let the uproar of life drown it. Circumstances can make a life-Do easy: a Work-Do is not easy—it is against life. Along with making the note Do sound more strongly in one's being, one has to reflect deeply—that is, in the Inner Man—upon why one is seeking the Work, for the two go together—or should do. If you have neither valuation nor aim, how can the strength of the Work ever be received? There is nothing to receive it with. If there is nothing in you to receive the Work, it cannot help you. If it does not begin to influence the way you think or feel or act, it is a sign that you have neither valuation nor aim.

Now, as I said, it may be that a person simply cannot understand what it means to increase his consciousness and feels helpless. This will be the case when he has never thought about consciousness. He has no doubt taken it for granted and so has never thought about what it is. The teaching that he is not properly conscious therefore puzzles him. He will agree that if a man is knocked out he loses consciousness and that after a time he regains consciousness. From this he might agree that consciousness is something that a man can either have or not have and yet remain alive. Consciousness, then, is not identical with life. The energy of consciousness is different from the energy of life; and in regard to this the Work says that no amount of life-energy will produce consciousness just as no amount of physical energy such as heat will produce life.

The diagram used in this connection is as follows:

Greater Mind

Energy of Consciousness

Psychic Energy

Life Energy

Mechanical Energy

No amount of one will produce the other. This means they do not merge into one another but are on different levels, in different degrees. For example, a baby has vital energy before it has a psychic life, and it has a psychic life before it has consciousness, but they are on different planes. They are as different as is the sight of the eyes from the sight of the mind. No amount of the one will produce the other. This diagram assists one to reflect upon the energy of consciousness and its high place in this scale of energies. It helps to make one realize that it is something distinct and definite and that, like other energies, it presumably can be decreased or increased.

The next thing we have to grasp is that consciousness is not memory, nor is it thought, nor is it feeling, nor is it sensation or movement. It is not a psychic process. Very complex psychic processes can take place without consciousness. The mind of the moving centre, for instance, makes very complex estimations in skating or piano-playing, etc., without consciousness—or practically so. All sorts of intelligent transformations and adjustments in the body continually take place without consciousness. Now it is especially important not to say that memory is consciousness. Memory and consciousness are not the same. This requires to be thought about. They are as different as the beam from your electric torch is from the path it illuminates. You do not think them the same. Similarly, consciousness is not the same as your thought, feeling or sensation. Through consciousness you become aware of them as contents, but it is not one and the same thing. In fact, consciousness can exist without any content.

The next point is that consciousness cannot be increased mechanically. No mechanical process will lead to an increase of consciousness. Since the object of the Work is to increase consciousness, it is as well to remember that nothing mechanical will bring this increase about. Something interesting lies here which you must find out for yourselves, so it is no use asking what it is. But one thing clearly follows—namely, that consciousness can only be increased by the use of consciousness. We are given, naturally, a little consciousness to start with. This can be increased, but only by conscious efforts. The mechanical efforts which belong to the routine of the day's work will not increase it. But going against mechanicalness consciously will increase it. Consciousness, then, is a very strange thing. It seems to be like yeast, which under right conditions can multiply itself indefinitely. But this comparison does not give us a right idea of what consciousness is. Consciousness is not like yeast, nor is it something that gradually evolves from vital or from psychic energy. It is something unique. It is something we come in contact with. It is a group of vibrations of high frequency and like light it exists apart from our contact with it. Like physical light it is still and always there though we shut our eyes or though we are blind. Of this light of consciousness we receive a very little. We are nearly blind. Now it is not the light that is to be increased but our contact with it. The receptive point of consciousness has to be changed. Then more consciousness is received. We have to begin work with the small consciousness we have. We seek not to squander it in identifying. But people throw away even the small consciousness they have. To awaken is to become more and more conscious by *letting* in consciousness into dark places. So it is said that self-observation lets light into the darkness within us. And also it is said in John that "the light shineth in darkness and the darkness comprehendeth it not". So it is with everyone who is given the Work, which is Esoteric Christianity—that is, its inner meaning—and does not open the door to it. He does not let it in. He sees the light but, not turning it inwards upon his own darkness, remains without comprehending it.

*Amwell, 1.12.51*

## THE IDEA OF BALANCED MAN

### Part I

The ideas of the Work penetrate us slowly. By now we may have realized that the way to Conscious Man lies through Balanced Man. Now, reflecting on the diagram of the seven categories of Man, we can see, if we want to, that No. 4 Man or Balanced Man actually is the bridge between Mechanical Mankind and Conscious Mankind and is therefore of the greatest importance. Formerly we may have chiefly regarded the diagram as referring to Conscious and Mechanical Man and ignored the significance of Balanced Man. Now, however, we should find it necessary to concentrate often on the meaning of this link that connects the lower and upper parts of the diagram and is significant to each of us. We can say at the outset that all the teaching of the Work converges on to this figure. The Balanced Man sums up the teaching and explains its existence, and, standing above the mechanical living of this life, is open to respond to another life, the living of which is our right—a right neither inborn nor acquired, but pre-existent in the Essence by creation. For we were created to become conscious; and to attain to a degree of consciousness sufficient to reach even the farthest outskirts of the Conscious Circle of Humanity is something incommensurable with anything that life offers. It makes indeed all the affairs and situations of life seem as nothing, or near to it. And if we could remember ourselves and did remember ourselves and did touch the Third State of Consciousness we would know this quite well already: and, knowing it, also know that our life lay above us, and not behind us or ahead of us—a knowledge that shifts the usual feeling of oneself which is horizontal and not vertical. By horizontal I mean what is based as on a horizontal line of past, present and future, and so on our idea of time: and by vertical I mean based on scale, and on above and below, on higher levels and lower levels, and so on values which are not connected with time but with states. Of this latter we have little or no coherent sense. We think of yesterday and the day before in terms of time, not in terms of our inner states on those days. We do not think that the day before yesterday we were in a state of abysmal sleep but that yesterday we had a small moment of awakening. Because we think in terms of time, we have so little memory of states. We seem to worship time. We say time is money and talk of never wasting time. We value it highly, but we do not seem to value states. Everything valuable gets swept away by time. Yet that small amount of awakening you had yesterday should have been put into the room of your inner memory which is outside time and is in shelves, arranged vertically in scale of value. Such moments eventually begin to lift us. They enable us to remember ourselves—out of time and its cares.

Whether I make myself clear or not, let us consider what kind of consciousness the Balanced Man has. We understand his consciousness cannot be one-sided. We can therefore think of him as two-sided, or other-sided as regards consciousness. He must have undergone, by work on himself, an increase of consciousness. His self-consciousness, his awareness of himself, must have widened. Or shall we rather say altered, changed. That would mean that the usual "feeling of oneself" in his case would have shifted its central position and a new feeling of himself would have taken its place; and this because he had increased his awareness of himself. He has become more conscious of what is in him, of what he had not quite admitted, or perhaps had even denied hotly. When you deny hotly you should take an observation and if you notice you often do it, take a time-exposure. Now the phrases used in describing the Third State of Consciousness are "Self-Awareness", "Self-Consciousness", and "Self-Remembering". We can see that Balanced Man must become far more conscious of himself to balance his one-sided consciousness of himself—that is, his self-awareness must increase and with it his self-consciousness. When the shift in the usual "feeling of oneself" in his case has taken place and one-sidedness has been replaced by two-sidedness or other-sidedness, then he will have reached a balance. Such a balance must certainly characterize No. 4 Man. He will no longer remember the feelings connected with his former one-sided or unbalanced state. By an extension of consciousness he will no longer derive his feelings of himself from what is false or imaginary in himself—that is, from False Personality or Imaginary 'I'. And by seeing in himself many of the faults he imputes to others, as well as some peculiarities of his own, his feelings towards others will completely change. While all this is taking place gradually, he may feel at times that he is losing something valuable. Life will not have the same taste. But if a man or woman changes, life cannot possibly have the same taste. If it does, then the man or woman has not changed. That is quite certain. Change of being means change in everything. You cannot change and remain the same. A man reaching the level of Balanced Man cannot remain what he was. As regards his being, he cannot be what he has been. To regret what one has been, in view of this Work, may only feed the self-pity. I believe that all regret about the past which is just regret is regressive or becomes so very easily. When in changing your tastes change, you will discover new tastes, finer and subtler. Identifying becomes less and less. That means a purification of the Emotional Centre and so quite different feelings. Thus the Balanced Man will not be tormented by the same feelings and emotions that infest the life of No. 1, 2 and 3 men. Through self-observation, through increasing self-awareness, through increasing the consciousness of himself, through attributing to himself in place of mechanically imputing to others, he becomes a different kind of man designated in the system No. 4 Man.

Now if we concentrate on these thoughts, giving our interest to them, we shall be able to reflect on the nature of Balanced Man and on our own situation in comparison to him. By this comparison we may perceive more clearly what it is necessary to ask for and estimate where to work on ourselves. For if we ask for nothing we get nothing. This is in the nature of the Universe, which can be thought of as response to request.

*Amwell, 8.12.51*

## THE IDEA OF BALANCED MAN

### PART II: THE FEELING OF ONESELF

We have seen how, in order to attain to No. 4 or Balanced Man, consciousness of oneself must be increased as well as a development of centres. We have seen how with an increasing consciousness of oneself the feeling of oneself is bound to alter. It is the usual feeling of oneself that contributes to our unbalance. These are very important points. With the feeling of oneself that one has now there can be no transformation of oneself, because, as I said, it is the feeling of oneself that keeps one just where one is, psychologically speaking. It is difficult to realize that this is so. One is not quite aware of the existence of this feeling of oneself and how one is limited by it. Now a balanced man cannot possibly have the same feeling of himself as he had formerly because consciousness of himself has widened. He will have lost his soul at one level and found it at another level of his being. However, we cling to our feeling of ourselves and indeed are blind to it. I advise you to try to notice it as often as you can. It helps one to connect so much of the Work together.

Let us take an example, step by step. Someone speaks and behaves in a way I resent violently. I make bitter retorts. I open a number of store-cupboards filled with carefully *preserved* bitter memories. I go on and on blaming the person, I cannot sleep, and so on. This is the life-way. The Work-way is different. *First step*: I observe I am violent and bitter. This is quite different from just being violent and bitter. It lets a ray of light in—that is, whereas I was unconscious, being identified with my state, I now am slightly conscious of it. I also notice and re-member a little what I am saying and usually say. *Second step*: I recall that no matter who is to blame *I* am to blame for being negative. If I value the Work this helps me to turn round and look for the cause in myself and not in the person. *Third step*: I must ask what is it connected with in the customary feeling of myself, that is behind the outburst. I re-flect in that quietness and strainlessness that comes when one is paying directed attention sincerely to oneself. For the cause lies either in some-thing that I include in the habitual feeling of myself: or it lies in some-thing that I do not include in this feeling of myself. Let us take the first case—namely, I have been aroused so violently because something I include in the feeling of myself has been injured. I reflect on what was said and done. I decide that it seems to be a criticism of my efficiency. Have I then a picture of being efficient and is this a component part of my customary feeling of myself? I did not quite realize it. As time goes on I become more and more conscious that it is so. To this extent I increase my consciousness of the sources of my usual feeling of myself. My task is then clear. I must notice where I am not at all efficient and slowly include this in my feeling of myself. Now this will change my feeling of myself a little. Why? Because my consciousness of myself is in-creased. Also I will be freed from being so touchy in this direction, by including the opposite.

Let us take the other possibility, namely that the cause lies in some-thing I do *not* include in the habitual feeling of myself. It will lie therefore in the dark—that is, the unconscious—side of myself. Now if this is so it will tend to be projected on to others. On reflection I find that this person always irritates me, quite apart from whether he criticizes me or not. There is something in him I cannot stand. Even when not present, he vexes me. Why cannot I throw him off? I begin to suspect what the reason is. I cannot throw him off because in some way he is me. But how can this be, when I love him so little and love myself so much. Well, certainly it sounds strange, but the reason is that self-love simply will not admit this part of me into my consciousness. I will not in-clude it in my feeling of myself. The solution is easy. I simply project this unpleasing side of me outwards and see it as being in another person *who is very like it*. So it comes about that the faults we dislike most in others are usually those that we display ourselves without being conscious of them. It would indeed seem that every precaution is taken to prevent us from awakening to what we are like. The first stage in regeneration, or being born again, not in the flesh but in the spirit, is precisely awaken-ing to what we are like, and this is only possible through increasing consciousness of oneself. But the approach to the first stage seems to be deliberately made extremely difficult. Pits and traps and barriers and many sign-posts and lanes ending in nothing are everywhere. And on the top of all this, the most extraordinary illusions about ourselves are pumped into us daily from early childhood, in addition to many stupid persuasions that almost submerge our perception of truth. In this respect would you not say that the power of self-justifying, so vigilant and inexhaustible, is not designed to help our awakening? (By the way, why are the devils so inexhaustible?)

To return: I have got as far as thinking that the cause of my outburst is connected with deeper things than an affront to my picture of being efficient, because this person arouses my ire in so many other ways. In fact, I am now willing to say that I must be projecting on to him some unpleasant side of me that I have not admitted into my consciousness. Others may have noticed it, but not me: and it certainly has never been included in my feeling of myself. Once more my task is clear. I must study this person in the light of being someone in me that I am unaware of. In general, he will be the *opposite* to what is included in my usual feeling of myself: and understand here that he may have qualities I need badly myself. As I admit him gradually into my consciousness I will become *whole*, instead of one-sided. This is something very marvellous. And, of course, the feeling of myself will entirely change.

We must by every means, method, trick and invention, increase the consciousness of ourselves in order to approach the level of Balanced Man. I say trick and invention deliberately. One can sometimes catch oneself out and one can also spy on oneself. This is not quite the same as observing oneself, or rather, it is a form of noticing oneself, as also is overhearing oneself. By the way, noticing oneself can be quite uncritical like casually noticing a passer-by in the street. But in every case the aim is to increase consciousness of oneself because when this begins the feeling of oneself begins to alter, and one knows it and thanks God. Now, remember, the reason why it alters is that you begin to include in your consciousness of yourself things you did not include before and so your former feeling of yourself *has* to change. Do get that clear in your minds. We live in a house with the blinds down. A little light gets in. This we call full consciousness: and so we, a parcel of little imbeciles, existing almost in total darkness, make a horrible mess of living and misuse or do not use our centres that can tune in to centres always working. As Ouspensky put it once: "We live in a house full of the most delicate and wonderful machines. By the light of a solitary candle we attempt to run them without knowing anything about them. If anything goes wrong, it is always somebody else's fault."

Do not think that these words of his are an exaggeration. If you require proof, look around—if you are incapable of looking at yourself. Now, pulling up the blinds a little hurts at first. Then one can stand a little more light and then more. What you took as yourself begins to look like a little prison-house far away in the valley beneath you.

## FURTHER COMMENTARY ON CONSCIOUSNESS
## AND A PRELIMINARY CONSIDERATION
## OF THE MEANING OF THE SOUL

At first, let us continue to expand the teaching on consciousness. In this respect, as we have seen, the Work says we live in comparative darkness—as it were by the light of a solitary candle, among complex instruments, the uses of which we do not rightly comprehend. These instruments are our ordinary centres and parts of centres, each having its own uses. A complete man would be therefore the embodiment of all these uses. We can see, then, that a complete man is far from us. We can see this, at least, provided we are not lamentably self-complacent and ignorant of our innumerable insufficiencies. Ignorance, by the way, is cited in esoteric literature as one of the most death-dealing vices. Neither men nor women should ever be satisfied with themselves. I am speaking here of psychological death, far more to be feared than the death of the body. The Work says we meet the dead everywhere, walking in the streets, sitting in houses, in offices, in courts, in cinemas, in clubs, in churches, in fact, everywhere—the living dead. This scandalous state of affairs is not revealed until we begin to glimpse it in ourselves. Looking in the glass are we sure we are not looking at the dead or, at least, the dying?—a strange question. The death of the body is necessary. It is destined. But psychological death is not and it is to this kind of death that I am referring. Now the increasing of consciousness will prevent it. Struggling with one's ignorance by efforts helps. But increasing the consciousness of oneself helps still more and this requires another sort of effort. The broader the consciousness of oneself, the more is the power of reception. A narrow prejudiced "oneself" takes in little. This makes overcoming ignorance by efforts, say, of study, nearly impossible. The person is not interested. There is no room in him. But of course there is plenty of room. His "oneself" has no room. But if he increases the consciousness of himself and thereby loses his previous feeling of himself, his power of reception will be also increased. Can it be said that we always knew this? I do not think so. It requires some considerable reflection to grasp its meaning.

Now the Work says that as we are we do not hear the continual messages sent out as high-level vibrations from Higher Mental and Higher Emotional Centres. When it is said that we do not hear them what is meant is that our ordinary—that is, our lower centres—do not pick them up. The term Higher Centres implies the existence of lower centres. The latter are not receptive of the former. Owing to the state of our three lower centres, our powers of reception are limited. It is for this reason that the Work says that our task is to prepare the lower centres for the reception of the vibrations from the Higher Centres. We therefore have to study by self-observation the state of our lower centres, and this is called the first line of work—namely, work on ourselves. Work on ourselves means work on our lower centres—on their state, their condition, their wrong working. With only one candle of light we cannot see them. Self-observation lets in more and more light. So the Work begins with self-observation. Now the condition of our lower centres not only renders them non-receptive to Higher Centres but is such that it would be dangerous to receive them. The state of the Emotional Centre for example, saturated with the emotion of identifying, and negative emotions, and self-emotions, is so bad that were the vibrations coming from Higher Centres to play on it directly it would cause us terrible damage. Only through its gradual purification can traces of the action of Higher Centres be received more or less directly. Even then a transformer must needs come in between and step down the high voltages that belong to the Higher Centres so that the lower centres are not fused.

Now a negative emotion will conduct wrong meaning just as a lie necessarily will. Thinking wrongly, from wrong ideas and illusions, demands *metanoia*, a steady and resolute changing of the mind by means of new ideas. Feeling wrongly through negative emotions, identifying and the self-love require much observation, constant personal work and intelligent decision. (There is nothing easier than to be negative.) This leads to the possibility of these centres being able to bear higher voltages. You may be certain they will receive them once they have been prepared—if you like, on the principle that Nature abhors a vacuum. And so the process will continue stage by stage. There is and must be a transformer in the three-storey house of our being. Although it will alter its ratio as we can receive more, I fancy we shall never be able to endure direct the high voltages of the influxes from the Higher Centres. In any case, all life depends on reception, for everything is reception. All Nature is reception. But we are created to receive far more than the vibrations of light from the Sun. Now if all that this "oneself" in us does *not* include is gradually brought into consciousness, our reception is correspondingly increased. The "oneself" that each person is clinging to at this moment (without quite realizing it) gives place to a wider self which eventually becomes the SELF. The narrow, over-sensitive bundle of pride, prejudice, vanity, illusions and wrong attitudes which make up the "oneself" disappears. The SELF emerges as a picture that has been restored by cleaning. The capacity of reception is then greatly increased—that is, much more influx from Higher Centres is received. But the former feeling of oneself is, of course, lost, for one is no longer the same artificial person that one clung to and suffered from as one's true self. Not only this. The previous "oneself" now has no power over you. You notice the process by not minding everything so much. This means the sensitive bundle of things you thought was yourself is merging into the rest of yourself and losing its outline. Now the Work teaches that we have a *soul* but that it is small and must be developed so that it includes far more than it does. As the

1533

undeveloped soul is, we are taught, it is nothing more than a shifting point of the most intense and violent identification. In a word, where you are most identified, there is your soul. The development of the soul is by a widening of it. You will at once see a connection here with the widening of this "oneself" which possesses us, as we are, but ceases to do so when it fades into the total SELF. We can therefore take it that the phrase "In patience ye shall possess your souls" has nothing to do with the meaning usually attributed to it. People think it means that we must possess our souls in patience. It means nothing of the kind and is merely one example of the degradation of meaning of every esoteric remark in the New Testament. Its point is that as we are we do not possess our souls but our souls possess us, and only through long patient work can we possess them and the nature of that patient work is what we have been studying—namely, the increasing of the consciousness of oneself which leads to the emergence of the broad SELF as distinguished from the narrow oneself or pseudo-self. Later we will make further reflections on the identity of the developed Soul and the SELF and the resulting increase of reception of the vibrations from Higher Centres.

*Amwell, Christmas 1951*

## NOTE ON TEMPTATION

At a small meeting here last Wednesday, the question of what temptation is was discussed, arising out of a remark made recently that it is only in regard to the Work that we can be said to be tempted and that other temptations are not really temptations because their result is a foregone conclusion. Now temptation is necessary in the Work. If people feel that they are never tempted in regard to the Work, they are not allowing it to join issue with themselves. It may be they work in a dream, and so merely dream they are working. Or perhaps they make no connection between the Work and their life, keeping them in two separate compartments. Or they may only sound Do in the octave of the Work, holding it in some degree of valuation, but not sounding Re and therefore may be incapable of sounding Mi. For without the application of the Work to oneself, which is Re, how is it possible ever to come to the realization of personal difficulties in the Work, which is Mi? In such a case one will not experience the meaning of being tempted in regard to the Work.

Now let us provisionally define temptation as a state in which a struggle is taking place in you as to what will take control. Put in terms of 'I's, it is a struggle between different 'I's. Put in terms of desires, it is a struggle between different desires. The outcome is what you do.

You call this your will or your deliberate choice, and so on, if you are liable to automatic self-deception and self-justifying and so of coarser psychological fibre. And once you do whatever you do according to the outcome, the temptation ceases. But if you are of finer material, you inwardly and secretly are aware that you did not really decide anything and it was all decided for you. In other words, there was no temptation. There may have been some anxiety but not temptation. Now put in terms of a struggle between different 'I's, the outcome was really a *compromise* between the 'I's, just as happens in politics between different parties. Put in terms of different desires, the outcome was really the *resultant* of these desires, like the resultant of forces acting in different directions in mechanics. In short, the thing was a foregone conclusion. It was not decision, but compromise or resultant. In other words, it was mechanical. As said, there may have been some anxiety or even perhaps doubts and the transient apparition of some ghostly resolutions, but the matter was eventually settled for you mechanically. Now you cannot attribute to a machine any power of being tempted. How can a machine possibly be tempted? You cannot say when your motor-car strips a gear that it was tempted to do so. If you do, you are using the wrong language. I will ask you now to consider the case of Man. The Work says that Man asleep is a machine. How then can he be tempted? You are using the wrong language surely if you say so. But if you are speaking of a man who is awakening from sleep, the matter is different. Such a man can be truly tempted. In fact, he is tempted, for otherwise he cannot continue to awaken. Now a man awakening is not entirely a machine. A machine has no psychology, but a man awakening begins to have a psychology and so can be tempted. In this connection, on one occasion when G. was asked a question about a man's psychology, he replied: "A man such as you are speaking of has no psychology. He is a machine. In order to study a machine, you do not speak of psychology. With him it is a question of mechanics and nothing more. Study him as a machine and you then will know exactly how he will behave in different circumstances." That is what G. said, in so many words. It shews one the reason why he so often said: "Which kind of man?" when people spoke of anyone. We forget the seven categories of Man and think too easily of MAN in the abstract instead of "which man".

Now in speaking of what is good and bad for the Work it is taught that whatever puts you to sleep is bad. It is only possible to observe what puts you to sleep when you begin to have a point in the Work within yourself—that is, when you have some 'I's in you that wish to work and are not much interested in the sort of things on sale in life. These 'I's group themselves on the level of Observing I and only gradually increase in number. Slightly below them are the crowd of life-'I's upon which the power of detachment inherent in that inner sense called Observing I enables us to look—at first only dimly. Many of these 'I's are not really life-'I's and should be lifted out of that sea. They will be if "the heat of the Work" in you begins to equal "the heat of life", as one ancient writer puts it. Heat means love. You will see that I am describing the state of a man awakening, a man who begins to have a psychology and not merely a machinery. This man has some choice. The choice is between two levels. Two levels are beginning to form in him—the Work-level and the life-level. Two sorts of 'I's are now being rightly arranged in him—Work-'I's and life-'I's. In place of disorder, order is being established in him. This is due to the power *behind* the Work; and, be it noted, the power *of* the Work in him depends solely on his own private secret valuation of the Work. Life will not and cannot bring about this order in him. That is why the Work has always existed, in one or another form, suited to the age. Now the strength of life, and its very clever but very simple ways of hypnotizing people and keeping mankind asleep, continually distracts us so that we forget to do the Work. But we *can* do the Work. It is the one thing we can do. So we have choice. And so we can be really tempted, just because we have these two levels instead of only one and can act from one or from the other. So, for many years, we are tempted in this fashion and mainly yield to life. After a long time we begin to yield more to the Work, but all that comes later.

*Amwell, New Year, 5.1.52*

## ON SOUNDING RE

### NOTE ON STARTING TO WORK

Often people who have listened to the teaching of the Work even for years do not understand what it means to work on themselves. They listen with their ears but do not hear anything with their minds. On many occasions O. said that people listened only to the words that he was saying, but did not try to hear their meaning. He said they were wasting their time. In everyday talk, however, we scarcely listen to the words another person uses but to their meaning. We hear meaning; meaning speaks to meaning, not words. Now meaning is on a higher level than words. This is shewn by the fact that the same meaning can be expressed in different words and also in the words of any foreign language. The words will be totally different. But the meaning will be the same. Meaning, then, stands at a higher level than words and so is prior to words. Now in order to make communication more practical, we learn a special language called the language of the Work. The Work uses special words with special meanings, such as Identifying, Internal Considering, Self-Remembering, Negative Emotions, Self-Observation, Sleep, Wrong Feeling of I, Waking, Death, Re-Birth, Real I, Mechanicalness, Chief Feature, False Personality,

Being, Essence, Multiplicity, Levels, Octaves, Scale, and many others. All these words *mean* something definite. As words, they can be registered and remembered. But this is not the purpose of this special language. To hear two people, not exactly friends, talking to one another, using Work-words without understanding them and each trying to silence the other, is something to be avoided. It can tempt one to think the Work must be all sheer nonsense. But of course it is only turned into nonsense by such talk. It is indeed taking the Name of the Work in vain. Now this expression when used of God—namely, "thou shalt not take the Name of God in vain"—does not refer to the word itself but to the meaning. To profane the Name of God is to degrade the quality of the meaning of God—and so to cheapen what is highest in yourself and therefore to injure yourself, for wrong attitudes injure ourselves. Esoterically, the name represents the quality, and the higher the quality, the greater the meaning. Now the quality of Work-words is very degraded when they are used anyhow, now one, now another, without any true appreciation of the special meaning of each. Understand that to juggle them around and have pot-shots with them in order to answer a question is not thinking. There is a great density of special meaning concealed in each Work-word. It is because of this density that, as one grows in understanding, their meaning grows and accompanies you. They come to mean more and more, just as the Gospels come to mean more and more as one's understanding of the Work increases, thus proving that this Work is truly esoteric Christianity. But here is what you have got to realize and realize again and again—namely, that the meaning of Work-words can never begin to be understood unless you start to work on something definite in yourself, whether you are a man or a woman. It is the same for us all. Now since so many do not comprehend what is meant by working on oneself, let it be repeated that there is no such thing. This has been said many times before. I mean, that to tell me you are working on yourself means nothing to me. But if you tell me that you are working *on something quite definite that you have observed clearly in yourself*, then I will be glad to hear it. Maybe I will have noticed it already for myself. For it is not difficult to see when a person is working on something definite. The look is different. The eyes and the expression of the face and the voice alter. The whole atmosphere of the person changes. It is not necessary to tell me or anyone what the quite definite thing is that you have observed in yourself and are working on. It is best to keep it in stillness, in silence. I mean, it is best not to talk in yourself about it, and so not to let your life-'I's know about it and start arguing, but to let only your Work-'I's know what it is. For then the Work itself will reward you secretly. This is what is meant by verses 3 and 4 in Matthew vi:

> "But when thou doest alms, let not thy left hand know what thy right hand doeth: that thine alms may be in secret: and thy Father which seeth in secret himself shall reward thee."

For some extraordinary reason the last line is rendered: "thy Father which seeth in secret shall reward thee openly." There is no mention of *openly* either in the Greek text or the Latin text of the Vulgate. When you do anything for the sake of the Work—i.e. through Work-'I's in you—you receive your reward in secret, which may take the form of flashes of Self-Remembering or flashes of positive emotion and certain states of inner peace. To be rewarded openly would mean at once that it goes into the self-merit and so into the Personality.

*Amwell, 12.1.52*

## MAGNETIC CENTRE

It was said recently that once you have valuation of the Work you do not need Magnetic Centre. It is necessary to understand that a thing may be useful in one place but useless or even a hindrance in another place. Nothing is valuable just in itself but only in its relation to other things. Now can you think of anything that is valuable in itself? Think for a moment. (Now think of a thing that is useful in one place but useless or even a hindrance in another.) We are taught that Magnetic Centre is valuable in its place. If strong enough it can lead us from life into the Work. Mr Ouspensky developed a strong Magnetic Centre and, to use his language, he went "in search of the miraculous". He did not find what he wanted in India. On returning he found this Work. Now Magnetic Centre is the power to distinguish two quite different kinds of influences which one can meet with in life. They are called *A* and *B* influences. *A* influences are created in life. They are the interests of business, of politics, of war, of sport, of rank, of power, of intrigue, of scandal, of innumerable forms of gambling, and of other interests such as food, drink, money, clothes, publicity, and so on. We are dominated by one or another or more of these influences through our attitudes. It is our attitudes that connect us with them as by invisible threads. Reflect on this and notice your interests. These influences (created in life and called *A* influences in the Work) keep the pot boiling. That is, they keep humanity on the move. They keep people going round and round, always thinking they are going somewhere, towards some goal. Until we ourselves wake up a little, we think the same; we suppose life is taking us somewhere; we imagine we are going towards some goal. We certainly are; but not to the one we expect. So we do not see our real situation; we do not appreciate its dangers; we do not see we are living in what the Work calls the Hall of Mirrors and are going in no direction whatever and are going nowhere. The mirrors are so arranged that it seems as though one were going straight ahead. Actually one is going nowhere; one is just going round and round. This is a simple but very clever illusion. But it only has any power as long as one does not observe oneself—and in life nobody does. It is unnecessary for life—in fact, nobody wishes to observe himself. This is due to a number of simple little illusions also all very clever—such as "Oh, I know myself through and through", or "It would make a chap introspective—morbid, you know", or "I'm far too busy for anything like that. I'm a practical person." They form an interesting collection. They are worth studying—I mean, in yourself. If you do not observe them—that is, if you do not make them conscious to yourself—they will do you a lot of harm by keeping you asleep in different ways, which of course is their object. Like much else, they only have power over you if you cannot let them into the light of consciousness by means of self-observation. If you *can* let them into this light, then you must look at them quite simply just as you might look at an orange on your plate. This is more important than I can say. However, you will probably begin identifying and self-justifying long before this happens and everything will slip back into your crowded darkness again and everything will be as before. You see, illusions are lies, and no one ever cares to admit to either illusions or lies. And there is always the master-illusion—namely, that one has no illusions. This lulls one to sleep. Is it not all very clever? Enumerate to yourselves the great illusions of which the Work speaks. See for yourselves, in yourselves, how simply and cleverly everyone is kept asleep and realize how it was unnecessary to build those fences round the sheep. Now a man with a strong Magnetic Centre already sees some of all this.

You have often heard it said that this Work begins at the level of Good Householder. It is not for freaks or abnormal people or useless people. It is necessary to be a responsible person, an educated person, a person of some good, and if possible a person who is, or is becoming, good at something. Please understand that for a person to be a Good Householder in the Work-sense, it does not mean he must possess a house of his own. A man is his own house. It refers to what is in that house. If all three storeys have something in them, it helps. Now the Work adds a few interesting things about Good Householder. It says that he does not believe in life. You will see that these are connected. The stronger is his Magnetic Centre, the fewer illusions about life he will have, so the less he will believe in it. You may not have noticed this connection before.

Now to return to Magnetic Centre, it was said that once Do is sounded, Magnetic Centre has done its work. It is also said that while it can bring you to the Work, it cannot keep you in it. I will try to indicate to you briefly how, indeed, it may become a hindrance unless it is let go. Early in the Work I was told by Mr Gurdjieff to put aside all my books and read no more. Now I had already studied at different times in the past the Gnostic literature, the Neo-Platonists, the Alchemists, some of the Indian Scriptures, the Hermetic writers, the Sufi literature, the Bible, the Chinese Mystics, the writings of Eckhart,

Boehme, Blake, Swedenborg and others, and had been a pupil of Jung for some years. I say all this on purpose to shew you how surprised I was to learn I had to put these studies aside. But it did not mean that my studies had been useless. It meant that now, having met the Work itself, they were no longer useful. They had played their part in forming Magnetic Centre. But they now enabled me to see how strong and clear and connected the Work was by comparison. What I had to do now was to study the ideas and the methods of the Work. Anything useful gained from the past would then fall into its place. Often I feel it is a pity that so few have made their Magnetic Centre stronger by the previous study of B influences. The Magnetic Centre, whatever its origin, can be made strong by thought and study. That is the main point. The stronger the Magnetic Centre, the greater is the evaluation of the Work. By those who have not done this the value of the Work and its unique formulations is not instantly seen. They have little or nothing to compare it with. In that case, they need to study esoteric literature some time later *after* they have heard and practised the Work in order to widen their minds. The esoteric parts of the New Testament, such as the Parables, are very valuable in this respect and continue to be all through one's development. In fact, I doubt if anyone can understand these without the Work.

*Notes for the Reader*

(1) The older education which gave a background of classical legend and an approach to Greek philosophy tended to form Magnetic Centre. The modern scientific text-books do not.

(2) The Work calls those who are not Good Householder—Tramps, Lunatics and Hasnamous. (There is the business Hasnamous, the political one and so on, big and small.)

*Amwell, 18.1.52*

## TRANSFORMATION OF MEANING

### Paper I

We think awkwardly, and personal emotions continually interrupt us. We feel resentment and our thought streaks and breaks up like a picture on a television screen. G. said: "You always think, think, think. I look." Of course, we are not thinking—not really. We feel we have to say something instead of looking, say, at the tree. We are unaccustomed to real thought. Our thought is so very awkward—so clumsy and confused, a fitting together of everything wrongly, in triumph, like an idiot child smashing up things with an evil pleasure. Some only have destructive thinking. Some can only disagree and call this thinking. Some always side with the minority out of a sort of cussedness and call this thinking. Many never know what they are thinking. Most call association thinking.

Then again, one's theory of life may be utterly wrong and all one's resulting thoughts wrong. For if the ideas of one's thoughts are wrong, one's thinking, which proceeds from one's ideas, will be all wrong. If you think from the ideas of the Work, your thinking will begin to be right. To think from the ideas of the Work instead of your previous ideas is *metanoia*—that is, change of mind (not repentance, as it is wrongly translated). To drive away your previous ways of thinking cleanses the dirt from the mind and you begin to catch its beauty. The battle goes to and fro for long. It is not really you who are fighting it. But it seems that you encounter one phase of tempting after another —or testing, if you prefer. It is one's Armageddon. Always reinforcements from natural thinking from the senses march up and seem to swamp you—and they will if you believe internally that Nature somehow created itself, and that there is no meaning, and only blind forces exist, and all the rest. Your thinking will be upside down. You will then be restless and unhappy, just because you see nothing above Nature. Where there is no meaning, you necessarily sicken and perish. Violence and ugliness and cruelty attract you—the lowest meanings.

Man lives by meaning. This Work transmits more and more meaning in proportion as the mind is cleansed from this dirt of wrong thinking and feeling, for it opens out. To think upside down is silly. It is to explain the higher by the lower. You then say that matter is first and the mind somehow arises. The Work says Mind is first. It says, in so many words, that before the beginning of time, Mind *is*, not *was*, but *is*, for *was* belongs to time. It indicates that Mind as the Absolute is outside and beyond all time, and so is free from all the imperfections of time experienced by our limited being. It indicates that the higher creates the lower on every successive level in the total Scale of Being. Nothing creates itself. All created things receive meaning according to their level of being, which determines their receptivity of meaning. All meaning is derived from Absolute Meaning which is infinite, and so is not in time and so is not created. To be created is to be limited, and the Absolute is under no limited conditions. The descent of meaning, from level to level, from higher to lower successively, never ceases, and is different at each level. Because of this, the *transformation of meaning* is possible, and can be experienced by Man as his level of being changes. Where he had seen one thing obscurely, he then sees a thousand things distinctly.

In this Work we seek transformation of meaning through self-change. This is possible and can be experienced, but not if we cling to former meanings, and indulge unchecked in self-emotions and negative criticizing and feeling. A definite line of work on our level of being is laid down in the Work-teaching. If it is genuinely practised over a sufficient time, we begin to look back with surprise on the former meanings we lived by. This marks the beginning of a change in our level of being owing to some degree of transformation of meaning.

As we are raised in being, so is meaning transformed. If we fall back the old meanings return. This up and down motion keeps on until a step is definitely reached. Then it will begin again, so as to reach the next step. At each step new meanings flow in and old meanings shrink. We begin to think differently. We see the awkward clumsiness of our former thinking—and know it was not thinking at all. We begin to see how wonderfully delicate and silent the movements of real thinking are, how nothing must ever be forced, nothing joined which so clearly does not belong, nothing put in out of order or scale. We see this tragedy of our previous thinking, the wrong connecting of things, the crude violence of it, the cruel muddling up of things. The same insight into our former feelings is also opened. But if the old habits of mind and feeling persist none of all this can take place.

*Amwell, 26.1.52*

## CRYSTALLIZED THINKING

Crystallized thoughts form attitudes. If you have continually thought in a certain way all these thoughts crystallize into an attitude. Let us suppose you have always thought that you did not get the attention you should have got. You have identified with this thought thousands and thousands of times. Eventually these thousands of similar thoughts form a solid deposit in the mind. This is called crystallization. Such a crystallization of similar thoughts forms an attitude, so you now have in you an attitude towards other people which has been formed out of thinking and thinking time and again in the same way that you never get the attention you should get from others. You will agree with me that such a crystallization forming this particular attitude is not uncommon and can be observed in many people you know. Very good—but how about yourself? Begin with yourself always in this Work. Have you observed it silently at work in your own life? It causes a lot of unhappiness both to yourself and others. It is a very powerful constituent of that form of internal considering called making accounts. It can eat one's force up daily and so produce a secret inner sickness of the spirit. It can make one extremely brittle or touchy ·or changeable or produce similar manifestations of weakness. But apart from all the evils that its presence can manifest in your psychic life—and also in your somatic or bodily life—the greatest evil connected with it is that it remains inaccessible to you, working silently in the darkness beyond your consciousness. Now here lies one out of several difficulties in the First Line of Work, which is work on oneself, beginning with self-observation. The difficulty is this: you can become aware of, and occasionally notice the qualities of, some of your thoughts. If later you learn to concentrate, by which I mean become very quiet in yourself, you then stand as it were motionless in the middle of the merry-go-round and witness an extraordinary throng, many sub-human and almost grotesque or deformed, or quite evil. These are thoughts which you usually mount. If you identify with any you move from the centre and go round yourself—that is, you and the thought become one and you now say: "I think."

But although you can more and more observe the various thoughts that can come to you and by this method take the feeling of I out of them more and more, you cannot observe an attitude. This is the difficulty. Once a system of similar thoughts has become crystallized into an attitude it is not directly observable. It has become part of you and acts invisibly and automatically without your knowing about it. Now a thought will not necessarily make you act, but an attitude will. In the given example, you will not keep *thinking* that you do not get the attention you should get, but you will keep on *acting* as if this were so and no matter what is done it will not stop this attitude not only from making you act in certain ways but from eating your force daily. The secret of its power lies in its situation—that is, it is operating slightly beyond the range of one's direct self-observation. It lies outside the small area of consciousness that one familiarly in life inhabits. In short, it is inaccessible to you as things are with you—that is, as long as you cling to the ordinary feeling of yourself which is the same as remaining (at all costs) in the small area of consciousness that you inhabit internally.

But the genuine practice of self-observation gradually draws into consciousness the things lying in the shadows and these in turn draw in things lying in the darkness. If you begin to increase the consciousness of yourself by observation of what is accessible, then after a time (according to your capacity to stand shock) you will find yourself becoming aware of the existence in yourself—your psychic make-up—of things you had not attributed to yourself but only to others. You will recall that we project on to others what we are not conscious of in ourselves—a charming device that we all have and one that contributes so much to the peace and harmony of human life on this planet.

Now, to take another example of crystallized thoughts. Let us suppose you have begun at some early stage to think that people do not like you. You have indulged in this thought freely and quite unchecked. You have had the same thought over and over again, year after year, until it has crystallized out into an attitude. You are now, let us imagine, a most successful person, surrounded by loving friends. But there is something wrong, a sad, far-away look, a sigh. Attitude is secretly at work, draining your force, unknown to you. Now there is another curious thing about attitude. As I said, you can observe thoughts but not attitudes: also a thought does not necessarily make you act, but an attitude does, without your knowing anything about it. You sigh, you have a sad, far-away look; or you act as if you are aggrieved, or you seem surprised when you are given anything, and so on. All this is caused by attitude operating from the background. The hidden attitude makes you act *mechanically*—in short it causes you to sigh, to look unhappy, to act as if you were neglected and so on—although there is absolutely no outer reason why you should. It consumes you. It eats your force, as the secret worm eats the rose. But the curious thing is that even though people assure you daily that you are liked or even though they give you irrefutable evidence that you do really receive attention, yet it makes no real difference, or only a momentary one. The attitude continues to exert its evil power from its dark abode. It is often accompanied by delicious forms of self-pity. It is indeed one of the powers of darkness: and every assurance, every proof, will be rejected without your knowing why. This kind of useless suffering is extremely common. It drains enormous quantities of force from humanity which is utilized elsewhere.


*Amwell, 2.2.52*

## TRANSFORMATION OF MEANING

### Paper II

We spoke in a previous paper on the transformation of meaning and about levels of meaning. There is greater meaning and lesser; or, put differently, there is higher and lower meaning in the total scale of meaning. Our susceptibility to meaning depends on the quality of our being. A low level of being will be susceptible only to a low level of meaning. It will receive inferior meaning. A man belonging to a more developed level of being will be capable of receiving meanings from a higher level. But it does not follow that he will do so.

Now our being is multiple in more senses than one. We have many different 'I's. They are not on the same level. We also have different centres, with different parts, lower and higher in function and therefore not on the same level. The different 'I's live in the different parts of centres. Inferior 'I's—that is, more mechanical 'I's, such as those connected with remembering small things or making small plans—live in lower parts. Higher 'I's, such as those connected with reflection or weighing evidence, live in the higher divisions of a centre. From this brief glance at the teaching on being, one can see that one's being is not all on the same level but is constructed on different levels. And from what has been so far said about the connection between level of being and level of meaning, we can realize that these different levels in our being will be receptive of different meaning.

Like the construction of the Universe itself as shewn in the Ray of Creation, a man is in levels. The descent of meaning, from higher to lower, from level to level successively, never ceases. Meaning at a higher level is not comprehended by a lower level. This is what is meant by the statement in the first chapter of John that the light shone in darkness and the darkness comprehended it not. The meaning of Christ's teaching was not comprehensible to the sensual, literal thinking of his audience. Sensual thinking, based on the level of meaning that the external organs of sense are receptive of, cannot comprehend psychological thinking. There is a gulf between them. They are discontinuous. We know from the three Octaves of Radiation derived from the Ray of Creation, and the Table of Hydrogens, which is further derived from the triple octave, that the Universe is an immense scale or ladder of vibrations which are discontinuous. That is, they do not merge into one another, but are distinct, on different levels. This was formulated by the Work before this century. Physical Science has since found that the observable physical Universe, regarded as energy, is a scale of descending vibrations. For example, our organs of sight are receptive of light which is composed roughly of an octave of vibrations whose frequency of waves lies between 750 billion (violet light) to 400 billion (red) vibrations a second. But these wave-energies are merely one octave of vibrations out of very many. Above and below the wave-energy that we see with the eye, say, as violet light (but which in itself is simply a vibration) lie many other vibrations of greater and of lesser frequency and wave-lengths. They are discontinuous with one another. For instance, vibrations just above violet light as regards frequencies constitute X-Rays. No amount of light will produce X-Rays. They are discontinuous. Also we have no external organ of sense for the reception of X-Rays. Similarly, we have no given organ for the reception of wireless waves which come far below light vibrations. Now, as regards the reception of *meaning*, apart from sensual perception, we have several internal organs of reception in ordinary centres and in parts of centres, which are given but not necessarily used: and also we have Higher Centres which our level of being is too low to hear.

In the esoteric teaching on re-birth of which fragments are preserved in the Gospels (although mixed up and in the wrong order, as G. said) we are taught that everything begins with change of mind *metanoia*. "Except ye change your minds, ye shall all . . . perish" (Luke xiii. 3, 5). This implies that the way we usually think, which is sensual, will prevent that possible inner development, that leads to re-birth, a New Man, the goal of each individual. Other levels of meaning are necessary, therefore, apart from sensual meaning. The mind must be given new ideas from which to think. The ideas of the Work are new. To think *from* them changes the mind. People, however, stick to sensual thinking, and at the same time try to listen to the ideas instead of really beginning to think from them. This is referred to in the Gospels as pouring new wine into old bottles, which is not the best thing to do as both are spoiled. Purely sensual thinking and psychological thinking cannot mingle. They are discontinuous—on different levels. Now the thinking of a small child begins simply from the senses —from appearances. It thinks from what it sees. Thinking, then, begins at the sensual level and is deeply ingrained. We take ourselves as our bodies. The mechanical or moving divisions of centres are turned to the senses. But the centres have more internal sides in the emotional and intellectual divisions. These *can* open on higher levels of meaning if they are purified. They can receive the Work-ideas and *think* from them, if the love and need for them becomes strong enough. The level of being on which some 'I's live—or can and should live, if we preach the Work to them—corresponds to the ability to become receptive to higher levels of meaning beyond sensual meanings. As long as the sensual mind grips and chains us, the Work will seem meaningless, because we have no level to receive its greater meaning. We continue in inferior meanings. We are then like people who are blind, having no receptive organ of sight. Yet if we strive and ask for sight, realizing we are blind, we will receive it and feel vibrations of new meaning. Then our relationship to and understanding of everything will begin to undergo transformation. Our lives will feel different. It is this Work, deeply pondered and gradually penetrating into our own living of life, that raises being so that it sees another level of meaning. New meaning is waiting there already, as are the vibrations from another station that a radio cannot pick up. We do not make the new meaning. We have to tune in. The Work is about how this is done—by psycho-transformism. Psycho-transformism leads to new meaning. A new level of meaning results from a new level of being. Change of being begins with change of mind. The ideas of the Work are new. Change of mind is when you really think in a new way and it means something. And finally—new thinking cannot be poured into the old bottles of the mind on the sensual level.

*Amwell, 9.2.52*

## TRANSFORMATION OF MEANING

### Paper III

When I see a familiar thing without associations it looks strange. I see it in a new way. Its meaning is altered. If I can look at my friend without associations he seems strange. I see him in a new way. It is not perhaps too much to say that I scarcely recognize him for the moment. In the same way, walking down a corridor with an undetected mirror at the end I may not recognize the person walking towards me. He seems to be a stranger. I see myself without associations for a moment. Ordinarily when looking in a mirror we see ourselves through the veil of associations that we have about our appearance. The point is that when momentarily the veil of associations is stripped away, something happens. What happens? Everything becomes alive. If you can by sufficient practice relax from the Personality, which is where the network of associations lies, and from, let me add, the wrong feeling of 'I', you find yourself in a different world—a world of another meaning. Actually the world is the same, but your reception of the impressions from it is different and so its meaning is different. When you are relaxed from Personality and Imaginary 'I' things are close to you. They speak to you. You are then truly taking in impressions. Impressions are falling on Essence. The level of Essence is higher than that of Personality. We understand that a higher level receives greater meaning. Now when you are blessed—that is, when you are relaxed from the Personality—you feel the intimacy of everything around you, as if things realized they could go on playing and you would not be angry. If you get angry you cannot relax from the Personality. Or it is as if you and everything around you felt quite suddenly at ease and something could creep out from each object and shew itself alive to you. And then suddenly life slams the Personality back into its place and everything is dead. Ouspensky describes how the significant meaning of everything changed when he reached a certain level or state into which his experiments brought him. Every object became so filled, so brilliant, with meaning, as to be almost unbearable. He writes:

"I remember once sitting on a sofa smoking and looking at an ash-tray. It was an ordinary copper ash-tray. Suddenly I felt that I was beginning to understand what the ash-tray was, and at the same time, with a certain wonder and almost with fear, I felt that I had never understood it before and that we do not understand the simplest things around us.

The ash-tray roused a whirlwind of thoughts and images. It contained such an infinite number of events; it was linked with such an immense number of things. First of all, with everything connected with smoking and tobacco. This at once roused thousands of images, pictures, memories. Then the ash-tray itself. How had it come into being? All the materials of which it could have been made? Copper, in this case—what was copper? How had people discovered it for the first time? How had they learned to make use of it? How and where was the copper obtained from which this ash-tray was made? Through what kind of treatment had it passed, how had it been transported from place to place, how many people had worked on it or in connection with it? How had the copper been transformed into an ash-tray? These and other questions about the history of the ash-tray up to the day when it had appeared on my table.

I remember writing a few words on a piece of paper in order

to retain something of these thoughts on the following day. And next day I read: "*A man can go mad from one ash-tray.*" The meaning of all that I felt was that in one ash-tray it was possible to know *all.* By invisible threads the ash-tray was connected with everything in the world, not only with the present, but with all the past and with all the future. To know an ash-tray meant to know all.

My description does not in the least express the sensation as it actually was, because the first and principal impression was that the ash-tray was alive, that it thought, understood and told me all about itself. All I learned I learned from the ash-tray itself. The second impression was the extraordinary emotional character of all connected with what I had learned about the ash-tray.

'Everything is alive,' I said to myself in the midst of these observations; 'there is nothing dead, it is only we who are dead. If we become alive for a moment, we shall feel that everything is alive, that all things live, feel and can speak to us.' "

You will notice that Ouspensky says that in our ordinary state we are dead. This was made evident to him from the level to which his experiments brought him. This meaning was opened to his reception. We do not at our level realize we are dead. We do not grasp the significance of the remark in Scripture: "Let the dead bury their dead." But if we can relax from the Personality we wonder at the antics and capers we were indulging in and why we were madly pressing, streaming, rushing along, both outwardly and inwardly. Who is this person who takes charge? Who is this person we have to serve, who dictates what we should think and say, and how we should behave and what things should mean, the person of whom the more we catch glimpses, the more is seen as stupid, ruthless and tyrannical? Is this person composed only of *imagination*? Is it possibly the Imaginary 'I' that causes us so much trouble and vexation and care and worry, where there need be none? Does to relax from the personality mean to relax from this Imaginary 'I'—the entirely wrong feeling of 'I' that tyrannizes over us and that only the whole armament of the Work and its teachings can destroy? Were I freed from the tyranny of Imaginary 'I' would I see everything differently? Let us see what Ouspensky saw about this tyrannous person when he was lifted above its sphere of influence into another level of consciousness:

"A very great place—perhaps the chief place—in all that I had learned was occupied by the idea of 'I'. That is to say, the feeling or sensation of 'I' in some strange way changed within me. It is very difficult to express this in words. Ordinarily we do not sufficiently understand that at different moments of our life we feel our 'I' differently. In this case, as in many others, I was helped by my earlier experiments and observations of dreams. I knew that in sleep 'I' is felt differently, not as it is felt in a waking state; just as differently, but in quite another way, 'I' was felt in these experiences.

The nearest possible approximation would be if I were to say that everything which is ordinarily felt as 'I' became 'not I', and everything which is felt as 'not I' became 'I'. But this is far from being an exact statement of what I felt and learned. I think that an exact statement is impossible. It is necessary only to note that the new sensation of 'I' during the first experiments, so far as I can remember it, was a very terrifying sensation. I felt that I was disappearing, vanishing, turning into nothing. This was the same terror of infinity of which I have already spoken, but it was reversed: in one case it it was ALL that swallowed me up, in the other it was NOTHING. But this made no difference, because ALL was equivalent to NOTHING.

But it was remarkable that later, in subsequent experiments, the same sensation of the disappearance of 'I' began to produce in me a feeling of extraordinary calmness and confidence, which nothing can equal in our ordinary sensations. I seemed to understand at that time that all the usual troubles, cares and anxieties are connected with the usual sensation of 'I', result from it, and, at the same time, constitute and sustain it. Therefore, when 'I' disappeared, all troubles, cares and anxieties disappeared. When I felt that I did not exist, everything else became very simple and easy. At these moments I even regarded it as strange that we could take upon ourselves so terrible a responsibility as to bring 'I' into everything, and start from 'I' in everything. In the idea of 'I', in the sensation of 'I', such as we ordinarily have, there was something almost abnormal, a kind of fantastic conceit which bordered on blasphemy, as if each one of us called himself God. I felt then that only God could call himself 'I', that only God was 'I'. But we also call ourselves 'I' and do not see and do not notice the irony of it."


*Amwell, 16.2.52*


## MAN WITH ONE SUIT

If a man were to be raised suddenly to a level of being above his own he would appear naked, because he would have no garments of truth belonging to that level. Imagine a man having only sensual truth brought into a place where only psychological truth exists. The senses are not guides to truth. There are far too many known (and unknown) fallacies of the senses, such as the one that Man stands on a motionless earth and the Sun and all the hosts of heaven humbly turn round him every twenty-four hours. People were angry when told this was a fallacy of the senses. Why? Because the discovery offends their self-importance. Many still believe it, I fancy, literally: very few ever feel it psychologically as a truth contradicting sense-given truth.

Notice how people dress their bodies up like children and what respect is paid to the body. The sensual life has so very great a power that the mind is dressed in its garments in most people and in nothing else. It possesses no garments of psychological truth. So if such a man, a man at the level solely of sensual truth, were to be raised to a higher level he would appear naked having no change of clothing for his mind. Now to such a man, with only one suit, the Work will be a continual stumbling-block. He will be scandalized by it, maybe secretly or maybe openly. The Greek word translated "offended" in the New Testament is σκανδαλίζω. People were scandalized when Christ taught them psychological truth, such as that to hate is to murder, instead of how often to wash and what not to eat.

Now everyone is his or her own truth and his or her own good. This means that a man or a woman taken psychologically is what each holds as good. There is the bodily man or woman and the psychological man or woman. Do not, for heaven's sake, think they are the same. What then, do you personally hold as truth and what do you hold as good? What are you psychologically? It is worth reflecting upon. If truth for you is only what the senses shew, then you are in falsity—just as if you think that good entirely consists in having your own way you are in evil. But we are speaking here of the sensual mind and in particular of a person whose mind has only one suit—that is, the sensual man. Since the senses are severely limited the mind solely based on their evidence will be severely limited. It will think, for example, that when a person is dead and buried and so no longer evident to the senses, he has not, and cannot possibly have, any further existence. Such a mind will say: "But how?—where?—I do not see him, or hear or touch him?" That is, relying on the senses only as the source of all possible truth, he can only conclude that the dead cease to have any further existence and are annihilated. This is sensual thinking and this by limiting us puts us in prison. A prison is what limits us. Now the Work teaches us that we are in prison but are not aware of it. What is the nature of the prison? The teaching that we are in prison is an ancient esoteric teaching. Pythagoras taught it some twenty-six hundred years ago. Now if we believe that our senses shew us all that is real and so, that they shew us all Reality and that no other realities exist, we keep ourselves in the prison of the senses. Reading some notes made years ago I came on this passage: "We should fear *not* to remember ourselves. We should fear to be under the power of the world. We should turn round from the moving shadows on the wall in front of us and behold the light. We should move out of the cave. It is true that we are in chains and can scarcely turn our heads round. But the Work can gradually release our chains. Eventually it can free us."

Now from what has been said we can see that we must be very much under the power of the world if we possess nothing but sensual thinking based on the world as it appears to the senses, and have no other part of the mind awake than its sensual part. We can see that such a sensual mind will make a very strong chain, fastening us in such a position that we can only see the shadows in front of us and remain in ignorance of anything behind us. Phenomena—that is, appearances—will seem to cause and move themselves, and truth and reality will seem to be centred in these appearances themselves. It will be just like the cinema which reproduces the situation. The darkened hall is the cave, the moving figures on the screen are the shadows cast on the wall, the film and the light that cause everything are behind us and are ignored. We gaze fascinated in front of us, hypnotized by the shadows, as completely tricked as we are by the trickery of life—or perhaps I should say, doubly so. Reflecting on the narrow slit of the senses we have, one wonders what sensual reality would be like if we were granted a new sense, say, one that opened the thought of another person to us, so making all deception impossible. Imagine the extension of reality resulting. If we all had this new sense our lives would become impossible at our level of being. No one could pretend. No one could say any one thing and mean another. Apart from what would obviously happen to certain professions, I still speculate about the medical profession.

This certainly makes one think that had we been given more senses, the resulting sensual mind, the mind founded on these senses—new and old senses—would be a very different thing from what it is now. Sensual reality—the reality common to all—would then be on a far higher level, embracing far more of truth, far more of reality and so far less falsity, far fewer fallacies and illusions. Now the internal senses open on realities other than do the external senses. This should make us pause and think. We know the Work teaches that we have more internal senses than external. On what realities do they open? If our present external senses shew us only a small part, could the internal senses if they were working shew us additional and greater parts of what is Real? We could not look to even a complete development of our Knowledge and Being ever revealing anything like the totality, the grandeur, and the fullness of all Reality. To think so is merely one example of the state of continual blasphemy that we live in, quite unperturbed, and as trite as when we say 'I' as if we had one— a form of blasphemy a little child avoids as long as possible. People believe they could understand anything if it were only explained. Now the sensual mind as at present is blasphemy by itself. It is a heavy chain round the neck that almost prevents a man even turning round enough to observe himself, for the sensual scarcely can observe themselves. Do not mistake it for a necklace of pearls. Do not pride yourself on your plain, straightforward, matter of fact and sensible approach to life. If you do, you will never get those inner unused senses to work that are so delicate and open you on to such new ranges of meaning, as the False Personality weakens its grip on you. Your suffocating opinions of yourself and your bad smelling self-meritoriousness, being false emotions, will drench and dowse their interior light. You will have a wet soul as the Ancients called it. A dry soul, they said, is better than a wet one—because it can hear and see more. A lot of work on oneself is necessary to begin with to dry these unused senses out, and to get them to work faintly. That is why we study and do this system for so long. The sensual mind, with its sensual thinking, has to undergo great changes. This only begins by thinking more and more from the idea of the Work, by constant accessions of thoughts born of the ideas taught in the Work, if possible daily accessions, which accumulate until *metanoia* is reached definitely and the sensual mind becomes only a part of the new mind. Do not trust the sensual mind. It is a useful servant. Do not let it be your master. Remember that the senses only work in the present moment. They do not shew you the past which lies in another dimension—as does the whole world. Do not trust the sensual mind.

*Amwell, 23.2.52*

## NOTE ON CERTAIN 'I'S

### WHAT DO YOU READ AND LISTEN WITH?

When you read a book alone you may use chiefly the Intellectual Centre or the Emotional Centre or the Moving Centre. If it is difficult to grasp, you read it chiefly with the Intellectual Centre and it will be necessary to use *directed attention*. You will remember it with difficulty or find you have scarcely understood anything and must re-read it. As a rule we don't re-read it and so we learn nothing new, unfortunately. If you read with the Emotional Centre the book will have to be exciting or romantic and you will read it with *drawn attention*. Your attention will be attracted, not directed, to the characters and the story and you will only need to use directed attention at moments where you do not quite follow the plot or the meaning of a sentence. You will remember it surprisingly easily—often years later. But if the story demands too much directed attention you will throw it aside. This is because it falls between centres. If you are pre-occupied with some domestic event and open a book to distract you, you will probably read it with Moving Centre which requires *zero attention*. Some people read large pieces of books with Moving Centre only, especially if upset, or if they think drearily that they ought to read. In that case, nothing is registered. You will have no memory of it. Zero attention gives no memory. Finally, a great many people do not read at all.

Now let me leave the question of centres themselves and come to 'I's in centres for I wish to-day to speak in more detail not only of how one reads (when alone) but how one listens to a person—for reading is a form of listening but different. I mean that different 'I's are used.

The question is: which 'I' is reading, or which 'I' is listening at any moment? And this will bring us once more to the question of the 'I's in general, and to the whole doctrine of 'I's which is of such importance in understanding and doing the Work practically. The Work teaches astonishingly that *none* of our thoughts or feelings is our own. It says that they are induced in us by different 'I's. But we take all of them as ourselves and think of them as our thoughts and our feelings and say "I think". This is an illusion. They are not our thoughts and feelings (and moods and emotions and desires and sensations) but those of different 'I's speaking through us. That is, they are the thoughts and feelings of, in my case, people who are not me but whom I take, without question, as myself. The extraordinary thing is that I never discovered that this is so, until I began to realize that I had been living all these years with this state of affairs open and plain to me if I had looked. Yes, but not open and plain to my external sight or any of the external senses. I had never discovered it before because I had never used an internal sense—namely, internal eyesight. *I never observed myself.* Yet I was given the power of insight but never used it. As a result these people, these 'I's, hitherto had played with my life as they pleased and I suspected nothing.

Now I have come to know several 'I's in myself whose approach and presence I can detect by various signs and symptoms. To take an example: one of them begins usually by affecting me physically first of all and then leads on to arousing certain feelings accompanied by certain trains of thought, many now familiar but all not yet completely so. That is, I still think that *I am thinking* some of the thoughts it induces in me, because I agree with them. I can observe the other thoughts it offers me as not being mine. This means I am not yet able fully to observe this 'I', since I take part of it as me—that is, I say 'I' to that part. So I cannot separate completely from it. This means that this 'I' is not yet thoroughly objective to me. I cannot see it as entirely distinct from me, as not being me at all, but another person in me, who wants me to take it as me. Now sometimes I listen with this 'I' and suffer much afterwards. This happens when certain conversations take place and this 'I' slips in and speaks suddenly out of my mouth. It manages this through what I think is true. Some of the things it says I can observe are clearly not true. They are lies, and so are not me. But as I said, some seem to be true and that is how it gets in. I fail to see that *the whole 'I'* is a bad person who seeks to do me evil, for when I listen with this 'I' it distorts what I am listening to and tires and disturbs me after it has eaten enough of me to satisfy itself for the time being. I cannot see yet that it uses bits of truth for its own purpose of overpowering me. Or again, when I am reading alone I may become aware that it is there, reading for me. Then I know there was something in the book similar to what it always wants me to think; and, turning a page or two back, I will probably find what it was and when this 'I' seized the opportunity to slip in without my noticing and start up its diabolical hypnotism. I speak gravely here because negative 'I's have to be taken with increasing gravity as one works. Some conceal their entry in innocent guise. But remember that all negative 'I's only wish to do evil and destroy your work. They seek to drag you deeper into prison. The trouble is that we continually strengthen these 'I's by listening by means of them and believing them, and do so little from our other 'I's. Now I am reading quite alone and not expecting anyone, the 'I's that read are not the same as when other people are around, or I expect to be interrupted. I mean that if I am deeply interested in the book, the 'I' that is reading it and the 'I's that are listening do not include in their circle the 'I' that I have been trying to describe above. You must do your own observation about this. I will now leave this example, quite aware that it is not adequately described, partly because of the difficulty in language.

We have then slowly and painfully to come to the realization that, as we are at our level, we have nothing that we can call I. It is pure imagination to speak as if we have. So we have only *Imaginary* *'I'*—that is, we imagine we have a real, permanent, unchanging I. But we have not. It is a terrible blow to one's pride to begin to see this psychological truth which our external senses contradict. Some ignore the very idea as preposterous. Try, therefore, to observe your 'I's. Try to see that it is 'I's thinking and feeling that are inducing these recurring moods and thoughts from which you suffer. The Work will look after your good 'I's. But, as regards your bad 'I's, the way of release is in stripping and skinning them, in tearing from them the precious feeling of I that you have been so foolishly squandering, allowing them to steal it from you all this time, and without which they would be formless. But incomplete observation will not free you. Gradually your observation must become complete observation so that all the feeling of I is withdrawn from them. Then they vanish. You are released from possession by them.


*Amwell, 1.3.52*


## THE WORK AND THE WRONG LOVE

The Work must become a reality to you. Unless it becomes real to you, it cannot help you. You must make room for the Work. If you remain full of yourself, the Work has no place to enter. If you give up nothing, it will give you nothing. It will give you nothing, because it cannot. If you give up nothing for its sake, it will never believe you, and if it never believes you, you will never will it. If you never will the Work, you will never do the Work. You will never believe it if you never acknowledge it and you will never will it if you never believe it.

If you never believe it you will remain in your present beliefs, which are no beliefs, if they are beliefs of the senses or opinions. If you do not believe the Work it will not believe you. It will not come into you and converse with you and shew you what you might possibly do and where you might possibly go. You will never know the extraordinary pleasure of these conversations which in my case were at first external and are now internal—the pleasure of knowing that the Work is yours, not as a thing in the world that can be stolen nor as your own jealous, exclusive property, but as something permitted you. I do not collect and dwell on these thoughts whose patterns are formed by such emotions as jealousy, envy and hatred, because these come from the self-love which is exclusive. The pleasure of gratified self-love is no longer pleasure but rather has a feeling of being suffocated. It is no longer self-love that makes me seek continuance in this Work. If it were, I could not continue in it. If your aim in this Work is only from the self-love, you will come up against a barrier. How could it be otherwise? If you have no pleasant places in your heart but those of the triumphing self-love, how can you love the Work? One is one's love. You may know that already, but that does not mean that you have seen the quality of your love. How can you reach greater meaning if your greatest meaning consists in having your own way, which is what the self-love always wants and seeks? When you reach the barrier due to self-love something has to yield, you know. Something has to cry, you know. Yes—but then, after, there is release. You will not resent as you did. Instead of your heart being in self-love and so always being hurt, there will be something more delicate and lovely. Instead of the self-love leading you, you will begin to be led by the Work. You will let something in, that, perhaps, you never realized you were keeping out. You cannot get to supra-sensual thinking—that is to psychological (or spiritual) thinking —through the self-love. Sensual thinking and self-love are conjoined.

*　　*　　*

The 'I's that have helped you reach to your position in life will not necessarily help you in the Work. You cannot take this Work in your life-stride, or your career 'I's. Some life 'I's will be useful, not as leaders but taking a second place. Your life 'I's belong to the parts of centres that life has developed in you—the 'I's relating to your job. But it is other parts of you that have to become receptive. Do you think of yourself as being fairly successful in life? Then do not imagine those 'I's will make you so in the Work. The 'I's that make or made you successful in life are not adapted to grasp the meaning of the Work. They belong to the customary, to what you know, to your main street. The seeds of the Work cannot grow there. They grow only at some distance from the wayside—out in your countryside. That is why you cannot take the Work in your life-stride, which puzzles many people. That also is why the Work teaches we have to strip off clothing—layers formed by life—so as to get to what is more us. The seeds of the Work

1555

sown in the self-love are not rightly rooted. Although they may grow formatorily on the Knowledge side, it will not be so on the Being side. The Work is to open something that was shut before which helps understanding. The self-love will not yield to love. This is always so in all things and in all directions, for love is at the expense of the self-love. So a barrier is reached that I have seen many reach, and one that I reached and stayed at until I was shewn the stature of the Work and my own, and something gave way. For long I wanted to be first in the eyes of my teacher. I wanted this more than I wanted the Work. You must understand clearly what I mean here. I wanted my self-love gratified. The self-love always wants to be first somehow and it can be pretty mean. When this did not take place I sulked or raged. Do you not see that I had to be treated indifferently and the reason why? We cannot suppose the Work can ever become a reality to any of us if we put other motives, interests and loves far before it or make it serve them. We cannot then expect it to help in our distress or fear, by turning towards it as a last resort. Its messengers will not hear. Since the self-love cannot think rightly psychologically or spiritually because it admits nothing higher than itself, it will keep us chained to the sensual mind. That means that we will give the outer or lower power and not the inner or higher. It will be our own fault. We will be governed by the senses. But the higher must be established beyond all doubt, for only this reverses us and makes Personality passive so that Essence grows. For this turns us the right way up. The self-love turns everything the wrong way round so one can never grasp what the Work is or why. The literal, which is narrow, exacting, brittle, and without grace, then crucifies daily the psychological. Sense crucifies daily the spirit. The self-love remains intact.

*Amwell, 6.3.52*

## ASSOCIATIONS AND NEGATIVE 'I's

"We see a man yesterday, not to-day." I will explain what this means. We take in nothing new about him because the impression of him always falls on and stimulates the same associations in us. We are not conscious of him but of our associations with him. We do not see him apart from associations. We are not aware of him objectively but of what we subjectively associate with him. So the father sees his son as a little boy and the mother sees him as a baby-in-arms. In the same way the son sees his parents, especially his mother, as they used to be. If he discovers, say, that his mother is not as his associations of her make him think, he may be horrified. He believes, of course, that he *thinks* of his mother. He does not realize that he does not think at all, but that his thinking is nothing but a process of mechanical association, that is set working in him whenever he sees or is reminded of her. She is never an independent human being outside him, having her own separate existence; nor is he to her. To live only in other people, to feel one's existence only in this way, is a weakness that seems responsible for much human error and misery. The physical basis for associations, both desirable and undesirable, both useful and useless, is the brain. We have to struggle against some aspects of the mechanical brain.

Now some people do not see the difference between impressions and associations. An impression comes to us from outside through eye or ear chiefly. The associations are within us, recorded, the Work teaches, on rolls in centres, like wax phonograph rolls. When we see a familiar object, one or more rolls containing past records associated with that object begin to turn. This is what is meant by the opening sentence: "We see a man yesterday, not to-day." It means simply that we see him through associations belonging to the past and do not see him now in the present. So we see him yesterday and not to-day. To-day we merely recognize him, just as we merely recognize everything else. We do not see things afresh. For this reason we cannot take in anything new. We resemble those savages who, seeing a great sailing ship for the first time, took no notice of it, but stared with interest at the little boat putting in to the shore. It was something familiar, something they could take in by association with their own boats. Like ourselves they could not take in anything considerably greater than what they were accustomed to. We do not like anything unfamiliar. For example, we do not like the idea that we are mechanical or asleep, or not properly conscious, or negative, or a cageful of 'I's. We have no pre-formed associations which can take in unfamiliar and offensive ideas of this kind. So we resist them and we resent them. Only by observing ourselves and all that goes on in us in the light of such ideas can we make new recordings on centres through which we can take them in and see the actual truth of them. These recordings are different from ordinary associations. They are made consciously because internal observation of oneself has to be a conscious act. It cannot take place mechanically. Also the impressions gained from self-observation are not from the outside world through the external senses but from an internal sense given but not used, a silent witness in myself, a spectator of what goes on in me, into which I must put more and more consciousness, more and more my feeling of I, by withdrawing it (tediously, with trouble), from what it observes. A gradual concentration of consciousness and the feeling of I begins then at this point, which then becomes Observing I in a practical sense, as a practical experience. One has then started on the difficult strange journey to Real I which lies above Observing I.

I wish to call attention now to how our emotional states can affect associations in us. You have noticed that when you feel in a pleasant state you tend to have pleasant associations with a person and smile and beam at him or her: and when you are in an unpleasant state you get connected up with unpleasant associations. In short, the emotional state alters the arrangement of things. But a powerful negative 'I' can not merely alter you but damage you. The ordinary swing-of-the-pendulum emotions, pleasant to unpleasant and back, do not seem to me like negative emotions, which stick often for a long time. Their characteristic, in fact, is that they *persist* and run on by themselves. Now negative states can be thought of as the opposite of anything that could be called positive art, which craves to transmit meaning from a higher level and so seeks what is from good and what is from truth, and cannot see only the worst in everything. To use a phrase, they transgress the limits of the probable and always in the wrong direction, making for greater falsity, ugliness, distortion, and lying, often beyond belief and remedy. A negative state only makes what is negative *more* negative and cannot do otherwise. Because it is basically evil in intention, leading down from hatred to violence, cruelty and murder, it can only transform evilly. Any negative state works on the associations recorded on rolls in centres so as to distort them, if it is not checked grimly. It endeavours to black out anything good recorded in them and to floodlight anything bad. Every negative emotion is therefore the opposite of any positive art, which is to transgress *within* the limits of the probable and always in the direction of greater perfection and greater meaning. The tremendous power and the number of negative 'I's that seek to do us harm by distorting associations and lying must never be treated lightly. You will have to meet them—eventually, when your Armageddon comes, if it does. They truly are *Legion*, as they defined themselves when Christ asked their name. He said to the evil spirit that was in the man dwelling among the tombs: "Come out of the man, thou unclean spirit."

"And he asked him, What is thy name? And he answered, saying, My name is Legion, for we are many." (Mark v., 8.9)

Yes, our negative 'I's are many and the sensual mind is their home, for it is like a tomb to the inner spiritual man. Now negative emotions harm us by many other methods also, as by darkening everything like the octopus ejecting ink. And like the octopus or the many headed Hydra of Mythology, they seize hold of you now on this side, now on the other, having many arms, fastening on every weak thing in your psychological make-up that you have not worked on or have not brought into the light of consciousness. When you hear the Work saying that it is not sex or power that governs the world but negative emotions, perhaps you do not take this seriously. And possibly even when you are in a negative state, you do not see what is meant. This is partly because you do not see quite that you are in a negative state. You see the state you are in as a reasonable state (under the circumstances) and so not negative. Here lies a difficulty, similar to the difficulty of seeing 'I's in oneself and one which we will equally resent. To feel you are right when you are negative, as one does in life, is to strengthen the state. In the Work, however, it is necessary to see that one is wrong. Remember that we put ourselves under more laws in the Work at first. Release comes later.

*Amwell, 15.3.52*

**MI 12**

If we could act consciously in every situation we would not internally consider. Internal considering sends us to sleep more than anything. It wastes energy. If we could externally consider only it would save energy. If we could act consciously in every situation we would create energy. To act consciously would mean to act without identifying. Identification leads to unconscious action. To act consciously in every situation would be to act without identification. To act without identification is one way to give oneself the First Conscious Shock. To give oneself the First Conscious Shock is to *create* energy. Two new energies are thereby formed in the human machine—the energy 24 at the early potential stage denoted by Re, and energy 12 at the note Mi. These two newly created energies appearing in the machine, by reason of the First Conscious Shock being given, strongly affect the working of the Emotional and Sex Centres respectively. The energies Fa 24 and Sol 12 are also created. You will notice that their octave position is not so potential as Re 24 and Mi 12, but they also influence the Emotional and Sex Centres, altering the quality of their working. The hydrogen Si 12, produced by the mechanical shock of breathing, by its position in the octave has the least potentiality for development—that is, for differentiation. It is old, so to speak, and more fixed. It has the least youth. The creation of these new energies, not present in mechanical and sensual-minded man, has to do with the ultimate transformation of the Sex Centre into the Higher Emotional Centre, and its very gradual withdrawing from the Instinctive Centre, the identifying, and the negative states and self emotions that characterize the working of Emotional Centre. All the three energies 12 can become Hydrogen 6 under the pulsations of the Second Conscious Shock which makes contact with the Higher Centre gradually possible. But for the Second Conscious Shock to begin to act in you Mi 12 must be present in sufficient amounts and retained at the wanted times. Here we miss much by sleep and habit. I mean we are not watching, not sensitive internally. There is a turning wheel of opportunities and some opportunity is not noticed when we are being helped. None of these conditions, of course, will be fulfilled if a person is chronically negative and identified or will not see insincerity—a bad fault—or follows appetite and self only and does not, in short, work. In that case, none

1559

of the special energy Mi 12 will be created; and the Work will not help. He will see nothing extraordinary in life; he will have no vision of the Work; he will not transform any impressions and will continue in the odours of the sensual mind and its dead works. *It is quite useless asking me questions about the Second Conscious Shock.* I say to you only that it is impossible to understand anything about it until Mi 12 is present and stored enough in you. In brief, you must give yourself the First Conscious Shock before you can get to know the nature of the Second Conscious Shock, and get to know what it is and all about it in its many aspects, and so create Mi 12, and prevent it falling downwards to the sensual level, until it shews you the direction of the Second Conscious Shock. For, like Joseph, it can interpret Pharaoh's dreams. Now to remember yourself in endlessly different situations is good. Also to act more consciously, which can only begin with noticing mechanical reactions after they have taken place and remembering them and then acting differently, is very good work indeed. As was said, that would be giving or seeking to give oneself the First Conscious Shock. I have watched it being done. But people stay in their dreary outworn psychological clothes—in their old reactions—and cling to them. To remember oneself is surely not to remember these garments? By doing that I fancy not a trace of the presence of Mi 12 will ever be found in you. That lovely youth will avoid you—like poison.

So we have to think about the First Conscious Shock and its primary importance in the Work, for without Mi 12 there is little change of being. I have said I speak only of the First Conscious Shock. In this connection I will add that people here must not be satisfied to remain as they are. There is far too much self-complacency or indifference. Consider carefully, if you are not, at bottom, satisfied with yourself as you are, and only would like another car. It is not necessary to point out that if you are satisfied any attempt at Self-Remembering that you make will go to make you still more satisfied with yourself as you are. The adoration of this mess called oneself is the commonest and most binding and limited religion. It is accompanied by often very funny rites. But it is inadvisable to make fun here. We explode, we flush, we pale, we are furious, and we never forgive. What a state we are all in without exception! Yet even so, it is possible to work, and to work afresh and often at the First Conscious Shock: and to discover it *for ourselves*, as we are at our particular stage. Our very violence indeed provides us with material for Self-Remembering. We surely cannot remain satisfied with ourselves after slowly perceiving these unstable foundations of our ramshackle being, which the least person in the Kingdom of Heaven could cause to blow up with a trifling remark. Yes, we sorely need to be born anew; and not of blood and flesh this time, but of Water and Spirit. That would mean another and quite new foundation: and so a New Man. The Work is all about this step.

## ON HAVING NO MIDDLE

Everyone, after a certain time, needs to begin to work on the pendulum in himself. A pendulum swings to and fro, from one extreme to the other. In the case of the emotions, there is the swing between, say, enthusiasm and its opposite. One is all for, and a little later all against, someone. You feel that at last you have met the friend you have been looking for all your life, a person who really understands your difficult circumstances and how you have suffered; and in a short time—perhaps only a week or so—you feel you have made a great mistake and you may add another look of resignation to your face. Now the pendulum is the great thief within. I only remind you that you have to find some method of managing it; or else it will take away anything it gives. It is uncomfortable to see a person totally asleep or unguarded, temporarily at one end of the pendulum, full of excitement, terribly happy, looking forward to a new life and so on. In this state the person is wholly identified with one end of the swing of the emotional pendulum. There is no sign of Self-Remembering. Notice this point. A few days later the pendulum has swung to the opposite side. The person is now dejected and miserable, bitterly disappointed, everything seems to have gone wrong and there is nothing to look forward to. The person is again wholly identified with one end of the swing of the emotional pendulum. Notice that there is again no sign of Self-Remembering. You will see in what sense the pendulum is a great thief. Also you will realize something of what was meant when it was said that we must work on the swing of the pendulum in ourselves and find some way or ways of managing it a little, after we have been connected with the Work for some time. Otherwise whatever you get will tend to be taken away and you will stick. At one time you will be for the Work; at another time against it; and so the swing of the pendulum will go on, with you its victim clinging fast to it, not seeing that you need not. Now as many of you must have often heard before, it is necessary to draw force from both the opposites—that is, from both ends of the pendulum. You will find by practice that it is not enough, or indeed possible, to draw force from *one* opposite. The two opposites are connected like the two sides of a penny and when in one you must remember the other. If you let yourself identify mechanically with each of the two opposites in turn—that is, with one side and then the other side of the emotional pendulum, wholly believing each with your whole feeling of 'I'—you will remain helplessly on the pendulum, swinging to and fro from excitement to depression, from depression to excitement. Emotionally you will be mechanical. You will not be living consciously in relation to your Emotional Centre but living mechanically and becoming every mood it presents. It is important to see this. People remain blind to it. They simply are their states and cannot separate. But if you are learning to draw force both from the excited side and the depressed side by remembering yourself in each and remembering its opposite and to some extent practise this in daily and in weekly life, you are *beginning* to live a little consciously. You must form a weekly memory as well as a daily one. Only you must not shew what you are up to, as by sitting motionless or staring heavily at nothing, no doubt with a beautiful picture of yourself being so steady, or hoping people will notice how calm you are. Anything like that ruins one's personal work on oneself, as I have often witnessed. The reason is that it strengthens False Personality—the very thing that has to be loosened and stripped away, garment by garment, before anything real can be uncovered on which the Work can truly found itself. You will have noticed how the 'I's composing False Personality demand an audience and how it tempts you to shew off, or to shew off by not shewing off. Very small children seem to me to be able to play in a silent absorption without an audience, but adults praise them and tell them they are clever so that essential phase is soon over. We can understand then that such an important form of personal work as drawing force from the opposites through Self-Remembering and remembering is to be approached with internal understanding and done in silence. Here indeed the significance of not letting the left hand know what the right is doing comes in. The external side of a man—turned towards life—the outer man composed of little 'I's, teeming and talking, in the small parts of centres—cannot possibly draw force from both ends of the pendulum swing. These 'I's swing with it. They have no anchor that holds. It is only Observing I that does not swing with the pendulum; and that has to be strengthened. I explained elsewhere that this means that one's relationship to the Observing I must be strengthened for it is not anchored to the waves. In short, one must practise, and daily at least, the exercise of observing oneself impartially without the soapy foam of self-justifying. As we are talking of the emotional pendulum, and taking it as one pendulum for the sake of simplification, it must now be pointed out that the observation of one's emotional state must not be limited to the emotional state of the moment. Mr Ouspensky used to emphasize that the whole swing of the pendulum must be observed from one state to its opposite and one of his customary replies to examples given at groups in this connection was simply "Incomplete observation". People did not grasp sufficiently that you cannot have one emotion without its opposite, which is often a curious one. I speak of the sphere of mechanical emotions, which is under the law of the pendulum—and this law operates in all things temporal, in the events of life as well as in ourselves. I remind you again of the phrase in Ecclesiasticus: "All things are double, one against another,"—that is, in sequence in Time. So you cannot have joy without sorrow—which I doubt as being opposites —any more than you can have positive electricity without negative, or a magnet without opposite poles, or a stick with only one end.

But in self-study by means of self-observation we find it very difficult to observe that any particular emotional state is connected with its opposite, or what its opposite is. A particular emotional state appears to be a thing in itself that has nothing to do with any other state. Now the inability to realize that it has, is one factor in rendering us so peculiarly helpless in face of our emotional life and so much under its sway. We are unconscious just where the pendulum, in its return journey, gains momentum, and, passing the mid-point, swings into the sphere of influence of the opposite emotional state—apparently, indeed, into another country. We fail to see any connection. There is, in fact, no logical connection. The two countries seem totally dissimilar. That is exactly why the Work tells us that we have to observe the whole swing from one extreme to the other in order to discover our particular opposites. This means an *increase in consciousness* of which we have often spoken before. An increase in consciousness in regard to our emotional life through the making of the opposites conscious by following the swing in Time, and so seeing how they are connected, shifts consciousness gradually towards the middle zone of the pendulum, to a third place lying between the opposites which becomes receptive of new emotions not on the pendulum. We acquire a middle. Let me add one thing. If you can observe the pendulum through a full swing you will be sometimes astonished at what the opposite of any particular state turns out to be and so realize why you could not get released.

*Amwell, 29.3.52*

## FIRST CONSCIOUS SHOCK

### SELF-REMEMBERING AND THE SENSUAL MIND

Essence comes down from above and clothes itself in a body which it builds out of materials obtained from both parents and limited to them. Through the body Essence gets in contact with the world. The body bears in it what is hereditary from the parents. The body itself is in three dimensions. What is hereditary is in the fourth dimension: that is, in time, in the line of ancestors. The Essence, though intimately connected with the body, is not the same as the body. The body perishes, but the Essence does not. When, through one of the many fallacies of the sensual mind, we take ourselves as our bodies, we get a wrong impression of ourselves. One result of this is that we cannot remember ourselves. This is because we take the visible body as ourself and cannot get any other idea of ourself but a sensual one, because for the sensual mind only what can be apprehended by the external senses exists. For it, therefore, the death of the body is the end of the man and anything said to the contrary is rubbish. I once idly began to make a collection of the epithets typically used by sensual folk. Rubbish, fairy-stories, poppy-cock, bunkum, drivel, sheer rot, absolute balderdash, damned phantasies, childish nonsense, and so on. Of course, the idea of Essence is non-sense. One cannot see it. One can never see what orders things. Now the sensual mind in us is not able to admit that the three-dimensional natural world definitely depends on and is ordered from a supernatural one in other dimensions. Nor can it grasp that Essence enters and leaves by a dimension not accessible to our very limited senses. But the mind that can think psychologically can grasp this. It also enables us to remember ourselves. I have pointed out to you often that the Lord's Prayer begins with Self-Remembering—for any prayer that does not is fraudulent and a pious waste of time. It says: "Our Father which art in Heaven." It ignores completely the father who provided half the building material for our bodies. It is speaking of Essence, which has no father here. Now when we begin to see all this with our internal understanding, we are beginning to remember ourselves. The sensual mind, based solely on the evidence of the senses, on being told of such matters will deny them and cannot do otherwise. Actually such things should not be told them, save in parables or in the rather indirect way that the Work uses. Here the following words can be quoted: "I speak in parables, because seeing they see not and hearing they hear not, neither do they understand." And another phrase, used elsewhere but again referring to the sensual-minded: "The world cannot receive the Spirit of Truth because it seeks not and knoweth not Him." We can realize then how necessary it is to develop psychological thinking, that passes beyond sense, so as to grasp that we have two sources of origin or two fathers, one connected with the body and the other with the Essence, which the sensual neither seeks nor knows. This makes Self-Remembering possible.

Now a man cannot change, cannot undergo psycho-transformism, unless his mind changes, and his mind cannot change unless the Universe changes for him, and unless his feeling of I changes. Register this carefully and reflect. To have the same thoughts and the same views of the world and the same feeling of I as you always had means that you are just the same as you always were and if you think otherwise you are deceiving yourself. This we all love to do. Change definitely means change; and in this case change means to change *yourself*—in every direction. If *you* change, the *Universe* will change and your feeling of I will change. Now if you think from the ideas that the Work teaches you, you begin to think differently, and that is the starting point of everything else. This Work is to teach you *to think in a new way*, both about what you are and about what the world is. How many hear that; but do not hear. Mr O. was told in his experiments on changing the feeling of I temporarily and artificially—after he had passed through the zone inhabited by confidence-tricksters, that is, by 'I's that lied to him and tried to entice and fool him, as they do so many—that he must "think in other categories". This means to think in a new way. He was shewn, for example, that he could no longer think of himself as he always had.

Another category was necessary. You may remember that when, under the influence of the drug, he had passed what he called the second threshold, he had the feeling that he had come in contact with another person who was himself. He says: "I came in contact with *myself*, with the self that was always with me, and always told me something that I could not understand and could not even hear in ordinary states of consciousness. Why? Because in the ordinary state thousands of voices at once are creating what we call our consciousness, our thoughts, our feelings, our moods, our imagination. These voices drown the sound of that inner voice." He adds that only when the clamour of these 'I's is stilled by some means can that other voice be heard. In my case this will be *myself*, not Nicoll. Now the sensual mind in ourselves is very powerful. It often masters us for days. It says: "I am Nicoll." For it, there can be no other self but the bodily self and the visible brain. There can be no self connected with Essence, distinct in origin from the bodily self. The piano and the pianist are the same. To think otherwise would be to think in a non-sensual category about oneself. Yet I know by experience that there is in me another person more essential and real than Nicoll. This person, which is *myself*, does not speak my language. For that reason I find it necessary to try to study his language, which is not a national one and which sometimes is expressed merely by changing feelings, delicate and coloured, like flowers (on which Nicoll treads with hobnails), and sometimes by things and people seen, as in a play, and sometimes by sudden meanings, without words, that connect things together. What this person, who is *myself*, communicates to me seems never to be put in clear simple unmistakable terms of *yes* or *no*, but presented in a high form of paradox very irritating to the sensual practical mind.

*Amwell, 3.4.52*

## AN EXERCISE IN THINKING ABOUT THE PENDULUM

Through the action of the Law of the Pendulum the violence that a man does to others returns on himself. History abundantly illustrates this. The saying, therefore, that "we should do unto others as we would that they should do unto us" is connected with one aspect of freeing oneself from this law to which mechanical Man is subject. One-sided behaviour, characteristic of mechanical Man, puts him under the Law of the Pendulum. It will excite the opposite in the sense of "what I do will be done to me". This must be the meaning of the saying that those who live by the sword shall perish by the sword. Now we are not to limit the action of the Law of the Pendulum to a single life. Mr O. told some of us that, when asked about Recurrence, G. had replied: "It is something like this: the executed becomes the executioner; the execuioner becomes the executed." In short, the situation is reversed. Passive becomes active and active becomes passive. The situation is turned the other way round. Now mentally it is possible to turn things the other way round, only most people obstinately refuse to do so. In this respect we are taught, as an exercise to increase consciousness, to try sometimes to take consciously the opposite view to the one we mechanically take. This is *including* the opposite, but not *rejecting* the other viewpoint. It is bringing the opposites together towards a middle, by including both sides in consciousness. It is not a conversion into the contrary but a recognition of it. It is a very useful exercise if from time to time one really does it. It widens the range of the mind. As an exercise it is related to the practice of External Considering. Among many other blessings, to be increasingly conscious of both sides of the Pendulum decreases violence. For example, one can be plagued by a sudden attack of violent thinking and feeling. When this occurs one is obviously identified with an extreme position of the Pendulum. What, then, is the opposite that one must summon into the consciousness to balance matters if one wishes to work on this unpleasant state? To call up the conventional opposite—that is, to picture oneself filled with gentleness and tolerance, as one remembers one was, say, yesterday, is not likely to prove the *effective* opposite that will give release. The effort may simply aggravate the state. Where is the effective opposite to be found? The answer is that it will be found in what you do not include in your feeling of yourself. In a recent paper on the Pendulum it was remarked that the opposite is often curious and not at all what one would suppose. For according to the common use of words one would expect a violent man to be in some sense the opposite of a man who is gentle. In the above example—taking myself as the victim of a sudden attack of violence— I find gentleness is not the effective opposite. If it were it should neutralize the violence through my Work-memory of gentle states in myself— that is, through my consciously remembering gentler states that I have observed and connected with the memory of Observing I. But I am supposing that this has had no result and that I realize I am in danger of descending into some really negative state or other from which I have learned to pray to be delivered. Now, my effort to save myself by making myself conscious in the opposite could not have any result because in this case the opposite is not gentleness, but *something that I am not conscious of* and so do not include in my estimation of myself. Therefore it is only when I behold in myself what has roused my violence in another person that the storm vanishes—as by magic. The opposites here are between what I am conscious of in *another* and what I am conscious of in *myself*. (If these two factors in two people were equal, they would cancel each other out, and the two people would be at peace with one another. But each would have to *include* far more in their own consciousness of themselves to reach this degree of conscious relationship to one another.) The opposites that I am dealing with here are therefore the great ones of Light and Darkness. For what I am conscious of is in the Light, and what I am unconscious of is in the Darkness, and these two are mighty powers at variance with one another.

Throughout ancient history you find myths about this struggle between Light and Darkness, of the hero as Light contending with the Dragon of Darkness or being temporarily swallowed by the monster and cutting his way out, and so on. The Work teaches that we are not properly conscious. It indicates that the supreme aim is to increase consciousness. As we are, we belong to "the people who live in darkness and shun the light". We will not face ourselves. We refuse to see. We change the subject or justify ourselves. Now what lies in your own darkness has a strange power over you. It keeps on influencing you and however you seem to resist, it overpowers you. At intervals its secret will paralyses the conscious will. Only the hero, consciousness, can contend with its dragon-power. The hero lives, to begin with, in that camera by which we can observe ourselves and thereby begin to widen and so increase our consciousness of ourselves. One is actually taught that to observe oneself is to let a ray of light into one's inner darkness—that is, into what one is unconscious of and so what one does not include in the customary feeling of oneself. Oh! this accursed artificial thing "oneself" —this over-sensitive bundle—this silly excerpt that causes so much trouble and which possesses us without our seeing it! Now the more one's consciousness widens, the more it includes, and the fewer will be the opposites and so the less will one's spiritual existence be at the mercy of swinging pendulums. This "oneself" is notably exclusive. It is extraordinarily exclusive. It will not include the "other side" of the penny in consciousness. Certainly, one should hate this oneself, which is a lie. The self-love runs into it. But the self-love should have a far better goal, for this "oneself", that gives rise to so many unnecessary opposites in us by its stubborn refusal to include anything more than it does in the consciousness, is not the Self that we ultimately come into when consciousness is widened sufficiently and the boundaries of the silly little oneself are swept away.

In conclusion I will try to make this exercise in thinking easier and will put the matter a little differently. The antithesis really seems to be between: "He is a fool"—"I am not a fool." I fabricate this pair of opposites so that the more I conceive myself as not being a fool, the more my violence is kept going against him for being so great a fool. Now the root of the matter is my feeling of superiority. To try to bring up gentleness or a vision of non-violence will not therefore neutralize my attack of violence. If I become conscious that the fool I behold in him is also in me the antithesis becomes; "He is a fool"—"I am also a fool". These are not opposites, so that the antithesis vanishes.

## THE CONNECTION OF ESSENCE WITH ESOTERICISM

In the Work it is necessary to think in a new way. It is repeatedly said that this Work is to make us think in a new way. If we do not do so, nothing happens. We remain dead to the action of the Work, for if we do not think the Work, it cannot think in us. To begin to think the Work is to begin to think in a new way. It is therefore necessary to begin to think for ourselves about some of the things that the Work teaches. This means that one must start thinking quietly and internally about, say, one or two of the ideas that belong to this system of teaching and follow a train of thought about them and make connections between them tentatively. People are so busy that very few do this. They are so much in external things. To listen is one thing: to think another. One is external, the other internal. Now the Work is made up of many different ideas, some of greater and some of less density of meaning. If one thinks about them, they open out their meaning to the mind. Meaning comes by thinking. These ideas, all of different colours, are blended together to form a single internal light as are the colours of the visible spectrum to form white light. To change the image, the Work can be thought of as something organized from many different parts as is the body to form an organic whole or unity. The Work is a unity. Actually it is a living whole, but it only becomes a living whole when it is taken in by the mind with some degree of grace and gradually connected up rightly by thought and memory and by hearing it taught time after time. Then it becomes a living whole, a light *in you*. Otherwise it remains something outside you, on the blackboard, and soon becomes jargon. It remains dead as far as you are concerned, for making contact with the Work is an internal matter. Now if it is muddled up and wrongly connected or if only random bits of it are taken in, it cannot do its work in you, save feebly, just as a radio cannot transmit vibrations clearly from a source not visible to sense, if parts of it are missing or wrongly connected, or the batteries exhaust themselves by various short-circuits as in our case negative emotions do, amongst other things. The matter, then, is as simple as that. The Work is a mental instrument to connect the human race with Higher Centres. It can be fitted into the mind and if rightly connected up can transform thinking by changing the powers of reception. Two sanctions, however, are required for this to happen. The first is that a man must be willing to take it in, otherwise it will not be able to enter him. If his mind is shut to everything save the cares and interests of external life, however hard the Work knocks at his door, it will not be permitted to enter. The man has freedom of *choice* here. In the second, if the Work has been permitted entry, then, after a time, which varies greatly in different people, the man must begin *to will to do it*. He must begin to *do* its truth. The man has freedom of choice here. These two choices depend on a man's inner sanctioning. Now all true esoteric teaching exists because man is asleep and can awaken. That is why the Gospels exist. That is why this Work, which is a re-formulation and called sometimes Esoteric Christianity, exists. But a man cannot be persuaded or dazzled by miracles or compelled by force to awaken. He himself can only awaken himself. And this he can only do if he gives the two sanctions mentioned —not externally but internally; not from the outer man but from the inner man; not from the surface man, the man of False Personality and the imitation-man, the man of appearances, but from the essential, hidden man. Otherwise the Work will only increase the action of Personality and render Essence more remote and passive than ever. Only the simplest and, as it were, most innocent, unsophisticated and real side of a man can receive esoteric teaching aright and this is what is meant by "Whosoever shall not receive the Kingdom of God as a little child shall in no wise enter therein" (Luke xviii.17). By the little child is meant Essence. Esoteric teaching must reach Essence. Esoteric teaching is always about the "Kingdom of God". It is always about inner development possible to Man—namely, the growth of Essence. And Essence cannot grow unless it is fertilized by the "Word of God". If you still expect some marvellous mystical experience, and that is the reason you attend the Work talks, you are working from the wrong love, and you will only neglect what your real work should be in preparing lower centres, and flatter your False Personality.

When the Work penetrates through layer after layer of the acquired Personality to the inborn Essence, the Essence begins to become active. The "spermatic word" of esotericism impregnates it and it begins to grow and develop. Essence in us is like the germinal spot in an egg. Personality is comparable to the yolk and the white. If the egg is fertilized the germinal spot grows and eats up the yolk and the white and a living creature results. But if it is not fertilized it remains an egg. So is the case with Man. Now let us think "in a new way" as we said according to what the Work teaches. What has just been spoken of can form a starting point of thinking from one or two of the ideas of the Work. We are told that Man is an undeveloped organism composed of born Essence and acquired Personality and that Essence is passive and Personality is active and that it is *life* as a neutralizing force that keeps this relationship going. We are told that if the Work becomes Neutralizing Force the position is reversed—namely, Essence becomes gradually active and personality gradually passive. If you think for yourself, you will see that this means that a man will live and die unfulfilled, like an unfulfilled egg, *as long as life only acts on him*, for his Essence is the germinal spot in him, and only esotericism can stir it into activity and growth. We have already spoken of the man who takes in and eventually wills and does the Work, through his own choice. In such a man the Work has now begun to become the Neutralizing Force and the relation between Essence and Personality has begun to become reversed. If you think for yourself from this Work-idea that has such a great density of meaning that I find it inexhaustible, you will be thinking in a new way. Your mind will begin to move, hesitatingly at first, along new paths, and you will see many things that you could not see before, when your mind only moved narrowly along its old habitual grooves. It is very good and very refreshing for the mind to think in a new way. It is like stepping off a noisy high road and wandering into the countryside. If your thinking is very conventional, you may feel quite awkward at first and perhaps even guilty. But after a time, you may meet a small child. Curiously enough, the child may seem to know you.

*Amwell, 19.4.52*

## SHOES IN THE WORK

### Part I

Each of you has a different life-memory, but you will find that your Work-memories become much the same. Our experiences in life are various, but our experiences in this Work are very similar. We can realize that directions in life are many; but this Work points in one direction. It is just because it points in one direction that Work-experiences tend to be similar, and thus Work-memories become more or less similar. Let us reflect on this for a moment. In life we are not taught we are asleep. We take it for granted that we are awake and fully conscious, and that we act consciously. In the Work we hear of a quite new and startling idea. We are, in fact, told a mystery. We are taught that we are asleep and do not know it. We are not properly conscious. We act mechanically. In the light of this mystery our life-memories are the memories of sleeping persons, of people wandering in the dark, of sleep-walkers. But when we begin to follow, and later obey, the Work, our memories become those of people beginning to awaken. Another memory is formed—a Work-memory. These Work-memories are not like our very different life-memories. They are similar simply because the successive stages of awakening are similar, like inns stationed along a common road—a road which leads eventually to an uncommon sea. This is the reason why we find in writers of all ages records of similar experiences. But when what I have called the uncommon sea is reached and embarked upon, a man disappears from human range. If he has left any records behind him, they are only about the journey as far as the shore. But once he embarks—if he does—nothing after is or can be recorded.

Now let us suppose he leaves some record, in his own language and symbolism, concerning the journey to the sea. For example, he might leave instructions saying it was necessary, first of all, to find a shop where real leather can be bought, out of which he must then devise shoes with which to walk on this journey, and that he must never let any mud on them touch his eyes, for it will endanger his sight; and also he must procure a musical instrument on which he must patiently learn to make and invent various harmonies and often play them, in different ways, and never forget them, especially when he is tired.

Now let us leave any discussion of the significance of each of these instructions for the moment in order to recall that in connection with the successive stages of awakening, the Work teaches that we are in prison, and that as long as we remain asleep we remain in prison. It says that there are some who have found the way out and left behind instructions in code for others who desire to follow them. This idea is not peculiar to the Work. It is a very ancient image of Man's situation on Earth. Now people do not see that they are in prison, just as they do not see that they are asleep. So they do not know that they have a prison-psychology and are sleep-walkers, though later they may come to see it. People may attend talks about the Work year in and year out and never realize the living truth of either of these two statements, partly because they do not observe themselves, and partly because they take them sensually. They see the discomforts of their lives, the lack of money, the shortcomings of others, and so on, but do not realize that the Work means that all people, high and low, whatever they possess and whoever they may be, are in prison and are asleep, and that this is why life goes as it does, like a tale told by an idiot. Not seeing any literal walls, or hearing snores, the very sensual-minded think the ideas are far-fetched. They cannot see their psychological meaning. They go on in their habitual ways, being upset and worried and negative and following illusory schemes and ambitions and worshipping endless varieties of false values, never seeing that these things form their prison walls and that certain 'I's are their gaolers. The sense-based mind blinds them and, as usual, sensual meaning crucifies psychological meaning. So they assert they are not asleep nor in prison. Nevertheless everyone is.

Let us now take the shoes mentioned in the instructions left by the man who reached the sea actually, and not in a dream. (If the image of a man getting out of prison had been used, the language or symbolism would have been different but the meaning the same.) First, what are the shoes? Of course, literal shoes are not meant, or literal leather. Psychological shoes are meant; not to be borne on the literal feet, but the feet of the psychological man. The psychological feet are where the psychological man touches life. In this Work we have to walk in life differently from the way we once walked. We are taught how to use the daily events of life as the means of work on oneself. For instance, we are told not to identify. Now it is obvious that a man practising non-identifying is walking through life in a different way from a man who is mechanically identified with everything. This can be expressed by using the sense-image of a man walking in self-made shoes of special leather. Like all parables, this will not appeal to the sensual mind. But the meaning is not sensual but psychological, and it is just here that the wholly sensual person fails to jump up to the psychological meaning. Now we are told that we gradually have to insulate ourselves more and more from the influences of life—otherwise we continually lose force. To awaken we must conserve force. We must always be working on one centre or on another or on another. A man without force cannot awaken. Life can completely exhaust us daily if we do not walk more consciously through it. In this connection, in addition to holding oneself away from the powerful attraction of states of being identified and not letting things constantly reach the blood, the Work teaches self-observation (which leads to increasing knowledge of our being) diminishing and stopping internal considering and finally, Self-Remembering, which is above all the rest. All these help to insulate us. If we *do* these things we walk through life in new shoes—in Work-shoes, not life-shoes. I repeat, *if* we do them. The first requisite then is to find where the right leather is sold. The second requisite is to make *for oneself* shoes of this leather and begin to walk in life wearing them—not an easy job. Try to grasp what these shoes mean. What I may term a code-word is being used here. Grasp that nothing literal is meant. Abstract from the sense-meaning. If this is never done, one will stick in the Work. Psychological thinking is necessary for this Work—as O. saw. If it is kept at the level of the sensual mind it cannot become alive in you. Both the Old and the New Testaments shout this aloud. When it is said, for example, that the horses of Egypt are flesh, not spirit, even if we are told that "horse" is a code-word for the intellect, we do not quite see what is meant.

Next time we will discuss the remaining instructions.


*Amwell, 26.4.52*

## SHOES IN THE WORK

### PART II: MUD IN THE EYE

Being by the bias of our senses sensually-minded, we accept the idea of the psychological man with the greatest difficulty. But the organized psychological man is a possibility as well as the given organized physical man, but quite distinct from it. We can admit that what a man is psychologically is distinct from what a man is physically, and that in this Work it is necessary to look at the psychological man or the psychological woman, even though there may be little enough to look at save a set of habits, conventions, clichés, and gramophone records. But when I speak of the psychological man I mean a person *organized* psychologically. Everyone has some kind of psychology but not an organized one. Now the organization of the physical man or woman is given free. Men and women are presented with their bodies, with their rather different and complex machineries, and their 15,000,000,000 brain cells and all the rest ready-made. At first they are open to the senses and so the sensual level begins to be formed. This sensual level as it were forms the feet or basis of the subsequent mind. It is made of psychological matters, distinct from the matters of the physical body, but unorganized. It is formed where the dawning of consciousness touches the strange, foreign, never grasped thing called the external world and is filled with the emotion of wonder. As the sensual mind grows, it relates the person more and more to external life. The child learns to get about, take things more and more for granted, and gives up wondering. In this manner the eventual thinking tends to become based mostly on the senses and, stripped of wonder, the seen world becomes the real, commonplace world. The sensual-minded man results—the man influenced by life-influences, by the evidence of the senses, by *A* influences, who has no window opening on to *B* influences. Having sensual thinking and no psychological thinking he is not balanced. He can never become No. 4 Man. He is unbalanced. Physically he is a man. Psychologically he is not a man. This is the man-machine the Work speaks of who has no real psychology. How, asked G., can a machine have a psychology?

A balanced man, in the Work-sense, must have both sensual and psychological thinking. Also he must try to perfect both as far as is possible to him. Throughout his life he must move in both these directions. Unless he does he will become one-sided in either one way or the other way. Put briefly, one relates him to the world, the other to Higher Centres. What we now have to understand is that sensual thinking does not and cannot relate us to Higher Centres or lead to the organization of the psychological man. We cannot remember ourselves aright if we have only sensual thinking and so cannot transform impressions by seeing things differently in another light than sunlight. Nor can we have any other aim than a life-aim, such as power, possessions, adoration, fame, and so on. Notice, in passing, that in the first recorded temptation of Christ, power and possessions are mentioned. Life and life-aims are personified as the *devil*, who says after shewing Him all the kingdoms of the world in a moment of time:

> "All this power will I give thee, and the glory of them: for that is delivered unto me; and to whomsoever I will, I give it. If thou wilt therefore worship me, all shall be thine." (Luke iv. 6,7)

This Work is to teach us psychological thinking, and Work-aims, and eventually, if lived, to organize the psychological man in us whom life does not organize. When we begin to assimilate some of the ideas of the Work and think from them about life we begin to transform the meaning of life by seeing it through the mental eyesight of Greater Mind instead of the sight of our sensual mind. We have to *imitate* the thinking of Conscious Man.

Last time we spoke of the necessity of making shoes for ourselves out of the special leather this Work sells. For example, if we are shod with the idea of inner separating from identifying, we will begin to walk through the day's events in a psychological way and not sensually only. The ideas of self-observation, non-identifying, non-considering, and so on, belong to psychological, not sensual, thinking. They are additions to and different from sense-thinking and put us on another level. But we are also beginning to form the basis or feet of the psychological man in ourselves. To do nothing towards insulating ourselves from mechanical reactions to life, to react to every object of the senses, and every situation, makes the organization of the second man—the man not given to us ready-made—that is, the psychological man—impossible. The sensual man will win every time. Psychological shoes must be made to protect us from life. The Work-ideas and teaching form the leather one must buy. The thinking and the living of them form the shoes. This can only be done by *you*. I cannot make your shoes. I can sell you leather. But to some extent I can tell you if you are making shoes wrongly, stitching them stupidly, or if you have not yet attempted to make any shoes at all, not having taken anything in even after years. Now since sensual thinking and psychological thinking are on different levels, one must not mix them. This is what that instruction meant, given in the previous paper, that we must not let any mud on our shoes touch our eyes. Realize, please, that the sensual mind is at enmity with the psychological mind. Life seen materially seeks to injure and destroy life seen spiritually. So later we become tempted by the evidence of things seen, by the obvious, in short, by life only, which seeks to hold us imprisoned in the sensual mind. We then begin to know what effort really means and where it lies.

That the senses will always war against the spirit is indicated in the allegory given in Genesis. It is said that God cursed the serpent after he had beguiled the Woman and said:

> "I will put enmity between thee and the woman, and between thy seed and her seed; it shall bruise thy head, and thou shalt bruise his heel." (Genesis iii.15)

The serpent doomed to crawl on his belly symbolizes the sensual mind separated now from all else. It bites the heel or lowest level of the psychological man and he bruises its head, the intellect based only on the senses. Now when I gradually develop my psychological thinking through the ideas of the Work, I see life in a manner quite different from what my sensual thinking led me to suppose. I see life as a thing *to work on*. I see it as a means to an end I had never realized. I no longer see it as an end in itself. The question, then, at any particular time, is: "Can I take this or that experience without being overwhelmed, totally identified, even broken? Or can I take it as work? Is the psychological man in me yet strong enough?" He will become so if you hold on to the rope, for then he will be given strength. But this needs effort and again effort. Only in this light, shed by the Work, can everything have present or future meaning for you; and all that happens to you will be the shock you need just then, and you will see this on looking back years later. What we cannot see with the sensual mind is that if we work, then something begins to work continually and closely on us, and often very drastically, for the issue is a great one and nothing trivial to be treated as of little account.

*Amwell, 3.5.52*

## PSYCHOLOGICAL THINKING
## AND THE KINGDOM OF HEAVEN

Contemplating the idea of psychological thinking as distinct from sensual thinking, we can see that the interpretations of the senses must not smear as with mud the understanding of what is not a matter of the senses. For example, we do not see God. His existence is not evident to any of our outer senses. I cannot see Him with my eyesight or hear Him with my ears or touch Him with my hand. Since God is not an object of the senses, my sensual mind will deny His existence, because sensual thinking is based on the evidence of the senses and none of my senses shews me that God exists. I will admit the existence of the Sun because I can see it, but not the existence of a creator, for I see no creator anywhere even with a telescope, so I can think in terms of the existence of the Sun and the Stars for I see them plainly, but the idea of their being created strikes me as nonsense. The existence of God, however, can be *understood*, even though it is not seen. This is where psychological thinking comes in. It is another level. It is distinct from sensual thinking. In this example, to mix them is like smearing mud on the eyes.

Now what does the mud mean and what do the eyes mean here? Not literal mud nor literal eyes are meant. Christ indicated to His disciples that for them it was only necessary to wash the feet and this was enacted for them. Notice this carefully. Their actual feet, visible to sense, were washed with actual water visible to sense. So a person might continue performing the ceremony for the rest of his life, thinking thereby to reach paradise in the end. While I think, from experience elsewhere, that washing the feet literally is an excellent and neighbourly practice, I do not think that it leads to the Kingdom of God. Nor do I think that any other religious ceremonial is of the slightest value in this respect if it is taken sensually, and not psychologically. Christ, who taught psychological thinking as the key to the Kingdom, and shewed that the Baptist had not attained it, had a good deal to say about this matter and said it sometimes in words of withering sarcasm. He also dumbfounded the sneering masses of surrounding sensualists, rigid in self-pride, by telling them that the Kingdom of Heaven was within them and not a visible thing. He said: "The Kingdom of God cometh not with observation: neither shall they say, Lo here! or, Lo there! for behold, the Kingdom of God is within you" (Luke xvii.20, 21). It was a state, not a place. Now if the Kingdom is within a man, the fulfilment of a man's development, which is the attainment of the Conscious Circle of Humanity, is in an inward direction. That is, it is in a psychological direction. It follows, therefore, that sensual thinking will not discover it and that only psychological thinking will. Therefore to begin with I shall have to ascertain what kind of man I am, psychologically, and not what kind of man I appear to be physically or socially. I will have to study what psychological things are in me that will prevent me from any development in the right direction and for this I will need instructions—often repeated, for they seem curiously difficult to remember—and occasionally expert advice. Whoever I am, I will be taught that what life has made me will not render me thereby acceptable to the Conscious Circle of Humanity because, for one reason, life will have made me one-sided. Now when—and if—I begin to make sincerely a psychological approach to myself and slowly—very slowly— make an inventory of various psychological things in myself—such as self-love, self-vanity, and self-pride, which are three very cruel lords that ruin one's peace of mind—I will realize very slowly that they may hinder my development and with the aid of the repeated instructions and repeated teaching of the Work may even see why this will be the case. I am then thinking psychologically. I am thinking psychologically about this thing called myself that I have taken for granted hitherto. I am even beginning to understand something of the meaning of the words: "The Kingdom of God is within you."

Now I will find that whenever I allow my previous sensual thinking about myself to mix up with my psychological thinking of myself which is being formed in me, it will swamp the latter. I must keep them separate or else there will be, as it were, a flood, and if one has not attempted to build an Ark, it may lead to one's psychological death. If the Ark that the Work eventually constructs with your help is not seaworthy, there will be a period of danger. One tires of the Work, especially when one is not tired. One has no time. It is all too vague—as if it ever were! The upper mill grinds more and more slowly—that is, one's psychological thinking slows and almost ceases. It is then necessary to play one's musical instrument and strike one or two chords that make harmony and remove dissonance. For it is a long time before the psychological mind is stronger than the sensual mind and the evidence of things not seen stronger than the evidence of things seen. But this reversal is possible. In regard to the musical chords that set the psychological thinking going again I will only say here that there are things that one can remember and things that one can forget and things that one can read and re-read and things one must simply hold on to until the life-thinking temptation leaves one—for a season. The temptation is, of course, intelligent and necessary. In dealing with Saul, whom you can perhaps recognize, David used a harp not once but on many occasions. Orpheus tamed animals with his lute. Also, I understand that the Angels often play on musical instruments and very beautifully. But I doubt if these instruments are to be understood sensually, any more than are Work-shoes that I have spoken about. They are not literal musical instruments nor are they literal leather shoes. As was once said, the devil is also necessary. The devil is the sensual mind. When you see the intention of the Work in tempting you and realize that it is necessary, you strike a chord on your musical instrument, which of course must have more than one string.

*Amwell, 10.5.52*

## PSYCHOLOGICAL SPACE

Man is both in time and out of time. Now the sensual mind is based on time and space, but not the psychological mind. We can say that only partial truth is accessible to the sensual mind. Truth is comparable to an inexhaustible sack of silver, from which a few coins have escaped, while the rest is guarded. As we shall see, this is only another way of saying that the sensual thinking cannot grasp what only the psychological thinking can. The more a man's thought can expand beyond the senses and their evidence, the more truth he gets from the sack. Now a word as to truth, whose quality is intimately connected with the good in a man. We can change good, such as charity, into truth—that is, esoterically expressed, gold into silver—so *Good* Householder is the necessary starting point for the Work. We cannot change evil, such as hatred, into truth. It breeds lies only. Now truth is only changed into gold by willing it and therefore loving it and and therefore living it— for we do what we love to do and will what we love. We have, therefore, to make Work-shoes so that we will, and love, and live the Work in daily life as simply as possible. I must say here in parenthesis that the level of Good Householder in a practical sense may not yet have been sufficiently attained, in which case a person's work will lie in adapting better to life through training the sensual mind, with effort, where it is lacking to a handicapping extent. This will be his or her work, for the time being. An important point to grasp here is that if the necessity of such an effort is personally observed, realized, clearly understood and accepted, results will very soon appear. This is partly because it is willed individually and therefore is not done from outer compulsion or from fear, or with a sense of grievance, and partly because the Work will find a way to help, if there is sufficient valuation of it. For when you do a thing from and for the Work it will be present with you in what you do, but not otherwise. From valuation comes affection, and affection attracts presence. Coldheartedness and cold-mindedness can only repel the Work. This is obvious enough on reflection.

Now, to return to truth. There is psychological and there is sensual truth. They overlap but are not one and the same. We shall have to discuss these elsewhere but it can be said here that it is psychological truth chiefly that can change our being and not sensual truth. Sensual truth is conceived in terms of time and of three-dimensional space, because the senses only register in the present moment of time and space. I cannot *see* you yesterday in your room. I can only remember a little. I cannot *hear* what you said upstairs a little while ago. I can only remember a little. I cannot touch you a moment ago when you were sitting in that chair, for you have gone out now. I can touch the chair, which is still in the present moment of space for me but not for you. Both time and space separate us. When I go out the street is now in the present moment of space and I see you again. We are now both in another part of space and in another part of time. Thus do my external senses work —always in the flitting present moment of time and in three-dimensional space, common to us all. All this requires thinking about often, for it is very strange, although people do not notice it. Now since I love you, you are always near or present to me—yes, but in some other world, some other space, not common to us all, quite distinct from the common external world registered by sense, but somehow quite or even more real. Now in which, or in what, dimension does this other world lie, in which you continue to exist "psychologically" for me, so that I seem sometimes even to be able to speak to you? Or how is it that I can dream quite clearly that we are walking or speaking together in the morning on a hillside? In what time and in what space does this happen? Certainly not in the time and space on which our outer senses open.

Now let us shift the line of argument. I will ask you in what dimension is your memory? Again I will ask how many dimensions has your thought. Has it length, breadth and height? Can you speak of a long thought or a broad one or a high one? Is it three-dimensional as your body is and the chair you are sitting on? Yet your thought is real to you. You may be plunged in thought without being aware of either time or space. Where are you then? Your consciousness is undoubtedly somewhere. Certainly your body remains in the dimension of time and space common to us all. It is visible and tangible to sense. But your thought is invisible and intangible to sense and yet it exists and is real. We conclude therefore that dimensions exist and are open to us inwardly apart from the dimensions on which our senses open outwardly and in which our bodies and the world exist. Each person has a private space. Now in this inner or private space, which each person has, thought and feeling and not muscles bring about movement. For example, affection brings about presence or nearness in this inner space.

Dislike will do the reverse. Affection is a state. Love is a state. Dislike is a state. Hate is a state. To feel affection or to love is to be in a particular state and the particular state you are in will be in this inner or private space of yours, and not in outer or public space. That is why I said above that valuation and affection make the Work present. Indifference or dislike removes it to a distance. Yes—but to a distance in this inner private space of yours, not in external space, for you may be sitting at a meeting, disliking it all and yet present in space. Now as long as I feel affection for a person I am in a certain state that continues and the person is present or near in inner space. Externally, to my senses, the person may be present at one time and absent at another time, but not so internally. It would seem therefore, that in this inner space that is private to me, there is no time as we understand it sensually. In place of ever-changing and ever-passing time there is state. We get, therefore, a glimpse of something in us that is outside time—namely, state and inner space. That is why it was said at the beginning of the paper that we are both in time and out of time. If nothing is transformed beyond the sense-based level, we are mainly in time. How much of us is outside time will depend how much we are governed by outer time and space and the external senses and sensual mind, and how much we can enter and organize inner space by good states and keep and feel this place separate and distinct from the jarring of everyday things. I will only add here that this inner, private space is sometimes represented by a room that we never discovered or knew to exist. We have, therefore, to distinguish by observation, thought, feeling, and inner taste, the two spaces.

*Amwell, 17.5.52*

## SELF-GLORY

We speak to-day of self-glorifying. For example, some use their sex for self-glorification. This increases their inner uneasiness and so makes them restless or tired. For this is always the result when every action is mixed with too much self-glory. When what one does is quite secondary to the satisfaction of self-glory one's life is uneasy. If you observe this feature enough in yourself, you will see it in others. Sometimes it looks like a bubble filled with a transparent glue in which the person is moving without noticing what he is in. Sometimes it appears as a top-heavy house being built on sand close to the sea or on a cliff-side. There are very many sensual images that are used to represent the psychological or inner state of doing everything mainly for the glorification of oneself. This is natural enough because it is the commonest psychological state on Earth. On the reverse side, accompanying self-glorification, are a great number and variety of pictures which stimulate us to the pursuit of self-glory. Do you see that gallant little ship beating up against the furious gale swept by enormous seas with the crew too terrified to come on deck? Do you see who is at the wheel? Well, that's me. Or again, do you see that handsome officer strolling about in No Man's Land, stretching and yawning and looking bored, and then turning back to his trench, coolly lighting a cigarette on the way, amid a hail of bullets? Well, that's me too. Both these pictures are exhibited in the same gallery. If you say you have outgrown these pictures, I will ask you in what gallery are you now standing, in the great Earthly Academy of Pictures? I should doubt you if you told me you had left the building. For example, you might without realizing it be standing before pictures of the loveliest or most witty or most fashionable woman, or even of the handsomest or of the best-dressed man, or of a great statesman or aristocrat or famous politician or a millionaire. (Of course, we are not speaking literally, for millionaires and politicians are not attractive to look at usually.) But, in any case, you are almost certainly gazing at some picture in your mind, and it is a good thing to get to work and make it conscious by means of candid self-observation. Why is it a good thing to make it conscious through candid self-observation? It is a good thing because if it is left in the shadows, in what is unconscious to you, in that region that you do not acknowledge and include in your inventory and conception of yourself, it will be constantly at work in you all the same and, being possessed of the uncontrollable power that unconsciousness gives anything in you—that is, all you will not face—it may complicate your life to the point of tragedy. Please do not make the elementary mistake of thinking that because you are not conscious of a thing it cannot possibly be in you. That is a really childish mistake in this Work, but some continue to make it and so get nowhere. They have, however, the consolation of retaining their own conceit of themselves and so of going out as they came in.

Now when self-glory is the main object, the quality of whatever work is performed will be second-rate. This follows because much of the energy that should be employed in the task will pass into grandiose self-imaginings and only a part into the task on hand. A painter, or writer, for instance, who works in the midst of phantasies of becoming famous, dissipates his energy and his work will suffer and its quality will reflect the being of the originator. Bear in mind that every psychic act takes force from you. Phantasies absorb a lot of force—they drain away force and exhaust people. Phantasies of being great, or having unusual powers or unusual charms, are commonplace. They are usually compensatory to commonplaceness and they take a lot of force and use it up quite uselessly. They sap you. For this reason they often prevent a person from attaining what he or she could well attain if he or she could approach things in a simpler or more direct and real way and make conscious and separate from all such grandiose imaginings. I have seen so much unhappiness and misuse arising from such phantasies.

They arise from 'I's in us which use phantasies to gain power over us so that they can absorb—that is, eat—our force and thus live like vermin on us. Some are far more dangerous than others. The only way to escape their power is to observe and observe and observe them more and more clearly, for by this means, by making them conscious, you will eventually separate from them, and once you are separated, by the thickness of a knife-blade, they begin to die, like a cut plant. Consciousness is often represented as a knife in ancient symbolism, because it cuts you clear of what is fastened on to you and draining your force. This image of the true action of consciousness is apt. One should reflect humbly at times on the depth of ancient understanding and the poverty of one's own. It gives right emotions, not complacent self-emotions.

Now whatever is done from the basis of self-glory is spurious. It is also unclean. It is dish-water, not the clean water of truth, but the dirty water of lies. All that you have done from self-glory counts for nothing. It is not real. It cannot raise your level of being. You may have apparently sacrificed yourself, visited and tended the sick—from a picture. You have leapt into torrents, rushed into burning houses to save people, bared your arm for a trial injection that may kill you—all from a picture. It counts for nothing. It is all founded on pictures and resulting self-glory. Understand again here that consciousness is our only remedy. It cuts away what is clinging to you. You are, unconsciously, acting from a picture without knowing it. You are unconscious of the fact. Let us reflect on pictures again. Many different pictures are in the galleries of the Earthly Academy—pictures of great and small heroes, and of martyrs and saints, a gallery devoted to pictures of those whose glory it is to be misunderstood, many pictures of hardworking grim people whose glory it is to hold the home together, upsetting everyone in the process, many pictures that are rather similar as of people toiling and slaving far into the night quite unnecessarily, many of people being so busy and rushed that you can scarcely see them, and thousands of other pictures, some unpleasant, some criminal. Each of these pictures appeals to different people's self-glory—you know criminals glory in their crimes. In every case the person is unconscious that it is a *picture* that controls him or her. As said, a thing in you that you are unconscious of has great power over you like an invisible magnet. I repeat that the remedy is the light of consciousness. This Work is based on increasing the light of *consciousness*. It is about our becoming more conscious—we who live in darkness—by self-observation and long work on ourselves. With the strength of the Work behind you you will gradually be able to make the secret and often dangerous picture conscious. Like a knife cutting a stem, consciousness will cut you away from that picture. You will be released at last from its power. When dragged into consciousness—painfully, at the expense of your self-conceit—it loses its power. You gain the force it was eating. Only as long as it is hidden in unconsciousness has it power. Legend says that fairies lose their power when their names are guessed. Try to see your picture and the forms your self-glory takes. Do both together over a long period. What do you glory in? What is your picture—this hidden picture you have been serving so long that has misled you and made you unhappy?

NOTE: This paper is about:
(1) *Self-Glory*, which arises from
(2) *Pictures*, from which only
(3) *Consciousness* can release us.

*Amwell, 24.5.52*

## THE MIDDLE LABORATORY

Because this Work does not consist in having one's own way in any centre, it becomes repugnant to the self-love and creates difficulties for everyone. Difficulties may appear at the start or emerge later. Since the mechanical divisions of all centres resent the Work, the Mechanical Man, made up of various habitual connections within and between these parts of centres, struggles to maintain his existence so as to prevent the formation of the New Man that would replace him. To express the situation more correctly, one should rather say that many 'I's in different centres whose power is threatened will resent the Work and so create difficulties by objecting, arguing or flat denial. Now a man, by his life, may have such a great number of strong, self-loving and world-seeking resistant 'I's that any 'I's in him that may possibly want the Work have little chance of forming a group and growing stronger in that man. This means simply that the Mechanical Man will murder any manifestation of the New Man. Others, a little better situated psychologically, through having doubted life and reflected and won-dered occasionally about its meaning, may take in the Work to some extent at first, so that a minute new living thing begins in them. This is the beginning of a new way of thinking and feeling. Then difficulties arise. Three things may then happen. Either the minute new living thing, which is the beginning of the New Man, withers because it has no depth of soil; or the Mechanical Man murders it by violence as Herod murdered the new babies, hoping to destroy Christ; or, thirdly, the man revalues the Work and starts again. Now let us speak of the three laboratories in Man and particularly of the *middle laboratory*, where the murderer can enter and work destruction unless you are watching. He will choose, like a thief, a moment when you are not awake. I do not here mean literal sleep.

We know from the diagram of the three foods of Man and their transformation that there are three transforming laboratories in us.

These transform gross into finer matters. You will understand that if you eat a beefsteak it cannot pass, say, into your brain as such. It has to be transformed into finer matters. Now usually the middle laboratory only is spoken of. This is because it is this one that is most liable to damage. But all can be damaged. The first transformation of food, symbolized by the figures 768 changing into 384, is carried out in the lower laboratory. The figure 768 denotes all substances that the human stomach and intestines can digest. We must recall here that the Table of Hydrogens is a *Table of Uses*. Things are classified and arranged in a vertical scale according to their uses. For example, anything that is of use for that form of food that Man digests in his stomach and intestines is termed 768. Thus substances of the most diverse sorts and kinds are brought into an at-first-sight amazing relation through this esoteric method of classifying a thing by the use of that thing. I may add here that we also are classified in a similar way. (So one should ask: "Of what use am I ?") Now if something is wrong in the first laboratory—and let us take only that part of it called the stomach—as, for instance, wrong food, too much food, too much or little hydro-chloric acid, weak or missing ferments, or chillness or a hundred and one other factors— then the transformation of 768 into 384 is interfered with. The whole food octave starting from passive Do 768 and proceeding mechanically by successive transformations to Si 12 will be to some extent affected. But in this connection we are told that we can accustom ourselves to far less food than we eat and that we have artificial appetite and that feeling hungry is largely a matter of habit, which does not reflect the real needs of the Instinctive Centre. When practising starving, the falling away of this artificial appetite on the second day or so can be clearly experienced.

I will not speak further here about disturbances in the lower laboratory, except to say that both in the first phase of digestion in the acid stomach and perhaps more particularly nowadays in the second phase of digestion carried out in the duodenum in an alkaline medium, persisting emotions of anxiety and fear, so typical of modern man, may cause the digestive juices to digest the living walls that contain them, and even eat through them, causing perforation. In other words, gripped by these negative emotions, a man begins to eat himself. Now to come to the *middle laboratory*, with which we are mainly concerned. The work carried on here is of a subtler kind. The matters dealt with in this laboratory are far finer and of a far higher order and so are capable of greater uses and of greater abuses. This middle laboratory, which we can suppose, by rough analogy, to be full of the most delicate and intricate chemical and electrical apparatus, demands, as it were, a constant temperature, complete freedom from damp, and absence of noise and vibration, in order to carry out its work. Notice that it receives substances for further transformation from the lower laboratory and also receives substances for further transformation from the upper laboratory. It has, therefore, most complicated tasks to carry out of the greatest importance to the food octave. Also the atmospheric food 192 called AIR enters here and is transformed into 96, passing on to the upper laboratory. Since it is situated in the second storey of the three-storey house that is Man, it is intimately connected with the Emotional Centre, which has its situation here. Therefore the quality of the work of transformation in the second laboratory will depend on the state of the Emotional Centre. If the state of the Emotional Centre is good, the middle laboratory will work well. The most damaging thing that can happen to it is an attack of violence. Violence acts like an explosion. In extreme cases it may be so intense as to damage the middle laboratory permanently. Owing to its repercussions on the upper laboratory it may affect the reason. Now we are taught that all negative emotions are based on violence and lead down to violence. We know also that violence only breeds violence. Nothing is settled by violence—as witness the world. Many other things have been pointed out, which can all be observed in oneself, concerning violence. One has, of course, first of all, to become conscious of one's own violence. We have many lesser recurrent attacks of violence. They must be circumvented eventually if we seek to prevent any new life in us from being murdered. All have to work on their violence for all have it though they deny it. These lesser attacks of violence arise from letting things "touch your blood". From this you get "bad blood" against one another. It is due to identifying. Try to observe in yourself what angers you in another person so much that you completely identify with that person and cannot stand him or her. This seeing the same thing in yourself *cancels* out the violence just as plus one and minus one cancel out. This is the true meaning of the Greek word translated "forgive"—as in "forgive one another". There is no trace of "forgiving" in cancelling. Nothing pseudo is meant. It is all cancelled out as by an electric spark passing between two oppositely charged bodies. The more conceited you are the less you can "forgive" by seeing the same thing in yourself so you will be more inclined to violence, for conceit prevents self-observation. You will be your own punishment as we all are. Now an attack of violence always disturbs the health. It is a wrong shock in the wrong place. The shock often works out days after in illness or physical trouble. It upsets the working of the middle laboratory, disturbing, among other things, the formation of the matter symbolized by the figure 96—whose use has to do with the balance and protection of what I will call the cushion of health between the psychic and physical life. Diminution of this fine matter lowers physiological resistance, while the identifying lowers psychological resistance. Both states let things in which should be kept out. The consequences are thus psycho-somatic. Now remember that violence arises from identifying. If we could remember ourselves—that is, draw our consciousness out of life-things at will—we would not identify and so would not be violent.

## INTERNAL ACCOUNTS AND FORGIVING

If we are told anything by the Work, we can be certain that the reason is connected with inner self-development. Everything taught by the Work has reference to the inner self-development that Man is capable of by creation. But for the development to begin and continue, a man and a woman must study and re-study, again and again, what the Work teaches. At first nothing is really taken in. Certain phrases are heard and certain words. They are scattered over the surface of the mind. But they do not take root and cannot do so unless the emotional factor of valuation becomes added. Otherwise they are not treasured, which is the same as saying they are not valued, and so the heart, which gives the necessary depth of soil, is not taking any part. Where a man's treasure is, there is his heart. If the Emotional Centre is not eventually in the Work, nothing will happen. There will be no change in the person. People will remain just the same as they were. There will be no psycho-transformism. Their hearts will be elsewhere. That is, their valuation will be in other things. They may give lip-service to the Work but no valuation. For this reason, the Work-Octave is said to begin with valuation. Notice that the *Work*-Octave is said. Much preliminary to and fro business, much starting and stopping, much argument, much struggling between yes and no, is necessary before a person comes into the path that is the octave of the Work. Some who have gained insight prefer to avoid the Work-Octave, and some, even wishing to avoid it, are made to go into the Work-Octave through the influence of the awakening Emotional Centre, the seat of Buried Conscience, which knows the Work already, and recognizes it. But such recognition is impossible if the phrases and words of the teaching are scattered over the surface of the mind and lie there without soil to take root in. Everything in the Work is germinal—the ideas, the instructions, the phrases, the words—that is, they are seeds. Now take a phrase like "making internal accounts". Have you studied and re-studied again and again what this phrase means? Can you say that you really do understand what making internal accounts means? Can you say with sincerity that you know very well what forms making accounts takes in your life? Have you observed them to-day? Against whom do you make them? Against God, or Fate, or Luck, or man or woman, or government, or your superiors or inferiors? You always personify what you blame. You don't make accounts against your damp house itself, but against the architect or builder, or the man who sold it to you, and of course your doctor who told you to live in the country. One can always blame one's doctor if no one else is at hand.

Now you have heard it said that a person may know the Work but not understand it. To know is one thing. To understand is another. The Intellectual Centre can know the Work and repeat it by heart, but it needs the co-operation of the Intellectual and the Emotional Centre to understand the Work. You may know it is necessary to cease making internal accounts, but do you understand why? Have you reflected not merely once but a hundred times why you have to give up internal accounting? If not, then you understand nothing about this particular bit of teaching that the Work offers us. You hear it—but do not understand it. Why? You do not connect it with yourself. You do not connect it through the first line of Work, which is work on yourself, in the light of the knowledge that the Work teaches. Listen to this conversation: some newcomer says: "What's all this about making internal accounts?" The self-styled old hand replies: "Oh, it's very important. You'll hear the phrase often. By the way, you know Atkinson, don't you? That man, I hear, actually said I was stupid. I've just written him a proper letter about it." "Have you? But surely I've often heard you say Atkinson is a conceited fool." "So he is. He turned down the job I offered him, thought it wasn't good enough." "But hasn't this got something to do with making accounts?" "My dear fellow, it has got absolutely nothing to do with it. Don't, for heaven's sake, start making wrong connections in your mind. I'm a seasoned veteran, very experienced in this Work, so I know what I'm talking about; do you imagine I am going to allow anyone to call me stupid? No, certainly not! I'll see he doesn't forget it, I assure you."

Well, now, I will not go so far as to say I overheard this actual conversation, but I have heard several similar ones. If you say: "How can this be?" I reply: "The answer is simple. It is just this kind of thing a person says who has never *understood* what the Work is about, even though knowing something of the phrases and words used in this special language, and so giving a superficial impression of understanding it. He has never connected it with his own psychology." Now I have been asked whether ceasing to make internal accounts has anything to do with what was spoken of last week, when the paper on violence was given. Well, of course it has. Last week the dangers of violence were explained in relation to the delicate work of transformation carried out especially in the Middle Laboratory. Violence injures new thoughts and feelings being formed by the Work in us. It injures the New Man. It was said that if one could see *what* made one violent with another person and if one could find by observation the same thing in oneself, the violence would vanish. It would cancel out, as do plus one and minus one, which add up to exactly nothing. Blaming another, making internal accounts against him, precipitates violence. Now it amounts to this—namely, if I become conscious of all and everything in myself, I could not be violent about any unpleasant manifestation in another, for I would see it also in myself. I would see myself in others and others in myself. I would reach this degree of objective consciousness. It was mentioned that the Greek word translated as "forgive" means to cancel a debt, to remit, to write off in one's account book what another owes. It has no sentimental meaning. To say one forgives another an injury or insult is not merely self-deception but also spiritual arrogance. It is as if one thought one could *do*. No, the only way is through a slow development of consciousness of what is in one by long self-observation, which will shatter one's pet idea of oneself, but will release one—and others whom one had imprisoned in one's hate and violence.

Now, in the original Greek, it is not said: "Forgive us our sins", in the Lord's Prayer, but "Cancel what we owe (in proportion) as we cancel what others owe us." Notice that emphasis not on what we have done but on what we have not done. This means that if, say, I never remember myself, I owe my Father who is in Heaven and continue to owe more and more as my life of being asleep goes by. I may worry intermittently about some things I have done but this is quite different from reflecting on things I have not done. If you consider the Work from this point of view you will discover several interesting things.

*Amwell, 7.6.52*

## REVENGE AND CANCELLING

You all know that something thirsts for revenge under "insult" and cares not a rap for cancelling. For it, cancelling is killing the other and not seeing the same thing in oneself. When you thirst for revenge, you are being led by wrong 'I's. They suggest this and that. If you can watch them, you will learn something about what is in you. But if not, you will identify with them. It is much easier to do so. Taking a short view of things, it gives you far more satisfaction. Revenge is sweet. Work is not. To go against oneself is never sweet. When you identify in this manner instead of separating, each of these 'I's will suggest that you say this or that, or write or behave in this or that way. *But it will seem to you that it is YOU YOURSELF thinking all this.* It will appear to you as: "I think I will say or write this. I think I will write that," or "I think I will do this. No, I think I will do that." What is happening to you is that certain 'I's which live in you in negative parts of centres have got hold of you. You have simply allowed them to get hold of you. You are asleep and enjoying negative emotions. You are thus moving into the slum-area of the great city of yourself. You are already in the hands of pretty unpleasant people. These 'I's are unscrupulous and nasty. But you do not see them. By a trick—and what a trick—they seem to be you—you thinking and you feeling. You take them as you, so they infuse you with their thoughts and feelings. You identify with them. You say 'I' to them. Whatever you say 'I' to, you take as being you and with that you are identified. You make it the same as you. Whatever you make the same as you, you make one with yourself. This is identifying. The process is not deliberate. It happens automatically and instantaneously. It is bound to happen automatically and instantaneously to everyone who takes everything that goes on within him or her as himself or herself. This mystery is not realized. I called it a trick a moment ago. The majority cannot see it. Some never can see it. If you begin to see it, you see to your amazement that it is a trick. It is indeed a trick. It is one of several quite simple and quite successful tricks that keep up the central mystery that Man is asleep but can awaken, and yet knows neither.

Now being already, through identifying, in the hands of some 'I's belonging to the less desirable streets of the psychological city in you, if you continue to identify, like the silly blind sheep that one is in regard to what goes on within, you will get into the hands of a rougher and tougher and nastier crowd of 'I's. They think nothing of blackmail, incriminating others and using minor violence. They, in turn, can hand you on to the lowest, murdering and most evil 'I's. All this can and does result from unchecked identifying with negative 'I's when you wish to retaliate and seek revenge. Now they only wish one thing from you. These 'I's wish to overpower you and take your force. Their method is to make you identify with them, so that your consciousness does not distinguish between you and them. But I will remind you here that it can be trained to do so. The Work desires you to do this so that you do not keep on losing the small amount of consciousness you have. Now this identifying with an 'I' is as if a man in the street suddenly became you. It is as if he vanished into you, and you never noticed anything. Of course, this can only happen when you are unconscious of all that goes on in yourself. The only remedy is to let a ray of the light of consciousness into yourself. This means to observe yourself—and to observe means to see things in yourself and to see eventually that many different 'I's live in you and use your name and voice. When you reach this stage of self-observation it is like being able to see many different people in the street where it has seemed that only you were. Now our relationship to the external world is such that when we see a person in the street we do not take him as ourself. We do not say: "I am this person, this person is me." Nor can this person approach us and say: "You are me and I am you." Such behaviour would be embarrassing. Indeed, we would be furious at such an attempt to take possession of us. Yet our relationship to the internal world of oneself is such that this is continually happening and it does not embarrass or upset us in the least. The trick works beautifully and silently and practically no one is ever aware of it. It is in use all over the world at this moment. The Work tries to make us aware of it, to open our understanding to it. But even with the help of the Work and all that it teaches people can remain unaware of the trick. Of course, if we already possessed inwardly that state of consciousness called Self-Awareness which the Work strongly recommends us to attain for our own good, we would at once be aware that some trick was being attempted when any 'I' approached us internally and said: "You are me and I am you", and then tried to vanish into us. We would be aware both of the approach of the 'I' and of its intention to seize control of us by turning us into it, like the prince in the fairy-stories being turned into a frog or Circe turning the sailors of Ulysses into swine. But magic of this sort is still being done and all the time people are being turned into what they are not. Surely Circe's island is this world. Now like Ulysses we are given a remedy from above, a divine counter-spell. It is the Third State of Consciousness. It is Self-Remembering, Self-Awareness and Self-Consciousness.

However we do not use this remedy because we are not forced to the necessity to do so. The Work is not actual and not serious enough to us and we do not yet see clearly what is happening to us. We have plenty of buffers within to smooth things over. As regards the Work, we can go about in a daze, and a haze, and a maze, day after day. We just drift. We may not see, for instance, that we are really being controlled by a majority of 'I's that are hostile or indifferent to this Work and to the whole teaching of esoterisism—by 'I's that either only some kind of amour-propre in us prevents from taking their logical course, or that are so cleverly concealing themselves that the real danger of our inner situation is not consciously realized. We have 'I's that are as antagon-istic to the Work as some narrow harsh people actually can be in life. Such 'I's can quietly poison us. They can hide behind a picture of virtue. If any 'I' does so, be sure that it secretly is your enemy. We little suspect how many 'I's in us are our enemies and only desire to retain their power over us.

Now when we come to the necessity of Self-Remembering it is like carrying in both hands a cup that is brimful of wine. So among other things it is then necessary to notice where one is walking in oneself. In the slums you certainly will be in danger of having the cup knocked com-pletely out of your hands. One will, therefore, be under the *sheer necessity* of finding some other way of dealing with "insult" than by mechanical retaliation and revenge or only being offended. For all the latter can easily make you negative and bring you into your slums. So you will miss an opportunity of work on yourself and spill some wine unless you find some way to deal with yourself. It is here that cancelling can come in. The case is different with those who have not yet reached the necessity of Self-Remembering. They carry no cup as yet. They are not cup-bearers. They can still try remembering themselves occasion-ally when they have time and there is nothing important to do.

## BELIEF IN THE WORK

In this Work we are told that nothing can change in a man unless he begins to think in a new way. It is also said that this Work is to make us think in a new way. Let us consider these two statements so that something of their meaning emerges and administers one or two slaps in the face. You will see that from these statements it follows that the mind *must believe* the Work. That is the first slap in the face. If there is no belief in the Work, nothing can happen. That is the second slap. The man or woman will continue to think as they always have and everything will remain the same. It is possible to remain "in the Work", as the phrase goes, for year after year and not believe it and so remain unchanged in one's way of thinking. This may, at first sight, seem impossible. But if a person has no belief in the Work and its authority and its teaching, that person will not undergo any change of mind and if anyone's ways of thinking remain unaltered, the Work cannot act on him or her. That is the point and that is the meaning of the two statements.

Consider the matter more closely, so that it engages your deeper attention and brings you face to face to some extent with where you are mentally as regards the Work. You can see that if a person has no 'I's with any attraction for or real belief in the Work, that person will not be occupied genuinely with what it teaches. One does not seriously occupy one's mind with what one does not believe in. On the other hand, if one believes that a thing is true, one thinks about it, particularly if it closely concerns oneself. Now this Work closely concerns oneself. I cannot indeed think of anything that concerns men or women more closely than the teaching of this Work. But if they do not believe it do you imagine they will have their minds miraculously changed by it and begin to think in a new way? I should have said not in a new way but in an *entirely* new way. Can you see, then, that since nothing can change in us unless we begin to think in a new way, and since this Work is to make us eventually think in an entirely new way, unless we believe what it teaches it can have absolutely no effect on us? Being mind-stuck we will remain just as we always were. There will be no change of being because there is no change in thinking. Without change of thought there can be no change of being. A man will remain the same man. The mind, with its former attitudes and habits of thinking will remain unaltered and so the rest of the person will remain unaltered. The knowledge taught by the Work will not enter the thinking and transform it. The man or woman will not even try to think from the new ideas that the Work teaches, and see life and themselves in a new way. They will not try to think from the ideas of the Work simply because they do not believe them. They will hear that they have many 'I's but not believe it —and so with the other ideas. For instance, they will hear that new knowledge, new being and new understanding are all connected and that one cannot have new understanding without the other two. But they will not believe it. Now reflect on this carefully. Notice if you have taken in what it means. *Do* you believe your understanding will remain at its present level if your knowledge does not change and that your being will not change unless your knowledge changes? I doubt it. But to continue, I may be given the new knowledge contained in the Work and often listen to it, but never really believe it. In that case I will not apply the new knowledge to the study of my being. I will make no attempt whatsoever to view the kind of man I am psychologically from the angle of the new knowledge. I will just go on chasing about as usual, pursuing my usual daily interests, running after my phantasies, satisfying my appetites, and voicing my usual daily imbecilities, with the utmost complacency. I will not, of course, see anything mechanical in all this. Privately I will laugh the idea to scorn that I am a mechanical man and fast asleep in mind and heart.

Now the Work is about a possible change inherent in Man by creation. You find this difficult to believe? No doubt you do. Well, this change is called psycho-transformism. *Now psycho-transformism begins with transformation of the mind.* It begins with metanoia, to use a word in the New Testament, which means change of mind and not repentance. A person, therefore, who does not really believe in the Work will experience no transformation of mind and so will not move internally into a position where changes can be performed by means of the influences of the Work. The Work will not be received. These influences act first on the mind so as to change the thinking. Otherwise there can be no psycho-transformism—no ultimate transformation of the person's whole psychology. There cannot be, simply because when it comes down to brass tacks the person does not believe in the Work or derides or mocks it secretly. There will be no change in the mind and therefore no change can result in the level of being and therefore no change in the level of understanding. The person may seem externally to change a little. This may be due to example, atmosphere and imitation, or vanity or motives of self-interest. But there will be no internal change, no genuine transformation, nothing so real and intimate that a man, turned and twisted in every direction, time after time, will remain always pointing to the Work. The mind, not being awakened by the Work, will not awaken the Emotional Centre. The underlying disbelief in the Intellectual Centre will be reflected as dislike and disbelief in the Emotional Centre. That is, self-emotions and not Work-emotions will remain dominant.

Now a man may *know* this Work and not believe it. *To know is not to believe.* Again, he may teach this Work and not believe it. That is quite possible for certain types. He does not deceive himself but deceives others. He may profess to believe, but very many profess Christianity, for instance, and do not believe it. That is why one has at times to observe oneself and see how much of one believes the Work and what the quality of one's belief is and how many 'I's fight against it. For according to the quality of your belief, so will the Work respond and act on you. A man may believe he believes this Work and find, by candid uncritical self-observation, that he does not. He sees that he has been deceiving himself. This gives him a good chance to go on. It is a useful shock as are all moments of sincerity with oneself. It clears away false 'I's that are like parasitic charmers in the mind. A man, a woman, are so very much their inner sincerity in this Work. Now I will add only one thing. To believe is to have confidence. To believe in the Work is to have confidence in something more than in yourself. To believe in the Work is to believe in something greater than oneself. It is to believe in Greater Mind—that is, in Mind greater than your mind. Now mind is invisible. Greater Mind is invisible. Your mind is invisible. To believe in Greater Mind is therefore for one invisible to believe in a greater Invisible. You will see that we are now speaking on the psychological level.

*Amwell, 28.6.52*

## FALSE PERSONALITY AND HAPPINESS

In what does happiness consist? Take your own case. Let us suppose you believe that there is an after-life and that you will go to Heaven and be perfectly happy. How do you conceive of this happiness? Have you thought about it? Some imagine themselves in a state of great magnificence, living in palaces, served by slaves, adored, admired and praised by everyone. They feel that this would make them supremely happy. Now this idea of happiness has to be completely eradicated. It must be torn out of the heart. The crudity and vulgarity of this widespread phantasy was commented on by Christ, when the disciples were quarrelling about who was greatest. He said that in the Kingdom of Heaven the person who served most was the greatest. This trans-valuation of world-values must have been a shock to them, as indeed the whole of Christ's life was. Another crude idea regards happiness as consisting in a continual gratification of one or other of the bodily appetites. This is entirely of self and for self and serves nothing but self. But I will pass on to the connection of the idea of happiness with the False Personality.

Consider for a moment people whose happiness is mainly to satisfy their False Personality. It cannot be said that they are made deeply happy by doing so. On the other hand, they avoid being made unhappy. By administering to the requirements of the False Personality they have their reward. Indeed, as we shall see, they are spoken of as having already had their reward in the very act of obeying their False Personality. This is interesting. The reward does not come later as it does, say, when a man works on himself over a considerable period and suddenly, apparently without any cause, something opens and in a flash of positive emotion he sees what Truth is. He may not have been, and probably was not, expecting any reward. He was not "working for a result". I mean that he was not making internal accounts against the Deity, such as: "Here, I've been keeping my temper in for over five minutes. When do I get a reward?" It must be said that some seem to expect a remarkably high rate of interest for making any Work-effort and some take a queer view of their importance. The quality of effort in the Work is poor when it is mixed with inner accounting and too much self-admiration. Since the nature of the False Personality is connected with instant reward, it will not gladly endure the Work, where rewards come by no means instantly. Let us take as examples some things said about False Personality and reward in Matthew vi:

> "When ye pray, be not as the hypocrites: for they love to stand and pray in the streets so as to be seen of men. Verily, I say unto you, they have received their reward."

Or again:

> "Do not practise your religious obligations before men in order to be seen . . . do not sound a trumpet before you in the streets as the hypocrites do when they give alms so as to have glory of men. Verily, I say unto you, they have received their reward."

Now you will notice that in these examples the reward is instant. No sooner have they sounded the trumpet and given money in public than they have received their reward. What have they done? You will realize that they have satisfied the False Personality and by so doing have had a moment of happiness. I mean that they have had a moment of that particular *quality* of happiness. Do you know its taste? It is a happiness connected with what other people think of you. It is derived from outside, not from within. In this sense it is external. I mean that its origin is from the world. It arises from audience. It demands an audience. This is due to the character of the False Personality. When you do a thing from False Personality, you expect at least praise of some kind. Even the wagging of your dog's tail may be sufficient. But if you have done the thing without a trace of love of doing it, or love of doing it for someone else—which latter is serving— then you will begin drawing up a long internal account if you get no acknowledgement. Yes, it is very difficult to make effort without getting any acknowledgement. Yet so much of the Work depends just on this. Why? Because, don't you see, otherwise it would increase False Personality.

Now the quality of happiness that comes from being first, or having most, or looking best, and so on, is not a genuine or deep happiness since it depends uneasily on what people think and needs continual re-stimulation, being over so quickly, as is indicated in the words: "they have received their reward." So, you see, they want it again and that makes them restless. But there is another quality of happiness which is independent of external things. It belongs to one's inner being. For that reason the False Personality, which belongs to one's outer being, cannot know it. One of its definite effects is to replace restlessness and its kindred anxiety and fear by peace. This peace cannot be shaken by external events if you keep awake. But it cannot be reached as long as consciousness is centred in False Personality and the latter is the active ruler within. That is why the successive layers of False Personality have to be stripped off, like skins. A stripping is painful to vanity, pride, conceit and self-liking, so it takes time, sometimes more, sometimes less. To get one skin off is wonderful. It does not kill you, for those skins are *not you*. It is the skins that are killing *you*. Stripping releases *you* from them, from what makes up the False Personality which is not you. It is a psychological prison. Every generation has its own kind. Observe its action in others, in intonation, in expression, in posture, in movement. Try to do so in yourself; and finally, observe it in life, in novels, in history, in the newspapers, in photographs, especially of yourself in the past, and also in the present. These are three powerfully interacting lines of work.

*Amwell, 5.7.52*

## WHAT IS A NEW WILL?

Let us begin by trying to understand something about what will is. In the first place, to will and to think are two different things, but we confuse them. It is necessary to observe clearly in oneself that we do not distinguish between them. They have different tastes. Willing is connected with the emotional side of us while thinking belongs to the Intellectual Centre. Now these two sides of a person do not work harmoniously together. You cannot say that you always will what you think, nor can you say that you think what you will. A man may think he should smoke less. But that does not mean he wills and does it. If we could see in a vision of expanded consciousness all our thinking throughout life and then in a second vision all that we have willed, we should be amazed at the difference. Actually these two records exist interiorly in every person. It can be added here that the level of a man's being or a woman's being is much more connected with what they have willed than with what they have thought. But since we confuse thinking and willing we do not observe and study the action of will in our life as distinct from thinking. So we do not see our life as will. Since the work of each centre and part of a centre in us has a different inner taste, we should really be able to do so. We can do so if we try. The result however is not flattering but very interesting. But if we cannot give up thinking how wonderful we are, we had better not try, but continue our life of illusion and vexation. But to-day I only wish to speak of what a new will can and does mean.

Will is connected both with what we like and what we love. What a man loves he wills and what he wills he does, either openly or secretly. If restrained, he does it in imagination, which spiritually—that is, psychologically—is the same. I mean that there is no new will formed. The dog will return to his vomit when occasion arises. A new will would mean to go in a new direction. But as you cease to like or love something —such as yourself—you will less and less will it. Now by observation you may come to dislike a part of yourself, something in yourself. Then you will not will it as you did when you did not clearly see it. But as long as your self-love remains the undetected, unexplored, prehistoric jungle that it is, you unknowingly let it will all of you, being ignorant of the enemies, the evil 'I's, it conceals, not being conscious of what is in the jungle. Amongst other things, that will mean that you openly or secretly always want your own way. This is will from self-love. This is undiscriminating willing, and really means that all things in this jungle, all calling themselves by your name—even man-eaters—feed their own wills. Some scream with rage if prevented. By the way, there are screaming parrots in everyone's jungle, that talk and talk and contribute much to bad daily human relationship if not destroyed. Now if one could through self-observation and self-study cease to love oneself *quite so much*, one would not so much wish to have one's own way. That would liberate energy. By seeing more what we are like we would not love ourselves so much. We would not be so critical and overriding (openly or secretly) of others. Self-love is the head love and draws in loads of energy at all times. Being more tolerant, through many private self-humiliations during the work on oneself and on self-love, we would also have some force released to give some attention to what others want in place of what we want. In short, we would have a little *new will*—like a small child—gained from diminishing the self-love. Now if a man continues to love the same things, he will continue to will and do them. In that case there can be no new will. His energies are fully used up in the circle of his interests. He will continue to go always in the same direction. For example, he will not be able to do anything new, being bound to the circle of his loves from which he wills. But if he works against mechanicalness—which is easier for those who observe externally—or against self-love—which is easier for those who have inner observation—or works against both, and both are difficult, then he may free enough energy to do something he would have thought impossible. I mean, he might go in a direction for which he had never developed any adapted function or of which he had not seen the use as long as he remained the machine he never suspected he was. I offer again an example in the following dream I once had, which was given some time ago. In this dream I was shewn quite simply a direction and state of will that at the time seemed impossible for me to follow or ever reach. I was shewn it only after crossing a certain barrier, clearly connected with what might be called the savage man of self-love, the prehistoric man (or woman) in oneself. This barrier, representing something psychological—that is, in one's being—was represented pictorially by a narrow deep abyss, difficult to cross and filled with ancient bones. Please understand that a literal abyss, literal bones, etc., are not meant. It is an allegory, intended to shew me something. The dream is as follows:

"Someone pushes me up a grass slope. There is a ditch. It is not wide but difficult to cross. The difficult-to-cross ditch at the top of the slope is full of the bones of prehistoric animals—the remains of violent things, of beasts of prey, of monsters, of snakes. They go far down into this abyss. There is a plank to cross by, but the air seems full of restraining power, like the invisible influence of some powerful magnet; and this, with the fear of crossing this depth—although the width is not great—holds me back. I cannot say for how long, for there is no ordinary time in all this. Then I find myself across—*on the other side.* What wonderful vision do I now behold? I see someone teaching or drilling some recruits. That is all. At first sight there seems nothing marvellous. He smiles. He indicates somehow that he does not necessarily expect to get any results from what he is doing. He does not seem to mind. He does not shew any signs of impatience when they are rude to him. The lesson is nearly over, but this will not make any difference to him. It is as if he said: 'Well, this has to be done. One cannot expect much. One must give them help, though they don't want it.' It is his invulnerableness that strikes me. He is not hurt or angered by their sneers or lack of discipline. He has some curious power but hardly uses it. I pass on marvelling that he could do it. I could not take on such a thankless task. Eventually I come to a place, perhaps a shop, where boats are stored. Beyond is the sea."

When I wake up I think of this man. To do what he is doing is so utterly contrary to anything I would do. I would need a new will to do it. It would mean that I would have to go in a direction I never went in. I thought much about this direction. How could I define it to myself? I would have been violent to these recruits. Yes, that was it. He shewed no violence. He had not a will of violence. He seemed purified from all violence. That was the secret. That was the cause of the curious power I detected in him. *A man without violence.* And then I reflected that to reach him I had had to get across to the other side of the deep gulf full of the bones of prehistoric beasts, full of the remains of violent creatures. This had been done for me somehow and I found myself in the borders of another country, only at the edge of it, but beyond the prehistoric beasts. Here this non-violent man lived and taught. It was the country of the non-violent, where recruits were being taught. They seemed to be an indifferent lot, but perhaps they represented people that could learn something eventually.

He had nearly finished his lesson. Beyond was the sea, and there were boats stored near it. No doubt when he had finished the course he was going on, somewhere, beyond the land. I had been given only a glance into the meaning of a new will—a will not based on violence or on having your own way. I repeat—only a glance. For I knew I had not, save in spirit, really crossed that deep gulf yet, filled with the bones of the violent past, and left it behind finally. There were no recruits for me—or were these recruits different 'I's in myself that he was trying to teach? Certainly none of the waiting boats was mine. But from this glance I knew more practically what going in a new direction is and what a new will purified from violence means. I know also that the possibilities of following this new will and new direction lie in every moment of one's life—and that I continually forget.

*Amwell, 12.7.52*

## DEFINITE, TOPICAL
## AND CONCRETE SELF-OBSERVATION

Let us try to get some of the energy contained in the idea that Man is asleep, and make some reflections by means of it. It is said often in these Commentaries that we should not remain unconscious of our psychology. One reason is that what we are unconscious of in ourselves we tend to see only in others. I mean, that we will tend to see, let us say, meanness, as outside of ourselves when it is possibly inside ourselves. If we are constantly seeing meanness in others we may be pretty sure that it is something we are blind to in ourselves. Now this tendency is one particular part of our general state of sleep. If we reflect on this particular part of our sleep we see that it gives rise to an incalculable amount of unhappiness in the world. We accuse and condemn another for what we also do and are. This is a failure or lack in consciousness due to the general level of our consciousness. It characterizes the second or "so-called waking state", which we believe—until we waken up to it—to be a state of full consciousness. The Work calls it a state of sleep. I ask in parenthesis here: "Do you, even after long, uncritical self-observation, truly begin to realize that you are not properly conscious?" Perhaps one has not thought of oneself in this way. Now let us imagine a person who says: "This idea that Man is asleep cannot seriously apply to me. I am far from being asleep. I agree others are. But I am unusually lively and always on the spot—and, by the way, I simply cannot stand that fellow X who is always shewing off and making out he's different from other people." Everyone makes remarks of this kind. It is due to a lack of consciousness. They are unaware that so often they are just what they are so critical of in others. They are unconscious of their own psychology. The consequence is that they see what is in them projected outside them like a magic-lantern slide on to another person. The imaginary person mentioned above does not see that it is he himself who is always boasting and making out that he is different from other people. Because he does not see it in himself, he is over-critical of it in others. If he saw it in himself he would not be.

Now the point that I wish to emphasize in this connection is that in the Work people do not practise self-observation in relation to something as definite as noticing the same thing in themselves as they are critical of in others. There is no doubt that there is such a thing as abstract, retrospective or remote self-observation. It can take more than one useful and necessary form provided it does not pass into useless unnecessary retrospective regret and negative brooding. One form is connected with taking time-photographs of oneself. But what I am speaking of here is *definite, topical and concrete self-observation*. It consists in observing in yourself what definitely irritates you in another person. It is definite, because it is about what you definitely notice in another. It is topical because it has to do with what is going on more or less at the time and it is concrete because it demands that you get down to the concrete job of finding in yourself what you find so irritating in the other person. For that reason I will call this commentary: DEFINITE, TOPICAL AND CONCRETE SELF-OBSERVATION. We can all admit that there is far too much bland, woolly, insincere self-observation; and too many never observe themselves. They open no roads into themselves and see no reason to do so. All within themselves therefore remains unknown and in darkness and the Work remains a conundrum. But the Work ranks self-observation as a prime necessity. Why? First, how can a man change himself unless he gets to know what lies in him? And second, by letting light into inner darkness—that is, the light of consciousness— certain changes take place through its influence. Unpleasant things grow in the absence of light. It is the darkness of unconsciousness that is a danger. We have heard time and again that the Work is to increase our consciousness. "The darkness of ignorance and unconsciousness is to be dispelled by the light of consciousness." Yes—that sounds very fine. Such language appeals to romantic, pseudo-spiritual folk. "Light!" they exclaim, looking upwards, "How wonderful!" Unfortunately this light is very painful in the way it operates. They find the letting of light into themselves not at all pleasant. They have to see what fools they are. It is just *that* that is an increase of consciousness. But in every case, whoever it is, it is a very tough business to increase the consciousness of oneself and not at all to one's self-liking. Far from it. An increase of consciousness of oneself is always at the expense of one's imagination of oneself, of one's vanity, at the expense of Imaginary 'I', at the expense of all the pictures treasured by the False Personality. For this light of consciousness, which illuminates things in us, seeks eventually to bring about the collapse of everything fictitious and unreal so that a new person can develop. Now to see one's own foolishness is an increase of consciousness if one hitherto regarded oneself as wise. I mean that an increase of consciousness extends one's knowledge of oneself. It is about something. It is not "empty". To know more about oneself is to become more conscious of things in oneself. It destroys the former feeling. This brings us back to the finding in oneself of the very thing that irritates us in another, of which we had been unconscious. When this is done, when we turn things the other way round, our irritation is dissipated. It vanishes. Now through being roused and irritated by things in others, by how they behave, what they say and so on, we lose energy by being made rather negative and are in danger of plunging into a fit of negative emotion. All negative states cause energy-loss. The Work says that we should act as mirrors to one another instead of disliking one another. That is, we can come to see ourselves in others and others in ourselves. The dog at the Institute in France was called "Kak vass!" *like you*. I was often irritated by its idle pretentious ways. The Gospels speak of seeing the beam in one's own eye as well as the mote in one's brother's eye. Let us recollect that the Work was defined as esoteric Christianity and look for a moment into this matter of beam and mote. The phrase is: "Why beholdest thou the mote that is in thy brother's eye, but considereth not the beam that is in thine own eye?" (Matt. vii.3) (considerest—κατανοεῖς). In the Greek the word used for the mote is simply *see*. That is easy to do. But the word used for the beam in oneself is interesting. It means "to take notice of, to detect, to acquire knowledge of, to take in a fact about, to learn, to observe, to understand". Obviously something far more difficult is meant than merely seeing another's faults. To turn round is not easy. But the Work expects it.

If you study what Christ said, you discover that nearly everything referred to what is within you. The Work also is about what is within. That is why it begins with self-observation and self-noticing.

*Amwell, 19.7.52*

**THE WORK**
**AS A SPECIAL FORM OF PHOTOGRAPHY**

We cannot admit the possibility of continuous observation. Just as it is impossible to observe any outer object continuously so is it impossible to observe any inner object in ourselves continuously. There is one advantage, however, as regards self-observation—namely, that we carry ourselves about with us so that we can observe ourselves at any moment if it occurs to us to do so. Yet even so we do not really observe ourselves afresh, but in a stale way, by associations. We observe what we always observe—a dull process without light. If we practised observing each centre, a little light would enter in. If we observe in ourselves what we see in another, much more light enters. In that case, it certainly ceases to be associative self-observation which of course is not observation but a mechanical process. All self-observation of any use to us is conscious. These conscious self-observations are, as was said, not continuous observations. They are to be regarded as discrete, discontinuous *events* of a very special kind that ordinarily people rarely experience. These discrete—by which I mean separate—discontinuous events, however, undergo definite arrangement. They are put in order and form a special memory to which I have called your attention before and which I have termed *Work-memory*. Without it, personal work is at a minimum. This ordering of conscious observations of oneself is the work of centres themselves, and must be left to them, because any interference by the formatory part of Intellectual Centre can spoil their right arrangement. Many observations are emotionally or sensationally connected, for example, that formatorily we would not believe possible. The result of all this inner hidden work of arranging is that we may come to have whole-plate photographs of ourselves—say one, or perhaps two, after many years. Nothing more valuable can come into our possession than one of these full-size photographs. By the possession of one of these photographs, pieced together by the work of centres from hundreds of brief, but conscious, snap-shot self-observations, we are saved from the unconscious power of everything represented in that photograph. We know that the object of self-observation is to let the light of consciousness into what lies in darkness within us. We are unconscious of all that lies in darkness in us. Unconsciousness *is* darkness, and darkness *is* unconsciousness. The only remedy is consciousness, which is light. Light overcomes darkness. For a long time we do not understand what this means, hearing the words with our ears and not with the mind. We know that whatever we bring into the light of consciousness loses the power it has over us if it remains unconscious—that is, in our inner, unexplored darkness. Operating from our darkness it can have very great power and extraordinary fascination. What would be the object of conscious self-observation so that it is dragged into the light if it were not so? Yet, as I said, people do not see what is meant. They cannot connect *light* with *consciousness*, because the words are different. And for that reason they do not comprehend self-observation or what it is for. They do not grasp that, unless we let the light of consciousness increasingly into ourselves, we cannot change. All that we are unconscious of within, all that lies in the darkness of unconsciousness in us, remains unchanged and as active as ever.

Now all the Work is based on Consciousness—on the power of Consciousness to balance and so heal us. For once a thing that we were unaware of is made properly conscious and is seen in relation to other things that are conscious already, it becomes its right size and fits into its proper place or is seen as ridiculous and so robbed of power. This is balance through consciousness. It no longer can play the rôle of some violent or evil bandit waging a guerilla-war in the hinterland of consciousness. These bandits often turn out to be naughty little boys dressed up. Exposed to full light they look silly. It is the same with the action of buffers which prevent full consciousness and so real conscience. Some of you must know by now that you have inner contradictions in you that are eventually bound to lead to a fall, like the house divided against itself, which cannot stand. The two sides of the contradictions must be brought together often into the light of consciousness. There is no other remedy. The remedy is precisely simultaneous light—not light on one and then on the other.

Now to return to the most valuable thing we can possess—this whole-plate photograph. It was said that we are saved from the *unconscious* power of everything represented in it. This is because whatever is represented in it we have, at one time or another, made conscious by a momentary beam of observation. That is, consciousness over many years has touched every part of it. Yes—but the organization of all these snapshot observations, these discontinuous personal events, into a full-size photograph is not one's own work. *We* did not see the connections of our observations. But something in us did and finally presented us with the photograph. "This", it says, "is one aspect of your life that can no longer imprison you." We did not see all the relations between one part and another that we can now trace in the big photograph. For the big photograph is the fitting-together of all these separate and apparently unrelated snapshots into a living whole. That which had power over us and which we had to serve as long as it remained in the darkness of unconsciousness has become objective. A living-time photograph of this kind is beyond any powers of description in words because, like everything else coming from Higher Centres, it has a double-significance and a double-use. It is enough to say that what was subjective has been made objective and what one was unconscious of has now become conscious. From this point of view it can be said that this Work teaches *a special kind of photography*. I know that if one became possessed of even one of these full-sized photographs one could never undergo an absolute recurrence of the life. With one photograph to study one could never be as before and objective consciousness would not be far away.

*　　　*　　　*

Now let me point out a few things that apply to everyone: If we were fully conscious we would not need this Work. It would not exist on this planet. But we are not fully conscious. If we were, we would be fully conscious of our neighbours and they of us. We would then see ourselves in others and others in ourselves and hatred and wars would cease, among other things. You must each reach and *are expected to reach* the state of insight into seeing that there is very much in you that takes charge of you and that you are unconscious of. If you cannot see this probably you will feel mutinous and resist the Work, openly or silently, as some do. Try to realize your need of the Work. Try to realize, even theoretically, that there are many people in you that you are not conscious of and so know nothing about, who continually overpower you and make you do and say just what they wish, so that you cannot call your life your own. Never believe you are a well-balanced person. That belief makes you stiff and slow. You are one-sided; and the more one-sided you are the more will you think you are balanced. Remember that a balanced man is many-sided and flexible. Notice you do not behave consciously all the time by any manner of means. If you believe you do, you are simply a fool and fast asleep. You are not what you think you are. But you are many things that you do not think you are and are not yet in the least conscious of. It does not require much increase of consciousness through self-observation for you to begin to suspect this actually is the case. One should suspect oneself, not others. Now it is useless holding out against these few general statements taken from the Work. To do so may point merely to offended dignity, which is commonplace, or to something more serious. The Work, of course, is the reverse of flattering to you or me or anyone else. Let me remind you finally that G. said we must move our brains every day, apart from other things. He also said that this Work is to make us *think* in a new way—both about ourselves and life on this planet. We tend to sit in the semi-foetid atmosphere of our small minds with every window shut, clasping an appallingly hideous Imaginary 'I' that is continually squealing or grabbing at something that does not belong to it. *This* is the extent of our consciousness. *This* is Man in the 2nd State of Consciousness.


*Amwell, 26.7.52*

**SELF-LOVE**

It is little use being on this disciplinary planet resenting everything. Like other negative states resentment makes bad chemistry. A negative psychology fitted on to a healthy body poisons it. Here you have at least to remember two things. The first is that your being attracts your life. In short, there is something wrong with the way you take things. The other is that since Creation comes from the inter-action of Three Forces, a Trinity composed of active, passive and neutralizing powers, there will always be a passive, second or resisting force to oppose you in the very nature of things. It is not just someone else's fault. Also, it is useless personifying Second Force as the Devil. These two factors, one inside, the other outside, we ignore. We don't really listen. Our self-love is deaf. We prefer *to take things personally*. At the Institute, although we were told that Personality had scarcely any right to exist there, no one grasped quite what it meant. I fancy we did not even know we had *Personalities* to separate from. It takes so long to see. I did not realize that one meaning of this remark was that I must not take everything personally. If I had known and practised "absence from resentment" instead of a sort of tolerant, weary, British patience concealing my resentments, I would have understood some practical things earlier. Instead I made a point of shaving, however unearthly the hour we had to be up at, because, of course, one had to keep up appearances. I was not separating myself from Personality, but the reverse. That is the worst of ideals. I was following pictures. Putting the matter in another way, I was following my self-love, not diminishing it. Moreover, at that time I was seeking the Work mainly from self-love, expecting to become a magician with supernormal powers.

Now I am not speaking of resentment that one does not shew, but of the practice of *absence from resentment*, which is another matter. Politely concealing resentment does not change the underlying love of self. The practice of absence from resentment does. The Work, with all its teachings, ideas and diagrams, seeks to transform the self-love. It is not enough to love oneself. One has got to love the Work also. What on earth is this self-love? What is it like? How does it act? It is indeed difficult to grasp that as mechanical men and women we are based upon it. Let us try to find illustrations, approximations and definitions. We can say of it that it has endless disguises. It is a wolf in many sheep's clothing. In itself it resents injury. It hates being laughed at. It cannot laugh at itself. It would like every event to reflect merit on itself and everyone to admire it, and if possible bow down to it. In the latter case it disguises itself as extreme modesty and is very humble. But if stung by something overheard it speaks with a voice like a wasp in a treacle jar. It is at bottom quite callous, save to those who enhance its merit. To these it may disguise itself as kindness, which becomes hard-faced if a criticism or mistake is made. One may be sure that whatever the self-love does it has its own interests in view—however you exclaim you cannot believe it. Public buildings, munificent gifts, free libraries, benefit others, but enhance the donor's repute, which is the real object. What the motive appears to be, and what it is, is not the same—just as it is with each of us. We should know all this in ourselves.

One writer speaks of the self-love in these words: "What is more restless at heart, more easily provoked, more violently enraged, than the love of self; and it is as often as it is not honoured according to the vanity of its heart, or when anything does not succeed, according to its pleasure and desire." Now no one can see his self-love directly. It is only possible to see the results of it. Resentment, restlessness, being very easily provoked or violently enraged, are results that one can perchance observe. One prefers not to; or rather, the self-love will not permit it. Again, all negative emotions are results of self-love, injured or dissatisfied. You know all negative emotions lead down to violence—to the prehistoric man, the prehistoric woman. What we want lies on the other side of all that. Now some transformation of the love of self would mean some release from violence and so something of a new will that is not self-will. Will springs from what we love. Self-love and self-will are twin. I described in a recent commentary a man with a new will whom I met beyond the gulf of prehistoric bones, beyond violence. He showed no resentment. His self-love must have been transformed—perhaps into love of God—Amour propre into Amor Dei—or love of neighbour. But you can't have the latter without the former, it so happens.

In any case, the point is that the basis of self-love makes us all unhappy. We all have this basis, and it is useless looking down on another and saying "Thank God I have no self-love like that"—for it is simply your self-love speaking once more in a thin disguise. Self-love, self-will, self-righteousness—such as "I keep all the commandments"—these three make an ugly trio. Another kind of righteousness altogether is spoken of in the Gospels and in the Work. It has nothing to do with the righteousness of the False Personality, with meritoriousness, with reputation, with outward appearances, with audience—which have all to do with the love of self.

Do you yet realize that you may do good and speak truth and practise sincerity and behave justly all from the love of self, and all for the sake of reputation, appearance, honour or gain, and in yourself *will* nothing good and think absolutely nothing of truth? It is the person *in yourself* that the Work seeks to change. This concealed inner man or woman is the subject for transformation, so that if all social and police fears and all external restraints were removed, it would not rush into every sort of evil that comes out of the self-love.

Now life-education is, or should be, an education of the self-love. One gets prizes. What else is there for school-masters to work on? It is both desirable and necessary. It is preferable to be among people who have an educated self-love than among boors. But, speaking paradoxically, although it is desirable and necessary, it stands in the way of the Work. The Work may find no point of entry and the inner perception of its truth may never be experienced. Given force from another, it may enter the person, but the underlying self-love will keep on casting it out and the Deputy Steward will scarcely be formed. The Deputy Steward opposes the self-love. The Steward himself makes war on it.

Now one way to attack the self-love is through self-observation. One or two of the stupid inventions of the self-love about oneself may be noticed. They may be brought gradually into the light of consciousness. Self-observation lets in light. Light illumines ridiculousness. One laughs at oneself, and thus begins to injure one's own self-love. It shews a considerable step forward to be able to laugh sincerely at part of one's self-love. What is conscious—that is, the light—meets what was operating unconsciously, in the darkness. The white and black meet, in however small a way at first. But each time it happens thus, self-love is diminished, and consciousness increases at its expense. It is wonderful to catch a glimpse of your self-love and be able to laugh at it. One loses the former highly-explosive over-sensitive feeling of 'I' more and more. That means more balance. That means becoming softer. You may by observing one clear aspect of your self-love over a long period be given a full-sized photograph of it as it has run through your Time-Body. But we have spoken of all that already. One word more. The untransformed self-love, as I indicated, prevents change in the level of being.

In one of the Epistles Paul speaks of the difficulty he has with people in his groups who do not really care for what he is teaching in itself, but come for other reasons. He says "they all seek their own" (Phil. ii.21). In another place (II Tim. iii.7) where he is speaking openly of "lovers of self" (φιλαυτοι), he says they are "ever learning and never able to come to the knowledge of truth". He means that having only self-love and no love for his teaching they cannot raise their level enough to perceive internally the truth of what he taught, and know it for themselves.

NOTE: The subject of self-love is so immense that only a few sides of it are mentioned in this paper. All life is based on self-love. Everywhere people are seeking to gratify their self-love in one way or another, or seeking revenge for what they imagine are injuries against their self-love. One or two things can be mentioned. One of the great dangers that threaten humanity is organized self-love. This is done by giving people a certain ideal and drilling the young in it, but I am not going to speak of that any further. You can think about it for yourselves.

Do you agree that the following is a simple universal illustration of self-love? "Smith despises Brown, and laughs at him. Brown despises Smith and laughs at him. But Smith cannot laugh at Smith nor can Brown laugh at Brown. That is the trouble with us all. That is why the Work tells us to separate from Personality. I have to work on Nicoll and be able to laugh at him. It is quite easy for others to laugh at him. But that is not what is meant."

*Amwell, 31.7.52*

## SELF-LOVE AND THE UNIVERSE

If a man changes himself, his view of the Universe in which he lives changes also. The one cannot change without the other. Just as what he was becomes something different, so what he lives in becomes something different. He no longer feels himself in the same way as he once did; and he no longer feels the world in the same way as he did. What is your view of the Universe in which you live? Perhaps you have taken it for granted just as you have taken yourself for granted. That is to say, you have not thought much about either. In my case, I could regard the Universe simply as a vast machine, so vast that a ray of light which travels at 186,000 miles per second would take millions of years to cross it. It contains billions of stars, far more than we can see with the naked eye. These stars are arranged in great masses called galaxies. Our Sun is a star in our galaxy, the Milky Way. Our galaxy is shaped like a disc. As we are in the disc, looking upwards we see a thick band of stars overhead. There are about 100,000 million stars, like suns, in our galaxy. The 100″ telescope at Mount Wilson in America has discovered that there are some 100,000,000 of these galaxies within the limits of its range, which penetrates to a distance of 1,000,000,000 light years.* Try to conceive for yourself the distance that light will travel in a single year going at a speed of 186,000 miles per second, which is a light year, and then try to conceive a distance of 1,000,000,000 light years. It is inconceivable to us, although it may not be to some greater mind.

A ray of light starting from the second nearest star to us in our own galaxy—the Sun is the nearest star to us—takes more than four years to reach us. This means that we see it where it was four years ago. We see the Sun, however, where it was eight minutes ago. None of the stars, owing to their distances and the limited speed of light which crawls through inter-stellar space, is where it seems to be. In this Universe, vast beyond belief, of incredible depths, the earth swims as a minute speck illuminated on one side. On this half-dark, half-light speck, you and I, full of self-love and self-importance, exist as two still more infinitesimally minute specks. This is our situation in the visible Universe in terms of physical magnitude, extended in a space of 3 dimensions. As regards the fourth or time-dimension, it has a peculiar relationship to our present moment of time because we do not see where the stars are, but where they were in the past. We see the Universe in the past—as it was. It would be awkward if the same thing happened to the objects in our room. We would see them, but not touch them.

Now what is the effect of all this on the self-love? Does it make Man "walk more humbly before God", as the phrase goes? Does it diminish Man's exalted idea of his own importance? It did once, but not now. Some centuries ago when Galileo asserted that the earth not only rotated but moved round the Sun, Man's self-love, not being able to adjust to this idea, was seriously offended, so much so that Galileo was had up by the Inquisition and had to recant in public. That was the occasion on which he muttered: "All the same it does move" ("e pur si muove"). Hitherto people had actually thought that the minute speck, our Earth, was the immovable centre of the entire Universe with all its myriad stars, which obligingly and humbly revolved round it, together with the Sun, once in twenty-four hours. But there is always a way to re-assert one's self-love if it receives a shock when faced by anything breath-taking or stupendous. One can scribble one's name on it. Seeing the Parthenon for the first time, one can at least scribble one's name on one of the pillars. By this bit of cheek the self-love, like a naughty boy, recovers its jauntiness. Some modern astronomers seem

---

* As the discovery of the wider range of the telescope has been made since the author's death it has been thought advisable to amend the figure.

to do much the same in regard to the Universe. It is a favourite technique of the self-love to disparage whatever threatens its supremacy. One can always sneer. Science tells us that the Universe, however gigantic, is nothing to feel any awe or wonder about. It came into existence accidentally and is meaningless. So that's that. Since self-love hates what is greater or superior to it one suspects that this hatred, originating in the self-love, is behind the modern scientific negation of purpose and meaning in anything. Everything can be explained away, even the exquisite *order* that can be discerned in the structure of the most minute things such as atoms, as well as in the vast things such as solar systems and galaxies. Nature is viewed as a series of Chinese boxes, one within the other, and the scientists are already saying: "We hope quite soon to open the last, smallest, innermost box of all." They do not add that it will certainly be declared empty, whatever they find. When Jung said to Freud that many dreams had other interpretations than those of retrogressive sexual wish-fulfilments and some shewed useful prospective directions for personal development, he was told that that kind of thing must not be admitted. Jung refused not to admit it. To-day the quarrel with science in general is with its interpretations, some of which are of amazingly poor quality. But many scientists are afraid to say what they think. To declare that there is intelligence behind the Universe means ostracism.

Now the idea of a mechanical, accidental, meaningless Universe will not help Man to raise the level of his being. It will have a contrary effect and naturally does. Feeling neither awe nor wonder, the self-love is not affected. It was said in the previous commentary that if the self-love remains just the same no one can change in himself (or herself). Although this was not much understood, I will only say that it is useless to argue about it. It is, of course, always the self-love that is arguing, being afraid to lose its power over you. Have you not noticed the self-love is very sensitive to attack? The Work mentions two Giants that walk before us and arrange everything for us beforehand. They are Pride and Vanity. These two aspects of the self-love are very sensitive to anything that might depose them. They are cruel lords to serve. The Work cannot walk before us (as it should in all things) as long as the strength of these two empty mindless and barren Giants is not diminished. Long observation of them does weaken them. But look for a moment at this: *it is the quality of your love for the Work that determines your valuation of it and its power to change you.* If this love is distinct from your self-love, then your observation of the Giants will begin to weaken them. The Work weakens them, but if your love of the Work is only another manifestation of your self-love, your observation of the Giants will not weaken but strengthen them.

Now we know, from the teaching of the Work, that the Universe is a *creation*, and not a dead, inexplicable, accidental and meaningless thing. It is a living thing of systems within systems, each with purpose and meaning, each living and capable of developing or degenerating.

We are created in it with purpose and meaning, living and capable of development or degeneration. Humanity on the Earth is, in fact, a special experiment in self-evolution. Something more is demanded of us than simply living and making our living. It is this something extra that we study by means of the Work-teachings. The Work is about this something extra. So on the one hand, as I said at the beginning, I can regard the Universe as a vast machine, accidental, meaningless and dead, or I can look on it in the light of what the Work says about it. Which attitude is likely to diminish my self-love and so change me? I leave you to answer for me and for yourself. I mentioned at the beginning that probably you have not thought much about the Universe and so have no view of it. You take it for granted. Yet it is what you exist in. The Work emphatically calls attention to it. But people are scarcely aware even that they live in the Solar System. It seems strange that they will not extend their consciousness even to this extent. Can you guess the reason?

*Amwell, 9.8.22*

## SELF-LOVE AND THE INNER MAN

We seek the gift of a new quality of will, which does not know resentment. Collecting in our minds everything belonging to our personal Work-memory and all we have understood so far of what the Work is saying to us, we will have no difficulty in seeing that this new quality of will cannot be the same as the self-will. The self-will is based on the self-love. The latter continually feels resentment if not flattered and cosseted. It demands to have its own way and won't listen to anyone. It can turn into that burning anger that is so difficult to put out without memory and mental agility and then into hate and finally into violent action. The advantages of receiving the gift of a new quality of will from which resentment is absent are so numerous and obvious that it is hardly necessary to mention them. But I will indicate one or two. To have a will characterized by absence from resentment would be to become a *New Man*—that is, *another kind of man*. Such a man, for instance, would move through the criss-cross confusion of jealousies and ambitions and the tangle of human relations in general without losing force. For us, our more conscious energies are soon used up and we plunge into mechanical reaction. For him it would be otherwise. Where we sank, he would continue to walk. I said that he would be *another kind* of man. Many years ago we used to be asked this question; "What do you think a man belonging to the Conscious Circle of Humanity would be like? By what signs would you know him?" Naturally some thought he would be tall and inexpressibly handsome, a commanding figure with beautiful dark penetrating eyes, perfectly dressed and with perfect manners—and all the rest of it. Some thought he would be very strong with enormous muscles, a jutting jaw, an unbreakable will and tremendous energy. Some rather naïve people thought he would be extremely well-connected. Their imagination went no further. Ouspensky pointed out that all these very human suppositions about a Conscious Man were based on an exaggerated ordinary mechanical man. He said that a Conscious Man was *another kind* of man—a man totally different from an ordinary man. In short, a New Man. Now, from what we know, and have heard, we might venture to think that a Conscious Man would not be impressed by any of the manifestations of the self-love so unpleasantly rampant in us. In fact, he might attack them. That would be one sign to know him by. He might tell us to strip all that kind of thing off. A further sign would be absence from resentment, pointing to the possession of a *new will*. You will see at once that a Conscious Man could not have a will founded on self-love. A Conscious Man is a man who has undergone a change of being—actually a transformation of being. As it was pointed out to you in recent papers, *no change of being is possible as long as the self-love remains unchanged*; and as long as the self-love remains the same, the self-will remains just what it was. You will continue to obey yourself. You will not inwardly acknowledge anything above yourself. You will not inwardly obey the Work, though you may pretend to it outwardly. You will not refresh your inner man with it because you do not inwardly believe it.

I wish now to speak more of the outer and inner man. I adopt these terms partly from a remark of Paul in one of his letters to his group at Corinth. He is speaking of his own faith though he had, of course, never seen Christ. He writes: "For which cause we faint not but though our outward man perish, yet the inward man is renewed day by day" (II Cor. iv.16). It is this renewing—or making fresh again, as the Greek word has it—of the inner (eso) man, accompanied at the same time by the perishing—or wasting away—of the outer (exo) man, that we should pay attention to. It reminds us of the Work-teaching about making the Personality passive and the Essence active. Through the gradual wasting of the Personality, through withdrawing energy from its mechanical reactions, which makes it passive, the Essence develops. That is, the Essence can only develop at the expense of the Personality. The Personality we can relate to the outer (exo) or external part of ourselves that surrounds the Essence, and the Essence to the surrounded inner (eso) part. (*Eso*-teric Christianity refers to the inner meaning of what Christ taught: *exo*teric Christianity refers to the outer literal meaning and ritual.) Now the internal Essence and its understanding can only grow through what is genuine. Lies kill it. Truth develops it. It has a high origin. What is false strengthens outer Personality, which has life on earth as its origin. Again, what is of the self-love is not genuine and so can only strengthen Personality. Paul is talking in his own way about how a genuine faith renews or stimulates or makes alive again the *inner* man and weakens the outer man, ". . . though our outward man perish yet the inner man is renewed day by day."

Now the whole of the Work may lie in the outer man or Personality. You then get a queer result. The Work, which does not come from life but from a high origin, instead of leading to a development of the inner man or Essence, which also has a high origin, strengthens the outer man or Personality which has a low origin and comes from life. Such a person may appear to believe all that the Work teaches although he sounds tinny. And since in such a case there can be no renewing of the inner man (*day by day*), there is no refreshment given him from within. The Work remains on the surface of his mind as mere memory and not as something working deeply, continually leading to a further perception of truth.

When Christ spoke of people who were whited sepulchres it was meant that the outer does not correspond to the inner. Christ said:

> "Woe unto you, scribes and Pharisees, hypocrites! for ye are like unto whited sepulchres, which indeed appear beautiful outward but are within full of dead men's bones and of all uncleanness." (Matt. xxiii.27)

We have to look, then, at the quality of the inner man. I spoke of this in the last paper. It is a very necessary and practical exercise, just as is practising absence from resentment. What would you appear like if the external were stripped off you now and only the internal remained? What lies behind your polite façade? If you appeared just the same after it was stripped off you might indeed congratulate yourself on having developed Essence. I am afraid that the external show of an average man or woman bears little resemblance to the internal show. Now it is the internal and its state that counts in the Work—not the façade. Speaking specifically of the relation of the outer and inner side of a person to this Work, there are people who may say they believe it and speak well of it and have taught others and so have done good for the sake of the Work. Yet if the *outer* man were stripped off them and they were left only with their *inner* man exposed the case would appear quite otherwise. More internally it would be seen that they do not believe one jot in the Work and what it teaches. They do not think well of it and, in short, have used it to produce some kind of outer impression on others, such as having great knowledge, or knowing all about esotericism and so on. The astonishing thing is that they do not observe their contradictions, one of the things which the Work tells us to observe. Being incapable of observing what is going on in their interiors, they may believe they believe, or persuade themselves they do, refusing to face themselves by a single glance within.

Now as regards this inner man in you: when your consciousness of yourself has increased enough for you to see better what you are like underneath the illusions of the self-love, then, for the first time you may see why Christ so often and so harshly said: "thou hypocrite." This had no real meaning to you before. You could not seriously believe you were the hypocrite. You could not—without any extra light of consciousness to help you. But when more light came and the grip of the self-love thereby began to be loosened through some experiences of genuine self-observation without self-justifying or self-pity, an increase of consciousness was gained and you began no doubt to understand this saying and probably many others. They meant something to you for the first time. You began no doubt to understand why the Work is called esoteric Christianity—that is, the inner meaning of the teaching in the Gospels —a thing impossible to attain without work on yourself, beginning with a self-observation that is without criticism or self-justification or self-pity.

A final word: you may say you inwardly believe the Work. Perhaps you do. You are your own judge of that. But I would ask you one thing: have you faith in your belief? If you are not faithful to it daily it will not, like a plant, grow.

*Amwell, 16.8.52*

## A REVIEW OF ESSENCE AND PERSONALITY

Let us review briefly what we can now understand about Essence and Personality at this stage of our study of the Work. There is first the teaching that Man is of two distinct parts called Essence and Personality. This is, so to speak, the first great mystery about Man (the second being that he is asleep). The next thing is that a man is born as Essence only and has no Personality. In this condition he is harmless like all very young things. The third thing is that Essence only grows a little and becomes surrounded by Personality. The next thing is that Essence and Personality are not under the same number of laws. Essence manifesting itself in the new-born child is under 24 orders of laws and Personality manifesting itself in the growing child is under 48 orders of laws. Man therefore has two lives possible to him, one belonging to Essence and the other to Personality. The fifth thing is that Personality becomes active and in consequence Essence becomes passive. The Personality and its life dominate the Essence which remains undeveloped. The sixth thing is that the object of the Work is to reverse this state in Man and cause Essence to become active and Personality passive. When this state is attained, the life of Essence dominates the life of Personality. The man is then from the Work point of view a developed or complete man as distinct from an undeveloped or incomplete man. The seventh thing is that life and the world act as neutralizing or third force to keep Personality active and Essence passive. It is only when the Work becomes neutralizing force that a reversal can take place and Essence become active and Personality passive.

Let us content ourselves at present with these seven points or teachings specifically given by the Work concerning Personality and Essence, and continue by way of commentaries. I will take, to begin with, the two possible major triads in Man just mentioned. Here, let us suppose, is a man having in him the triad made up of Personality as active or first force, Essence as passive or second force, and Life as neutralizing or third force. This is his great configuration. Or, put in another way, this determines his relation to life. This configuration or relation is necessary and inevitable for so-called civilized Western Man. It happens to us all. Now let us suppose the existence of a man in whom the major triad is made up of Essence as active or first force, Personality as passive or second force, and the Work as neutralizing or third force. Such a configuration or relation is not necessary for a man to get along in life and certainly is not inevitable. It does not *happen*. It is not mechanically brought about. To attain it at least two things are needed. The first is to find a teaching designed precisely to lead to this state in which a new neutralizing force exists. The second is to live this teaching *in oneself* and so *do* all it teaches. Such a teaching will be *against life:* because life has produced the first triad and cannot produce the second triad. That is why it is said that the Work, *not* life, must become neutralizing or third force for the configuration of the second triad to take place. Notice that it will be useless merely to seek to change one's life by taking up a new profession or by playing the harpsichord or living in another country. All that is *life*. This becomes seen better as one begins to awaken. It prevents wrong or useless efforts or efforts to avoid real effort. Inner taste, in short, develops. Again, it will be useless merely to give up going about, or going to theatres, or reading novels, or playing on the harpsichord, and so on. No—what is important is to do what you did *differently* inside—for example, observing what you are like without identifying as you did, without always making accounts against others or getting so negative or feeling so resentful. The inner work can lead to change of the Life-triad eventually.

Now people often talk too glibly about the Work being a new neutralizing force, without realizing what this means. They see the Work-triad put up on the blackboard and nod their heads. They have seen that diagram before. Let us consider what it may mean and begin by considering what it does not mean. If a man or woman continues to live, speak, feel, think, act and behave as they always have, although they are being given the Work-teaching, then Life remains their neutralizing force and not the Work. They do not really value and so do not obey the Work. They value and obey Life. There is nothing reprehensible in this. Why shouldn't they? Why begin to strip off their clothes which they believe comfortable, on the vague promise of being given new ones that will suit them better? It is true that, remaining based on the self-love, which is a necessary characteristic of the Life triad, and therefore always liable to resent anything and everybody, they often experience distress or anger or unhappiness. But they will not perceive that this is because they wear a cruel hair-shirt underneath their surface-apparel without knowing it. They cannot perceive it because they do not value self-observation and change. All the familiar life-giants that spring from the self-love, the giants of pride, of vanity, and envy, all their innumerable attendant giants of jealousy and power and covetousness and hate that keep human life as it is, will prevent them. Such is the power of the first or the Life-triad. It is something that we, asleep in the apparently soft cocoon of self-love, only begin to see when we stir and begin to awaken and to emerge from the illusions that we are free and conscious and can do as we decide. I advise you always to observe self-love in yourselves and realize what it does to you, whether subtly or crudely. We are riddled with its evil poisons. Let no one tell me they do not have any or do not know what it is. That is the voice of self-love speaking. But let us leave the matter there and say a word as to what the Work as third force does mean and why esoteric or inner teaching must exist, as well as life-education, in view of the two distinct and discontinuous parts of Man—namely, Personality and Essence. Personality is developed by Life and has to be. But Life does not develop Essence. Why not? This is what the attention must be focussed on. Why should not Life bring Essence to its full development? How is it that a man in whom Life has developed a full Personality cannot proceed smoothly to a full development of Essence? Surely, if Life can do the first it can do the second equally easily? Not at all: Life cannot. Life can provide the food for the development of Personality but not the food necessary for the development of Essence. The secret is that Personality and Essence need *different* foods for their respective development. They need *different kinds of truths*. For example, the education of Personality is developed by a knowledge of the truths of science, but Essence is not. A knowledge, say, of the world-markets and the political situation develops Personality, but Essence is not developed by knowing truths of this kind. Essence, before it is manifested in a human body, derived from the parents on earth, comes from a much higher level than the Planetary World under 24 orders of laws. It is said that it comes "from the stars". Our Sun is a Star in our Galaxy of Stars called the Milky Way. Whether you say it comes from the level of the Sun or from outside our Solar System does not matter for the moment. The point is that it has a very high origin, in vertical scale. By comparison, Personality has a very low origin, whatever one's ancestry in the past in horizontal time. Now Essence ceases to grow because it has not the right food from Life to grow by. But if a man, imbued with a knowledge of this Work (whose origin is the Conscious Circle of Humanity, which in the Gospels is called the Kingdom of Heaven) continually steeps his mind in its Truths and thinks and thinks again from them and perceives their depth and acknowledges them and applies them to his inner states, Essence will begin to grow. He is giving it the right food that the business of Life does not supply. His energies will cease to flow only downwards into his personal reactions but begin to flow upwards, like the mythical Jordan, to another level, where Essence lies. For Essence and Personality are on different levels. *We* are also. One is under fewer laws than the other. This means it is on a higher level. Only the kind of Truth that the Work teaches develops Essence. If a man loves it, he eventually wills it, and if he wills it he does it. It is this willing to do this Truth of the Work that forms the New Will in a man—of which we have spoken recently. It is this willing to do the Truth of the Work that develops Essence. This is its right food, which it came down to receive. Essence is deathless. When the body of flesh and bones is laid aside it returns to the place from which it came, taking what it has received. This willing of the Work is not from the self-will, which comes from the self-love. The will of the Personality takes second place to this will. The will of the outer Personality obeys the Will of the inner Essence. It is content to say: "Not my will but Thine be done." Having made the Personality passive through the developed Essence becoming active, by the power that comes from doing the Truth of the Work, which is stronger than life, the man has now attained the secret *end* and hidden meaning of his creation. From being the semi-man that Life made him he is now a complete MAN.

*Amwell, 23.8.52*

## ESSENCE AND THE RETURN JOURNEY

The following quotation is of some interest in view of the subject of recent papers. It is as follows:

"I dwell in the high and holy place with him who is of a contrite and humble spirit." (Isa. lvii.15)

Whatever this means, it suggests that a man filled with the love of himself, who never questions his own importance, is not likely to be able to ascend in the Scale of Being to any higher level of development. Presumably the speaker in the above quotation is on a high level because he says that he dwells in the "high and holy place". To ascend to his level, a person must apparently be humble and contrite. We know that there are ascending and descending lives in this world; and no doubt in any other world also. But we know specifically that some definite thing is meant by *ascent* in the Work. I mean that we know that an ascending octave—Do, Re, Mi—proceeds from what is coarser to what is finer, and that it always begins with passive Do. Now do you imagine that the self-love is a passive thing? Would you say that it is humble and contrite? Obviously self-love and all its children—pride, vanity, power, egotism, and the rest, have nothing contrite or humble about them. A man will not ascend by their aid to new being. Now, a passive Do means that whatever it refers to can be acted on by something above it in scale. *It yields to what is higher than itself.* On the other hand an active Do means that whatever it is, it acts on something else, and is not acted upon. Consider the food 768 taken into the body. It is acted on by digestive juices. That is to say, it is passive, because it submits to their action which breaks the food into finer and, therefore, cleverer and more useful matters which pass into the blood, while all that is useless is cast out. This is what the Work should do to us psychologically, if we only would allow it to. But the self-love will do all it can to prevent this from happening. In the case of the Food-Octave, the first step consists in passive Do 768—which is ordinary food—being transformed into the higher matters classified as 384; and so on upwards stage by stage to matter 12. If 768 entered as an *active* Do it could only go downwards in the scale of matters becoming denser and denser and, therefore, more stupid and more useless. So it is psychologically with anyone whose unregenerate, unfaced and unfought self-love is dominant, for this blocks the way to any ascending octave. Self-love is not passive and it refuses to be acted on.

Now since Essence descends from a "high place" and becomes ultimately encased in a body of flesh and bones, an ascending octave must exist in Man connected with this descent. The idea here is that Essence having descended may be able to re-ascend—that is, to retrace the path of its descent. If Essence re-ascended and the centre of gravity of a man's consciousness and being were truly situated in Essence instead of in Personality, then the re-ascent of Essence would be the ascent of the man also to the level of his origin. It would be the return journey. This idea of the "return journey" is mentioned in many places in ancient esoteric literature, as in the Hymn of the Robe of Glory in Gnostic writings, and it is obviously referred to in the parable of the Prodigal Son in the Gospels (Luke xv). The Prodigal Son, who was in all probability a man who had attained all the desires of his self-love and found that everything tasted like husks and nothing was real—perhaps he has been a multi-millionaire—is described as "coming to himself". He became aware in some way or other that he was not going in the right direction and had come to the end of things. Everything had become meaningless, as it does easily when only the gratification of the self-love and its ambitions is the object. So he says, after having *come to himself*: "I will arise and go to my father and say to him, Father, I have missed the mark." So he arose and came to his father. It does not mean his earthly father. His father rejoices and says: "Make merry, this my son was dead, and is alive again; he was lost, and is found." You will see some significance in these words *dead* and *lost.* When a man turns round and, leaving Personality behind, begins to move in the direction of Essence, he ceases to be dead or to be lost. Seeking the development of Essence through the internal man, and turning away from the falsities and insincerities and shallow professions of the external man, he begins to become alive instead of being *dead* inwardly, in spirit. He begins to see what he has to do, what is spurious in him, what he has to observe and make more and more conscious and work on, and what he has to strip off and leave behind. So he is no longer *lost*, aimlessly drifting through the years. He is going somewhere now. He is going on a real journey. It is a long journey, but he will soon begin to feel he is being helped. This is why in the parable it says: "But when he was yet a great way off his father saw him and had compassion" and ran to welcome him. The phrase "a great way off" indicates that the journey from Personality to Essence is a long one. Compassion and welcome indicate help. It is as if the Work were speaking, and saying that when a man really comes to himself—that is, when he remembers himself and recognizes himself—he knows that he is not the person he is always pretending to be, or has taken himself to be, and that he is going in the wrong direction in trying to keep it up. It is curious that this parable is called the Parable of the Prodigal Son. What was he prodigal of? Some people seriously think it refers to money. They take it sensually, literally, and imagine it was used by thrifty parents who unknowingly were eating husks themselves. You will notice that the word "Prodigal" does not occur in the parable. It is really a parable about a man who, however successful, finds that life does not give him what he expected and who, realizing that he must have some other origin than life, which does not make sense taken by itself, and something else to do apart from the business of living, sets out to unlearn all the falsity that life and its fashions have filled him with, and to strip off all the attitudes that his vanity and self-illusions have formed in him. It is really a parable about the *return to one's origin*—not to one's mother, but to something beyond and different. The man has discovered his true origin. He has discovered Essence. His whole emotional life begins to change. He has caught the rope overhead—not by being merely told about it, but by jumping for it himself, by an effort of his very own, by an inner act of his inner man. In connection with the realization of our vertical origin, as distinct from our temporal origin, and the resulting *recognition* of oneself, I will give a few quotations, without comment. Christ said: "Call no man your father upon the earth" (Matt. xxiii.9). When his mother speaks to him at the miracle of water into wine, he says: "Woman, what have I to do with thee?" (John ii.4). Elsewhere he says: "Know ye not that ye are all sons of God?" I will give a brief extract from the Hermetic Literature (*Hermetica Bk.* 1). The writer is speaking of the Creator setting the cycles of birth and death of all living things on earth going, including Man. But Man is different from all the rest of Organic Life—about which we shall speak in a moment. Man has within him something more than animals and this he must get to know. He has *mind* over and above sense.

"Let Man, who has mind in him, recognize he is immortal. . . . He who has recognized himself enters into that Good which is above."

He adds that those who do not, wander in the darkness of the sense-world and repeated rebirth into it. Lastly, there is Jacob's vision of the ladder stretching between Heaven and Earth, with figures ascending and descending:

> "And he [Jacob] dreamed, and behold a ladder set up on the earth, and the top of it reached to heaven: and behold the angels of God ascending and descending on it." (Genesis xxviii,12)

You must think for yourselves what these few references must indicate.

Now we can see that none of what is said above can be similarly applied to the Personality. I mean, that there is no return journey *via* the Personality, because it is on the level of life and created by life. There is, therefore, no *ascent* in the Scale of Being through the Personality. It did not descend into this earth-life as Essence did, but was made by this life. The main problem with Personality, eventually, is to make its power almost *negligible at will*. It can then be used. Now, let us return to the origin of Essence. We understand that Organic Life originated from the level of intelligence represented visibly by the Sun. It is simpler just to use the term "Sun". It became necessary for the Sun to create a sensitive living film on the earth capable of receiving influences coming down the Ray of Creation and passing them on to the terminal point of our particular Ray—namely, the Moon. We will have to speak in terms of allegory. The Sun was willing to undertake this task, only it made the condition that it must receive something for itself as a reward for all the labour of planning, creating, experimenting and maintaining the sensitive film of Organic Life on earth. For this purpose, after having made the conditions on earth suitable for his existence, it created Man *as a self-developing organism*. That is, it gave Man more than was necessary. This special creation was purely experimental. It may fail. The point was that if a sufficient number of human beings developed themselves beyond what was necessary for mere existence and survival on the earth, they could rise in the Scale of Being to the level of what is represented as the Sun. The Sun would then receive something for itself. For this purpose also, a certain kind of teaching, giving directions for this self-development, was sown in suitable places and times on the earth. Owing to the level of Man's intelligence it could not be presented except in a difficult and seemingly distorted way. This is what is meant by *C* Influences coming from the Conscious Circle of Humanity inevitably changing into *B* Influences on the earth. The trouble lies in our ordinary thinking, which cannot embrace the opposites although our Higher Centres can. For the rest, Organic Life was made a kind of pain-factory in which everything has to make continual effort or suffer in different ways, and all this birth, pain, death, suffering and fear, and also negative emotion and anxiety, produces vibrations which are food for the nourishment of the growing Moon. Such, very briefly, is our situation in Organic Life on earth.

Paul speaks somewhere about the *whole of creation* groaning together, awaiting the birth of the Sons of God. He says:

> "For the earnest expectation of Created Nature waiteth for the revelation of the Sons of God . . . for we know that the whole creation groaneth and travaileth in pain . . ." (Rom. viii.19, 22)

It is not known in what school Paul was taught, but this phrase seems similar to what the Work teaches. You also find similar hints scattered through the Gospels. Man, therefore, as distinct from other forms of life, has a chance in this difficult world of suffering, pain and danger, and his position is not hopeless. He has that in him which comes *from above*, although being asleep he has forgotten his origin and believes only in his senses. If he develops his relationship to that which comes from above, after first developing his necessary relationship to that which comes from life, he can ascend to the level of his origin. We can suppose that the term "Sons of God" refers to those who have undergone this development, and ascended to another level of experience.

Both the Gospels and the Work give directions about how to begin this ascent. If you ponder on what is said, for example, in the Sermon on the Mount, you will become convinced that it is not the self-love and the various crude or subtle forms in which it can manifest itself that point the way to this ascent. Some other love is the starting-point.

*Amwell, 30.8.52*

### THE ANTAGONISM
### BETWEEN THE SELF-LOVE AND THE WORK

Can some of you not yet observe and not yet laugh at even one manifestation of your self-love a little? Are you still too proud or smugly self-satisfied or just blind to yourself? Remember that no change in your psychology can take place as long as your love of self remains unchanged.

When the body of flesh and bones is laid aside you can take nothing with you except your psychology. You become your psychology. You become the victim of it. If you hate, you find yourself in hatred, with all those who similarly hate. You then all hate one another. Hate springs from the self-love that has been offended or slighted or made fun of. The person who is always feeling insulted is full of the love of himself. He hates people. There is an extraordinary amount of hate in the world to-day. Hate makes people sub-human in behaviour, as we have witnessed in recent years. To begin to grasp what you are psychologically, ask yourself frequently what your relation is to the good of the Work, to the truths it teaches about ourselves. What is your relation to its good and to its truth?

I speak of one's inner—that is, one's real—relation, not what one's False Personality pretends or displays or imagines. Your psychological body is rightly organized according to your inner relation to the Work. Let us make some reflections on this inner relation. When people secretly feel they are doing a kindness to the Work by associating themselves with it, they have no inner relation to the Work and actually are in psychological danger. A man or a woman must truly want the Work more than the present state of their lives to begin to have an inner relation to it. They must be careful never to patronize it outwardly or inwardly. I have witnessed the ruthless consequences of doing so. To connect the Work with the personal self-love is to value oneself more than the Work. Is that plain? The psychological body is then in disorder and cannot be formed. One sign of this is that these people who at bottom love and value themselves and their present lives before all else never get hold of anything clearly that the Work teaches. Everything is muddled and confused and obscure to them. The reason is that the thought has no clear direction. It is as if opposing currents meet in a stream and stir up mud in the swirl. They go round and round. Why? Because the Work threatens the self-love. How do you suppose you can think clearly about the Work when your self-love secretly detests it or ridicules it? Your thoughts will not take it in. In this connection I quote again a remark made by Paul in his second letter to Timothy. He is speaking about what happens when the self-love meets esoteric truth. He is referring especially to the end of the age in which we are now living, "when every thing is cracking—little by little", as G. said. He mentions various signs and symptoms of the general breakup of all good and truth and the rise of evil and falsity. Among other things he says: "For men shall be lovers of their own selves (φιλατοι) . . . ever learning and never able to come to the knowledge of the truth" (II Tim. iii.2, 7). You should be able to see the reason why they cannot perceive truth for themselves. The self-love fights against the truths of the Work. The truths of the Work can waken us. The self-love seeks to keep the man or woman asleep. Awakening is thus rendered impossible for them. They are "ever learning and never able to come to the knowledge of the truth". It must be clear to everyone by now that no one can awaken without self-observation. To awaken, a person must see more and more clearly what he or she is like. This is painful. But it gives us courage to die to ourselves and our self-love. When the self-love is strong it prevents all self-observation. A person simply cannot see what is meant when told he is difficult, slow, self-satisfied, lazy, smug, conceited, and so on. The self-love will not accept it. It may get violent. If you cannot see by your own observation, step by step, over a long, accumulating time, what you are like, you cannot awaken to what you are like, and so will never desire to die to what you are like. Your consciousness of yourself will not shew any increase. And unless you begin to awaken to what you are like, the self-love will continue to have full undisputed power over you. You will think,

of course, that you are having power over yourself. You will be griev-
ously, tragically wrong. It will be your pride, your conceit, your vanity,
and the annoyance or violence you feel when these are wounded that
have power over you. It will be the idea of your own charm and excellence, your self-esteem, self-valuation, self-importance, your polite
superiority, and contempt of others, that will direct you. It will be your
inner indifference and downright selfishness and meanness, your envy,
jealousy and your desire for power, that will control you. All these
giants, the offspring of the self-love, *have power over you*, not you over them.
This silly little imaginary 'I', this imaginary thing you call 'I', makes
you imagine that you are marching through life in the multitude of
your own cleverness and strength, and that is what is so tragic in us all.
No, you are being marched along by these tough, merciless giants. A
good subject indeed for a cartoon—as are so many things in the Work.
(For example, try to draw your False Personality.) Yes, these giants
are cruel lords. A man much governed, say, by his vanity, suffers often
and uselessly from this particular giant. So he is perplexed, often hurt.
As I said recently, it is just as if he wore a hair-shirt and did not know
it or why he was uncomfortable. All the aspects of the self-love can
torment and make us suffer in hundreds and hundreds of ways, all
of them useless. They spoil our lives. *Therefore we must observe, and again
observe, our self-love, and bring it into conscious perception and acknowledge it.*
This I will call the direct method. *Or we must observe time and again what
we are really like.* This steadily diminishes the love of self. We begin to
lose our admiration and love of ourselves as we continue to observe our
behaviour and what is in us. This I will call the indirect method. At
points they merge. In both cases, however, you must not justify yourself. Or rather, since this is impossible, *you must also observe how you
justify yourself.* I mean, that you must include in your observation of
something in your self your justifying of it *as one complete observation.* This
we continually forget to do, although we have been taught it often
enough. Ouspensky used to emphasize that people's observations of
themselves were always incomplete, for one reason because they did
not observe how they criticized or justified themselves afterwards. When
you observe also the result on yourself of what you observe you have
brought into consciousness what otherwise you would have identified
yourself with. Remember that what you observe distinctly you are not
identified with. When you identify with all you say, feel, think and do,
you are not observing it. You are then asleep. Now to continue; let us
consider a little more the difficulties of seeing the self-love.

Your inner relation to the Work, whereby it will nourish you,
depends on two things. One is your own perception of the truths it
teaches. Some of these truths are that Man is asleep and his special
task is to awaken from sleep, that one is a multiplicity and not a unity,
that one does not remember oneself, that one identifies and internally
considers, that one constantly submits to the power of negative emotions
and False Personality, that one has only Imaginary 'I' and makes the

fatal mistake of taking it as Real I; and so on. These are a few of the truths of the Work. I mention this because I was asked recently what I meant by the truths of the Work. The second thing that determines your inner relation to the Work is *doing the Work*. If you connect yourself *by your own inner perception* with the truths of the Work and by doing them *realize their good*, you will receive the two foods necessary for the development of Essence. Just as the physical body requires literal food and drink for its nourishment, so does the psychological body require the two psychological foods of good and truth, which the Work can supply.

Now one of the things *to do* is to observe oneself and realize most thankfully the *good* of it in process of time. One of the difficulties in self-observation is to bring home to yourself the meaning of a word applied to you. Let us take the word *vanity*. Someone might say to me: "You are vain." Let us suppose the meaning of the word does not come home to me, owing to my never having observed myself, I might reply: "I am not in the least vain", and feel vexed. There is a gap here, which can only be filled in by oneself. When G. told someone years ago that his chief feature was *Peacock*, the person was incredulous. He could not see what was meant, and I believe never did. Yet others could easily see what was meant. This illustrates one of the difficulties of *doing* the Work on the side of observing oneself. You are given a word—such as self-love—and cannot find any application of it to yourself. On the other hand you may observe at times something you cannot find a word for and recognize only by inner taste. Perhaps, years later, you realize it is vanity, about which you were incredulous. This is a characteristic experience in the Work, and is a sign of the self-love weakening and letting in some truth about oneself.

Now to return to the antagonism between self-love and the Work and the question of the quality of one's inner relation to the Work. The matter can be stated simply. If your relation to the Work is mingled with self-love you will receive nothing real and the danger is great because the seed of the Work may be destroyed. This is the theme of several parables. The seed falling on rocky ground and being destroyed by the heat of the sun is one:

"And when the sun was risen, it was scorched; and because it had no root it withered away." (Mark iv.6)

The sun here is the heat of the self-love. The great parable in this connection is the one dealing with the Cleansing of the Temple. It means that the inner relation to the Work must be cleansed of the element of the self-love and its interests and ambitions. The Work is not a business proposition, nor has it to do with life-aims. These things cannot develop Essence which has come down from another level. *The inner relationship to the Work*, cleansed from the self-love, forms *the temple in ourselves*. Through this "temple" communication with a higher level is possible, but not if it is defiled with the self-love and its interests:

"And Jesus went into the temple of God, and cast out all them that sold and bought in the temple, and overthrew the tables of the moneychangers, and the seats of them that sold doves, and said unto them, It is written, My house shall be called the house of prayer; but ye have made it a den of thieves." (Matt. xxi.12, 13)

You will notice how harshly the Work in the person of Jesus deals with the mingling of the love of self with one's inner relation to it. It is a mixing of two levels which, if not separated in the mind and heart, are mutually antagonistic. It is the psychological meaning of this parable that is important for us to-day.

*Amwell, 20.9.52*

## A NOTE ON THE MEANING OF FAITH

### WORK-INTRODUCTION

We return for the time being to the necessity of psychological thinking in the Work as distinct from sensual thinking. The idea, briefly expressed, is that nobody can develop *internally* by means of sensual thinking. The kind of thinking based on the senses alone, however logical, carries us only so far. It does not and cannot open the inner mind. Only psychological thinking can do so. In this connection we have in the first place the scale the Work gives of levels of thinking:

GREATER MIND

Psychological Thinking

Logical Thinking    Sense-thinking    Formatory Thinking

A-logical Thinking    Superstition

I will remind you that we were told that unless we believed in the existence of Greater Mind we could not assimilate the Work—that is, take it in so that it becomes a part of us and thus influences us. The ability to reach the level of psychological thinking depends on the conviction of the existence of Greater Mind. Without psychological thinking we cannot make contact with Higher Centres. In the second place we have the three primary divisions of the Intellectual Centre and the Emotional Centre, termed the moving part, the emotional part, and the intellectual part.

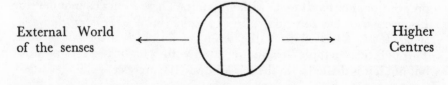

External World
of the senses ⟵                              ⟶ Higher Centres

I will take the Intellectual Centre and call the moving part the site of the outer or external mind, the emotional part the site of the middle or intermediary mind and the intellectual part the site' of the inner or internal mind. This latter mind is turned to Higher Centres. Sensual Thinking cannot open it: only Psychological Thinking can open the inner mind. Now try to notice the points of contact between what has been said above and what follows, which is taken from a chapter in the book being written, provisionally called *The Mark*.

★    ★    ★

### FAITH

The word translated as *faith* (pistis) in the New Testament means more than belief. It means *another kind of thinking*. Let us take an example from the Gospels. In Matthew xvi (5-12) it is said:

"And when his disciples were come to the other side, they had forgotten to take bread. Then Jesus said unto them, Take heed and beware of the leaven of the Pharisees and of the Sadducees. And they reasoned among themselves, saying, It is because we have taken no bread. Which when Jesus perceived, he said unto them, O ye of little faith, why reason ye among yourselves, because ye have brought no bread? . . . How is it that ye do not understand that I spake it not to you concerning bread, that ye should beware of the leaven of the Pharisees and of the Sadducees? Then understood they how that he bade them beware not of the leaven of bread, but of the doctrine of the Pharisees and of the Sadducees."

In this incident it is clear that the disciples took something said by Christ in its sensual meaning—that is, according to the literal sense of the words. Christ told them that this was a sign that they had little faith. It is not a question of *belief*. They may have believed greatly in the seen Christ. Yet they had little *faith*. What does this mean? It means that faith is something more than belief. In this case, faith means understanding on a level other than literal understanding. Sensual understanding cannot make contact with the meanings contained in Christ's teaching. He was not speaking of literal leaven but of psychological leaven. Christ was not speaking sensually but psychologically. His words had no sensual meaning but only psychological meaning. The leaven spoken of was not literal leaven nor was bread literal bread but falsity infecting good. Sadducees and Pharisees are always within us. The Sadducees can be compared with the scientists of to-day. They did not believe in any life after death. That is their leaven of falsity. The Pharisees can be compared with people who are in appearances, who, so to speak, think the important thing is to go to Church on Sunday "to be seen of men". That is their leaven. They were stigmatized as hypocrites—without inner belief. Now Christ here connects the disciples' lack of psychological understanding and consequent inability to see what was meant with littleness of faith. In other words, Christ connects the capacity of *psychological understanding* with the possession of faith; and sensual understanding with littleness of faith, or even elsewhere with blindness, with complete absence of faith and inner death. *Faith is necessary to open a part of the mind not opened by the senses.*

Let us turn now to some other passages concerning faith and its high meanings. Many may have believed in Christ as a visible miracle-worker. They believed through what they saw, through the evidence of the senses. But in Hebrews xi.1, faith is called a *basis* for belief in what *is not seen.* "But faith is a basis for things hoped for, a conviction of things unseen." It is not only a conviction of things unseen, but is a basis or plane on which another world of relations and values can be reached, one that is above the seen world and the cause of it. So the unknown writer of Hebrews continues in these words:

> "It is faith that lets us understand how the worlds were fashioned by God's word; how it was that from things unseen all that we see took their origin."

The writer goes on to describe how through the possession of faith certain things have been done. Now although it may be true that nowhere in the Scriptures is faith exactly defined, but chiefly its effects, certain things are said about it—as above—to shew it has to do with an inner perception of scale. If faith causes a man to perceive in his mind that a world, invisible to sense, lies above the seen world and is the cause of it, then he perceives things in scale—that is, in terms of higher and lower levels. When the centurion said that he was a man who was under those above him in authority while he himself had those who were under him in rank and added that it must be the same with Christ, he was speaking in terms of scale. He meant that Christ only had to give orders and his sick servant would be healed. On hearing this Christ exclaimed that never before had He met any one who understood better what faith meant. It is related that a centurion sent messengers to Christ asking Him to heal his servant:

> "And Jesus went with them, and when he was now not far from the house, the centurion sent friends to him, saying unto him, Lord, trouble not thyself: for I am not worthy that thou shouldest come under my roof: wherefore neither thought I myself worthy to come unto thee: but say the word and my servant shall be healed. For I also am a man set under authority; and having under myself soldiers; and I say unto this one, Go, and he goeth; and to another, Come, and he cometh, and to my servant, Do this, and he doeth it. And when Jesus heard these things, he marvelled at him, and turned and said to the multitude that followed him, I say unto you, I have not found so great faith, no, not in Israel. And they that were sent, returning to the house, found the servant whole." (Luke vii.6-10)

To return to Hebrews, the writer goes on to say: ". . . it is impossible to please God without faith." That is, it is impossible without the basis or foundation of faith, which makes it possible for a man to think beyond the evidence of his senses and realize the existence of invisible scale and understand psychological meaning. To realize scale means to realize that there are different levels of meaning. Literal meaning is one thing, psychological or spiritual meaning is another thing—although the words used are the same. For example, we saw that the word *yeast* used in the incident quoted indicated two levels of meaning. The disciples took it on the lower level and were told it was because their *faith* was little. Their thinking was sensual. They had difficulty in thinking in a new way on another level. And their psychological thinking was so weak just because they were based on sense and not on faith. Thus *sense and faith describe two ways of thinking, not opposites, not antagonistic, but on different levels.* For without the perception of scale and levels, things are made to be opposite when they are not so, and Man's mind is split into "either"—"or", which leads to endless confusions and mental wrangles and miseries. The writer goes on to say: "Nobody reaches God's presence until he has learned to believe that God exists and that He rewards those that try to find Him." It is apparent that if scale is behind all things, if *order* is scale, and if to set in order is to set in scale, then what is higher and what is lower must exist. To everything there must be an above and a below. A man who cannot perceive scale, visible or invisible, as did that centurion by means of his psychological understanding due to his great faith, will be shut to the intuitions that only faith opens out to every mind that hitherto has been asleep in the senses and the limited world revealed by them.

NOTE

(1) According to the Work-diagram, there is an outer, middle and inner mind. Call them what you like: only the outer mind is related to the senses and the inner mind to Higher Centres and their mode of thinking.

(2) The inner mind cannot be opened by the love of self for then a man thinks only about himself and always looks to himself in all things and to nothing higher.

(3) If the inner mind is not opened the man lives in externals and has only the senses and sensual thinking as his basis of understanding. He has no power of psychological thinking—or at least very little—because he is not in touch with Higher Centres.

## HOW WRONG ATTITUDES PUNISH US

The Work emphasizes the importance of attitudes. In self-study we are told we must observe our attitudes. It is said that we cannot change unless our attitudes change. A wrong attitude distorts our relationship to things. The Work teaches us that we are connected with outer things as by threads through our attitudes. When you have no attitude towards anything you are not connected with it. If you are completely indifferent, for example, to religion, you may imagine you are very tolerant, but it is really due to your having no attitude to it. The influences that are created in life, such as politics, war, and all its intrigues, riches, social position, business, sport, breaking speed records, drink, gambling, and so on, are called *A* Influences. Our attitudes to them connect us with them and hold us to life, not merely as by threads, but often by ropes. According to your attitudes so are you connected to these life-influences. Other influences of a different order are sown into life by the Conscious Circle of Humanity and they have to do with psycho-transformism—that is, with the possible transformation of Man through inner development. They are not created by life. These influences in themselves are called *C* Influences, but they become changed by life into *B* Influences. This is because to understand *C* Influences directly we should have to understand the language of Higher Centres, which think in terms of Yes and No. We think in terms of Yes or No. That is, we think formatorily. Formatory thinking has no third or connecting force as have Higher Centres. Third Force relates the two opposing forces. Formatory thinking is like asking whether in riding a bicycle you should turn the front wheel to the right or to the left and insisting on having a definite answer.

Now this Work primarily comes from *C* Influences and it can open up Higher Centres. Our connection with the Work depends on our attitude to it, and to the idea of Greater Mind or Conscious Man. Attitudes can be negative or positive. If you have a negative attitude towards the Work, you will not be able to take it in. This may happen if a man has no Magnetic Centre, because Magnetic Centre is actually defined as the power of distinguishing between *A* and *B* Influences. For example, one should be able to distinguish between the influences contained in the *Financial Times*, and the influences contained in the Gospels. One should be able to see that they are about quite different things. A man seeking to enter this Work should study over a considerable period through self-observation what his attitudes are towards it. It is an interesting and necessary part of self-study. Some of his attitudes will be negative and some will be positive. As his study of the Work increases through its application to his own being, and the seeing and acknowledging the truth of it, his attitudes will then become more positive and less negative. Truth changes him. If, however, he does not study the Work in relationship to his being through self-observation, and sees no truth in it, his attitudes will not be altered. He will remain the same. Since we are not directly conscious of our attitudes, we must try to discover them by some method, as by noticing the effects they produce. The trouble is that we are at home with our attitudes, but the Work will inevitably make war with many of them if we let it in. If you do not wish to change and see no reason for it, the great thing will be not to let the Work in so that you can continue to remain as you are. (I give you this as a profound secret.) I must repeat again that people do not know they have attitudes. They just dislike these people, and like those people, dislike these interests and like other interests, and so on, without realizing that this is all due to attitudes in them. Very naïve people tell you that they have no attitudes and really believe it—they imagine they have open minds.

Now by way of commentary I want to speak about how wrong attitudes injure ourselves. We cannot have wrong attitudes without in some way harming ourselves. As I said, a wrong attitude gives one a wrong relationship to a thing; for example, a wrong attitude towards other people gives us a wrong relationship to ourselves. I will try to explain by taking the attitudes we have towards the opposite sex. There is a woman in a man, and there is a man in a woman. As long as we are one-sided and so unbalanced—that is, as long as we are No. 1, 2 or 3 people, there is disharmony in the man with the woman in him, or in the woman with the man in her. That is to say, the woman within the man punishes the man, and the man within the woman punishes the woman. In each case, they are at variance with themselves. When the man brings the woman in him into consciousness, or the woman brings the man in her into consciousness, then this inner variance ceases. It is long work, but from it comes peace and acceptance of the sexes. I am, of course, speaking psychologically here. This is what Christ apparently meant when He was asked when His kingdom should come and answered:

"When the two shall be one, and that which is without as that which is within, and the male with the female neither male nor female."

This saying of Christ is reported in the Second Epistle of Clement. We can notice here that in the case of a man, that which is without is the man, and that which is within is the woman—and vice versa. Now if a man has a bad attitude to Woman, then he has a bad attitude to the woman in himself. If a woman has a bad attitude to Man, then she has a bad attitude to the man in herself. It is exactly the same with everything. You can have a bad attitude to life, to the world and to the Universe itself—but you are in all these things and these things are in you. In the same way, if you hate your fellow beings you are also hating something in yourself, and some part of you, and in fact a very important part of you, will be dwarfed and crippled. The more one reflects on attitudes, the more one realizes how important they are, and how dangerous wrong attitudes can be. When attitude is right, the fullest connection is made. If we had *objective consciousness* we should see things as they really are. If we saw things as they really are we would have right attitude to everything. This is far from us at present. If a man became conscious in the woman in him, he would then see things both from the woman's point of view and the man's point of view. This would obviously make him less subjective. But although we do not possess anything like objective consciousness at present and see everything through our own prejudices or illusions, such a man would certainly have no illusions about women, knowing the woman in himself, and the same would apply to the woman who knew the man in herself. Meanwhile we can at least work on wrong attitudes—especially wrong attitudes to the Work itself and as far as possible on wrong attitudes to one another in the Work. For the latter we require to study the meaning of external considering which must never be neglected in favour of having one's own way.

*     *     *

A wrong attitude gives a wrong relation. So a wrong attitude to the Work will give a wrong relation to it. Let us take an example. Suppose we hear that the object of the Work is to clean and purify lower centres for the reception of Higher Centres. Suppose also we are taught that Higher Centres exist *in* us, fully developed and always working, but we cannot hear them because of the clamour of 'I's, of negative states, of internal considering, of identifying, of self-justifying, of phantasy, of vanity, of pride, and all the rest, as well as the silent obstruction of buffers. Let it be supposed that I hear all this taught but that I cannot for a moment accept the idea that Higher Centres are *in me* already. I believe that I have to search and find something *outside* me. I will then have a wrong attitude to the Work. Owing to this wrong attitude, I will never properly grasp what the Work is teaching. I will be looking out—not in. The idea of the Conscious Circle of Humanity being *in* me will seem extraordinary. When it is said—as it was in the recent paper on Faith—that the inner divisions of centres can communicate with the Higher Centres within us, and the outer divisions can only communicate with the world of the senses outside us, then I will not believe a word of what is said, and shall go on looking for a "stone god" of some kind outside me. I fancy many, owing to this particular wrong attitude, stick in the Work. Not accepting Higher Centres *in them*, they still worship an external god, in tradition, in social customs and opinion, in convention, even in certain people. They then have a wrong attitude to the Work. Unless there is a *change of attitude* they will get stuck and remain so. Beyond a limited point, the Work will be unable to grow *in them*. If the Work cannot grow in them, it cannot connect them with Higher Centres.

It helps to compare attitude with bodily posture. Right attitude is like right posture. You cannot pass a narrow low door in a wrong posture—with head erect. You will stick. It is the same with wrong attitude.

*Amwell, 4.10.52*

## UNDERSTANDING THE WORK

To know this Work does not mean to *understand* the Work. There is all the difference in the world between *knowing* and *understanding*. After "Tertium Organum" was published, G. said to O.: "If you understood all you have written in your book, I would take off my hat to you." At first sight it seems extraordinary that knowing and understanding are not the same thing. People say of someone with a reputation for learning that he knows a lot. They do not think it necessary to add that he understands a lot also. They think that the one implies the other. Yet it might be perfectly correct to say that he knows a lot and understands nothing. Also it might be correct to say of someone that he knows very little but understands a great deal. If you reflect on this latter example, you will see that he thoroughly understands what little he knows. In life the confusing of knowing and understanding and the mistakes that arise from it does not concern us here. But in the Work we have to try more and more to grasp the essential difference between knowing and understanding—otherwise a barrier may arise that will bring us to a halt. To *know* the Work is one thing: to understand the Work is altogether a different thing. Knowing the Work involves a part of a single centre. Understanding the Work involves the Whole Man. By the Whole Man I mean the whole Psychological Man—the Man of Thought, the Man of Emotion and Will, and the Man of Action. All the centres in Man have eventually to participate if anyone aims at a deep *understanding of the Work*. A small part of a single centre will not be nearly enough. How can anyone expect to *understand* a gigantic thing like the Work, with its immense background in time, with a little part of a little-used and possibly badly-furnished centre? It is like expecting to become a great musician by learning a few notes on the piano—and not all the notes, mind you, but a few in the middle. Such is our conceit, which must make the gods laugh or weep. For, as G. said, we are like monkeys in the sight of Conscious Man. And I fancy it does not take long self-observation—provided it is sincere, uncritical and without self-justifying—to catch startling glimpses of what he meant. Now a man or woman must know the Work before they can begin to understand it. Knowledge comes before understanding in the day-by-day horizontal passage of time, but in the eternal, vertical scale of values understanding is far higher and so far greater than knowledge. The Work says that there is no greater force we can create in ourselves than understanding. It also says that anyone in contact with the Work must continually seek to increase his understanding of it. It is the parable of the talents over again. For otherwise the Work gets cold and begins to die. I will remind you that the Work judges your own work, because the Work is hidden in you. It is in you in the form of Buried Conscience. If it were not, no man would work. You are not aware of Buried Conscience. But it is quite aware of the sincerity or otherwise of all your Work-efforts and your thoughts and emotions about it. Sincere work *begins* to bring Buried Conscience into your consciousness, little by little, as you can bear it. Insincere work buries it more than ever.

Now if your *knowledge* of the Work, such as it is, remains only laid up in your memory like the unused talent, you will never *understand* it. Indeed, you will never really know what on earth it is all about. You will hear again and again phrases such as Self-Remembering, internal considering, identifying, self-observation, and be really quite bewildered by the whole thing. It will become so much jargon to you. This is because you do not yet *understand* any single thing in the Work. You have not thought for yourself about it, so you do not understand why it exists or what it is for or what it means or how it can possibly apply to yourself. Meetings will be a strain. You will be glad to escape into the pure air of God's simple world and have a chat about why the Valentine-Osbornes no longer speak in their cramped corner of this colossal universe. Well, in that case, it may be the best thing to do. But let us speak seriously once more. What has to be realized is that no one can do this Work without *understanding* something about it. What is the good of doing anything without understanding? If you try to work without any *understanding* of the Work you can get no result. Only when the Work becomes *emotional* can you begin to *understand* it. The knowledge of it in the Intellectual Centre and the dawning emotional need for it and the increasing valuation of it in the Emotional Centre, together with the growing perception of its truth, unite to give the beginning of the *understanding* of it. The Work is then no longer a matter of mere memory or of words. It is no longer merely knowledge. It becomes a living experience affecting the Being of a man and entering into his Will. Thus Knowledge and Being unite to form Understanding. Suppose you attempt to work from memory of what you know of the Work and without any understanding of it. It is quite possible that you could say to me after a time: "I observe myself three times a day after meals for one minute. I remember myself before breakfast and after dinner for two minutes, if I remember to. I read the Commentaries—two pages a day—before going to bed. But I do not seem to get any result. I have not had any higher emotional experiences." No—you would not. You will see at once, surely that such a person is not working from any *understanding* of the Work, but by a sort of rule of thumb. Nothing of the Emotional Centre participates. It is just cut and dried stuff—like a daily dozen of bending and stretching, prescribed by the doctor. Efforts of this kind are useless. Indeed, every effort you make without understanding is useless. Only what you do from your understanding counts. If you cannot *understand* why you should observe yourself, if you cannot *understand* you are a mass of contradictory 'I's and have no Real Will but many wills and are *nothing*, if you cannot *understand* that you pass most of your life asleep in your inner spirit and do not remember yourself but mistake yourself for your Personality, if you cannot *understand* that negative emotions are evil and harmful and destroy your happiness, if you cannot *understand* that identifying spoils all the enjoyment of real emotions and that internal considering makes you weak and self-pitying—if all this and more—then why, in God's name, do you work, and whatever you do, *is it work?*

<br>

*Amwell, 11.10.52*

## CONJUNCTION WITH THE WORK

No conjunction is possible without reciprocal affection. If the Work seeks to enter into a man's understanding, it will be unable to do so if there is nothing reciprocal coming from the man. Real conjunction with the Work needs affection for it. Affection is that which opens, while non-affection shuts. There is no real conjunction between a man and a woman if there is not reciprocal affection. He must have affection for her—yes, but she must have affection for him, otherwise there is no conjunction. It is only a true conjunction when mutual affection conjoins. Affection on one side without reciprocal affection on the other effects no conjunction and produces a commonplace human situation. Now, if a man or woman seeks conjunction with the Work but has no affection for it, conjunction is impossible. Unless there is conjunction with the Work, it cannot begin its alchemical work of transformation of psychological lead into gold. Only according to one's affection for it can it work its gradual changes in a person's being and understanding. A little affection effects little change. Why? Because there will be little conjunction on your part. Adequate conjunction is not possible without adequate reciprocal affection from you. According to the extent of the reciprocal affection so will it make conjunction. Now, in relation to the Work, no one can tell straight away the quality of his or her affection. That is to say, it is impossible to know whether your affection is good or bad. But though direct knowledge of the quality of one's affection is not possible there is a sign by which you can judge it.

If you remain the same kind of person never quite seeing or caring much what this Work is about, then the quality of your affection for the Work is bad. By this is meant that the quality of your affection is of such a nature that it is impossible for the Work to make any adequate conjunction with you. Your affections and the interests, thoughts, and occupations arising from your affections lead in another direction than the Work. It is not the fault of the Work that it cannot make adequate conjunction with you—and by adequate is meant sufficient for it to enter you and root itself in the soil of your being. If it did, as it grew so would your understanding grow, and you would see more and more the inner meanings of the Work which are endless. But if it cannot root itself in your being your understanding will not grow. It is your own fault. You do not really value it. Therefore you give it, and I mean here the living Work itself and the spirit of its meanings, little or no genuine affection. It is common to love oneself. This affection is the most vulgar of all emotions. But it is rare to feel affection for the Work and all that the Work implies in its teachings. Such affection does not belong to the mechanical division of the Emotional Centre in which people live as a rule. It is not a manifestation of the vulgar, common self-love, which can only hate the Work once it clearly perceives where it leads. Conjunction with the Work is only possible through emotions of a higher order which belong to the non-mechanical division of the Emotional Centre. These make it eventually possible for the Master, that is, your Real I, to take charge of you. This is the object of the Work. The pathway of the Work leads interiorly to Real I. It leads away from your *name*—in my case from Nicoll. The Master cannot draw near anyone unless the many coatings of self-love are stripped off. How? By the method of seeing what one is *actually* like through uncritical, non-justifying observation—in place of what you *imagine* you are like. A man, a woman, must *awaken* to what they are like. *The cause of self-love is that we are asleep.* As we awaken self-love diminishes. The Imaginary I and the False Personality must give up the ghost. But a man will not try even to observe himself seriously if his affection for himself, like thick glue, adheres far more strongly to him than any attachment he has for the Work. The Work teaches that there are three lines of Work. Now, we are apparently told of three qualities of affection in the Gospels. A man must love God with all his soul and heart and mind; and love his neighbour as himself. There is love of God as the supreme thing, and then love of neighbour, and love of self. I have always thought, and still think, that this second injunction is not easy to understand. I will give the absolutely literal translation of the passages in Matthew xxii.37, 39.

> "Thou shalt love Lord the God of thee, in whole the heart of thee, and in whole the soul of thee, and in whole the mind of thee", and "thou shalt love the neighbour of thee, as thyself."

The last injunction cannot mean that you must love your neighbour *in proportion* as you love yourself, for then it would seem to follow that as your love of self diminished, your love for the neighbour would also diminish. The neighbour, however, does not necessarily mean whoever is nearest you in space. Your neighbour is not necessarily the person next door. That would be the sensual meaning. But if we lift the idea of neighbour to its psychological meaning, your neighbour would mean the person who is nearest to you in some altogether different sense. It could mean the person psychologically nearest to you, nearest in understanding or quality of being. Your neighbour could also mean the person with affections similar to your affections. We have seen that reciprocal affections conjoin. All people having similar affections could then be your neighbours through reciprocal similar affections. Theoretically, the love of God should unite all people. But it obviously does not. Religious sects hate each other. Who can say he loves God? People have different qualities of affection. They love quite different kinds of things. Dissimilar affections do not conjoin. But those with similar affections, who love similar things, form one definite category of people invisibly connected and capable of conjoining themselves. They are neighbours *psychologically*. They would love one another more easily. One should find one's neighbour—or neighbours—so as to escape solitary confinement in the lonely and sad prison of self-love which is indeed a cruel lord.

The second injunction seems to be usually explained as if it read "Thou shalt love thy neighbour". It is the addition of "as thyself" which is not quite easy. Paul says:

"The whole law is fulfilled in one word, even in this; Thou shalt love thy neighbour as thyself. But if ye bite and devour one another take heed that ye be not consumed one of another." (Gal.v.14,15)

But how can the unredeemed self-love stop biting another? I have never noticed it can. Paul leaves out the love of God as the first necessity. After the two injunctions are given in Luke x.29, the Lawyer wants his moral duties exactly defined and precisely labelled. Literally translated, he asks: "And who is to me neighbouring?" The parable of the Good Samaritan follows, in which the Priest and the Levite successively pass the man lying on the road wounded by robbers. The third person is a Samaritan who pities him, picks him up, and looks after him at an Inn. Christ asks the Lawyer; "Which of them of the three, neighbouring seems to be?" The Lawyer replies: "He having shewn the pity towards him," not using the hated word Samaritan owing to his extreme attitude to the Sect. Christ says briefly: "Go and do in like manner." Do what? The parable is taken as meaning chiefly that one must be kind to those in distress. But it seems to mean more, it refers to the necessity of working on wrong attitudes. Why otherwise bring in a Samaritan, so hateful to a Jew? The parable implies that freeing oneself from fixed prejudice and wrong attitude is needed before the stage of development called love of neighbour can be possible. And this means discarding a considerable amount of encrusted self-love. Christ advises the Lawyer to go and do just this.

The love of self, if it is primary, not only destroys mutual affection but would, if it had its own way, destroy human society. It wants all power. It does not and cannot love the neighbour, though it apes this rôle and many others both pious and sentimental. It cannot form a conjunction with the Work. It loves nothing higher than itself—and the Work is much higher than it. Real I is higher; and behind Real I is God. It is generally agreed that one cannot love one's neighbour save by means of a love higher than self-love, and that is why the love of God is put at the head of everything, in the primary position. But this love belongs to the *inmost* division of the three divisions of the Emotional Centre and so needs no external idol to worship. It knows God is within a man. (Inmost is the same as highest.) The self-love can *never* open this inmost mind. It keeps a man skating uneasily about on the surface of his being. By itself, putting the matter as simply as possible, self-love is hell. Hell is inverted order where things are upside down like the reflection of a tree in water. To put one's self-love in the highest place is to put this commonplace, vulgar, stupid and silly love where a quite other quality of love should be. In my case it would mean putting Nicoll, and all he imagines himself to be, first. How, then, could I have affection for the Work? How could the Work make conjunction with me if nothing reciprocal comes from me? Self-love will not be of any use, for self-love is love of self and not love of the Work. It may be attracted at first through some form of conceit or vanity. But the Work will not accept that quality of love for long. It will not root itself in the soil of your being so that its growth is at the same time your own development. Shut up in the love of yourself you will remain little changed. And your understanding of the Work will be obscure because the Work needs reciprocal affection of a fine quality to conjoin itself to—and feed—your understanding.

*Amwell, 18.10.52*

## CONSCIOUSNESS AND LOVE

In the last paper reciprocal affection was spoken of as being necessary for conjunction with the Work. If a person has no affection for the Work there can be no conjunction with it. If there is no conjunction with it there is no understanding of it. In short, affection for it opens the way to the eventual understanding of the Work. Indifference or dislike closes the way to understanding it. If a man values many other things far more than any value he puts on the Work in his inner self—apart from what he pretends with his outer self—it will be unable to make a conjunction with him. He will not resemble that merchant seeking goodly pearls "who, when he had found *one* pearl of great price, went and sold all that he had, and bought it" (Matt. xiii.46).

1634

Notice he had to sell first before he could buy. He sold what was value-less in comparison with the pearl. The merchant is yourself in relation to the Work. To sell means, psychologically, to get rid of former interests you have valued by drawing energy out of them through not identifying. The released energies can then go to the "pearl"—which for us is the Work and the attaining of consciousness. All this will take very many years. It is a mysterious process like a seed that grows no man knows how, and it leads to a gradual transvaluation of one's previous valuations. To buy means to appropriate a thing, to make a thing one's very own psychologically. Psychic energy is like money. With little free psychic energy one can buy little new understanding. Now to want a thing is to value it, realizing one has not got it. Not to want it is not to value it. This is either because you imagine you have got it already, or because you do not care. To want a thing with all one's mind, soul, heart and strength is to value it supremely and want it with all centres. It is to love it, to feel the most powerful affection and emotion for it, before all other things. But the Work says that we cannot love like this. We are not one but many. Our being is characterized by multiplicity. We have many different 'I's, pointing in all directions. One 'I' wants something, another 'I' does not. One 'I' likes, another 'I' dislikes. One 'I' has affection, another is indifferent. When a person is in the Work all this confused strife of 'I's goes on year by year under the fitful light of self-observation, and within hearing of the Work. This is the period when the Deputy Steward is being formed. All those 'I's that eventually decide that their lives are silly, and that they value the Work more than their former pursuits group themselves around Observing I and begin to point *more or less* in one direction. They form a transmitting medium for influences coming down from above, from the Steward who is in touch with Real I. But at first this transmitting medium is an imperfect one. Some 'I's ought not to be there, and some important ones are still missing. But the man, the woman, feeling only the general mass effect of the Deputy Steward can then say they value the Work and have reciprocal affection for it. They will *not* say they love it. They might, however, say they are very often *conscious* of it. The reason is that the Work is now in them and not on the blackboard.

The question arises; Is love in its true sense consciousness? This brings us again to the injunction "Thou shalt love thy neighbour as thy-self" (Matt. xxii.39), the meaning of which was discussed a little last week. I said then that I had always found it uneasy to understand. Apart from the meaning of neighbour which is difficult enough, what does "as thyself" mean? Which self? From letters I gather that some find no difficulty in this passage and do not regard it as needing any explanation. One says it means simply that one must love one's neighbour and anybody knows what that means. Very good. But even so, why add "as thyself"? Mechanically we are built on self-love which painfully has to be separated from us layer by layer as we awaken to our real condition. Most of what we call love is a veiled extension of the self-love. The only relevant commentaries I can find are those of the Early Church Fathers who chiefly dwell on the illustrative parable of the Good Samaritan, given in Luke x.29-37 that follows the injunction. They take this as signifying Christ, who came from above to be neighbour to those in this world who are spiritually wounded almost to spiritual death. The symbolism is interesting. He gave them "oil" and "wine", and paid for them at the Inn. Certainly anyone having understanding of this Work might be able to help those who are to-day similarly wounded by this age of materialism. They would then clearly be neighbours, psychologically speaking.

Now the Work speaks of three kinds of love. There is physical love, emotional love and Conscious love. It says that emotional love easily turns into its opposite. It is love-hate. For this kind, the Greek word φιλειν seems to be used in the Gospels. It is a torturing jealous love— and not love at all. For Conscious love the word ἀγαπειν seems to be used. It is never used of sexual love. Christ asks Peter which kind of love he has for him. Peter only understands emotional love (John xxi.15-17). This is the word used in the passage under discussion. Suppose we substitute consciousness for love. It would then read: "Thou shalt be conscious of thy neighbour as thyself." This could mean "Thou shalt be conscious of thy neighbour as thou art conscious of thyself." To me, at least, this rendering would be considerably more understandable in the light of what the Work teaches about the need for increasing our consciousness. We are not nearly conscious of ourselves. We behold the mote in another's eye, but do not see the beam in our own eye. We do not put ourselves consciously in the position of another person. We do not do unto others as we would have them do unto us. Owing to a general lack of consciousness, human relations in the world are what they are. As you become more and more conscious of what you are really like, you become less and less critical of what the other person is like. Arrogance, superiority and intolerance fade, because they are seen by you to be ridiculous. The object of this Work is to increase consciousness in every direction. Observing, in quiet, the same fault in yourself as you have heatedly or bitterly pointed out in another seems to me to be practical love. For by the Work method of finding the same thing in yourself, you eventually see your neighbour as yourself, and yourself as your neighbour. But you must know yourself to begin with. You must begin to be conscious of yourself. This is the most necessary part of Conscious Love, which is not blind.

## THE WORK AND THE LOVE OF SELF

It was said in the previous paper that the external part of the Emotional Centre is the seat of self-love. Why it is so necessary to speak often about the love of self is that as long as this love completely dominates us it cuts us off from the middle and interior parts of the Emotional Centre which the Work seeks to awaken. When the Work says that its object is to *awaken* the Emotional Centre eventually, this is what is meant. When the emotion of self-love dominates a person, the Emotional Centre is asleep. It cannot awaken. What has to be understood and re-understood is that the external side of a person is dominated by self-love. The psychological site of this self-love is in the external division of the Emotional Centre. As long as a person is dominated and therefore guided by the love of self, he cannot be guided by anything else. That is the first point. The second point is that as long as anyone is dominated by his or her love of self, no development of the inner divisions of the Emotional Centre is possible in that person. It is not merely that the love of self cannot connect a person to the internal side of himself or herself. It is more than that. The love of self actually disjoins the external side of a person from the internal side—that is, from the side of a person which the Work seeks to awaken and develop. The Work does not seek to develop the love of self. On the contrary, it seeks to diminish it. It seeks to draw energy out of the self-love so that the freed energy can find a new direction. The action of the Work on a person is not to make him or her more proud and conceited or selfish or self-centred or negative. It is designed to have the reverse effect, provided a man *does* it. It is designed to make people feel more and more, in proportion to their powers of endurance and in different ways, and after different periods of time, a process of *depersonalization*, so that they no longer have the same feeling of who or what they are. This gradual withdrawal of energy from the customary narrow, easily resentful and brittle feeling of 'I' is accompanied by a gradual new and broader feeling of I—as if one were living in a large place. This gradual new and broader feeling of I is not centred in the love of self. It is not situated in the external division of the Emotional Centre. It is internal to the external division. It can hear, feel, value and understand the Work. In short, it can do what the self-love cannot. This new feeling of I is highly desirable. It is like being introduced to a new civilization, to another form of life. But for a long time the old feeling of 'I' reasserts itself temporarily and seeks to resume its dominion. This is where it is possible to speak of temptation, in the esoteric meaning of temptation. If one ceases to keep the Work warm and viable in oneself, if one lets it get cold too long, punishment comes. It takes the form of a cessation of meaning, of a deadness inside. One is back in life. One starts complaining again, feeling old grievances, making accounts against others, and, in short, singing one's song. This is easy. It is mechanical. It is not Work. Of course, there is no one who is punishing you. We punish ourselves—by casting ourselves down to a lower level because we allow ourselves to fall asleep. The remedy is to begin to work again —seriously. For this, you must sacrifice your suffering. Of course, it is easier to sleep—and suffer uselessly, and "feed the Moon". Are you aware that a *single sentence* uttered by a negative 'I' and *consented* to in your inner talking can let in a rush of negative 'I's? Just a sentence such as: "It's all very well her saying that . . ." Down goes the lift, bang to your basement, and every devil of the night emerges ready to eat your force, as it did formerly.

Now the self-love can imitate affection for others. One cannot, however, help another through imitation affections. They are not cognitive—that is, they give you no knowledge, no insight. Cognitive emotions—that is, emotions which give you knowledge both of yourself and of others—belong to the middle and inner divisions of the Emotional Centre and not to the external division. A man or woman powerfully affected by the love of self will have no love for anything so abstract as knowledge. Why should they? They regard themselves as everything. The self-love always regards itself. It cannot look up. Underlying the love of self there is, inevitably, hatred. This is why mechanical emotional love turns into its opposite when it is affronted. What the self-love really wants in its heart of hearts is to have its own way and dominate everyone else and make everyone a slave—the whole world even, as history shews. However, it takes many forms. One ought to observe some of the forms it takes for oneself—I mean, in oneself. If you do not have too many false attitudes about yourself and too many buffers, you can occasionally notice it at work in you and catch a glimpse of some of its ways of concealing itself and pretending to be something quite different. Notice if you can how everything you do for merit is self-love. Very much of what people call love—such as love for their friends—is an extension of self-love. If you are nice to those who are nice to you, do not think that the self-love has nothing to do with it. Wait till the other person is not at all nice to you and then observe your self-love blowing up for a storm. The life of self-love is death. People immersed up to the neck in it are really dead. They are only external. There is nothing internal. The most dangerous and unhappy form of self-love is to love power for its own sake—social, professional, political, local or domestic. The love of ruling seems extraordinarily destructive of any justice or peace of mind and certainly ruins the Work. A mother who loves to rule can harm her children very much, especially her sons. The love-pattern is wrong. Also this evil attribute can lay down early bitterness or sadness in the children. I have seen many such examples. When the love of ruling at all costs for its own sake comes first, that person is really a devil inwardly, whatever the outward appearance. You can feel it by experiencing a cessation of everything in you, a drying up of all thought and feeling. Such people may seek to appear as if charming. They worship themselves. A man imprisoned in his self-love regards himself in everything. He is surrounded by himself. His mind is placarded with his own image. Even if he lifts his thoughts to heaven, he sees *himself* there and thinks of *himself* and of how he should comport *himself* and what conventional remark he should make—such as "Jolly nice place up here." For how can the self-love raise itself above itself? It would cease to be self-love. How could it cease to care what happened to it? How could it cease always internally considering? You might think *self-knowledge* —for which one life-time is not enough—naturally springs from self-love. If a man is interested only in himself and his own and always regards himself, will he not necessarily know himself? On the contrary, he will be blind to the kind of person he is. Self-love is not cognitive. It lays down no memory for "next time". It makes darkness, not light, within. The man will therefore hate self-observation which is to let a ray of light within. The first commandment of the Decalogue says: "Thou shalt not worship other gods." To the sensual, literal mind this means one must not bow down to idols. The psychological meaning is that you must not worship yourself. You can cease to do this only by observing little by little what you are really like. A man who loves himself before all things, adores himself. He (or she) makes himself a god to himself. Now what you love most is your God. Think for a moment. What do you love most? What is your God?

*Amwell, 1.11.52*

## THE WORK AS THIRD FORCE

In the paper of the week before last something was said about the formation of Deputy Steward. It was explained that Deputy Steward was gradually formed at a higher level than the 'I's turned to life. This collection of 'I's of variable strength of character surround Observing I, and they become, in the course of time, in sufficient number, a transmitting medium that can receive, although obscurely at first, the influences of the Work which come down from a higher level. The task of Observing I is to observe its owner from the point of view of what the Work teaches. This is the application of the Work to oneself. Without it, no inner connection is made between oneself and the Work. In a person who can perceive the difference between *A* and *B* influences —that is, briefly, in a person who has Magnetic Centre—there exist 'I's that either do not believe in life or are not content with it. They feel there must be something else. It was indicated in the paper that a wrong 'I' may be in the Deputy Steward or some may be missing or —let me add—an important 'I' in you may enter and then stray away.

Deputy Steward is exactly like the formation of a group in the Work, only it is internal, invisible, *in you*, and not outside you as is a visible group of people. You can find the authority for this in some of the parables in the Gospels. I remind you again of the fact that this Work is Esoteric Christianity—that is, the inner meaning of the teaching given in the four Gospels. In regard to an 'I' straying from the Deputy Steward there is the parable of the Lost Sheep. Ninety-nine sheep are on the mountain, but one is missing. As was said, the Deputy Steward is formed at a higher level—that is, on the mountain—out of those 'I's which can hear the Work. The parable is as follows:

"How think ye? If a man have an hundred sheep, and one of them be gone astray, doth he not leave the ninety and nine *on the mountains*, and seeketh that which is gone astray? And if so be that he finds it, verily I say unto you, he rejoiceth more of that sheep, than of the ninety and nine which went not astray." (Matt. xviii.12-13)

The phrase "on the mountains" is translated literally from the Greek. It was evidently misunderstood by the translators responsible for both the Authorized and Revised Versions who render the phrase "and goeth into the mountains".

In regard to a wrong 'I' being present in the Deputy Steward, one of the parables dealing with this is that of the man having no wedding-garment. The relevant passage is as follows:

"But when the king came in to behold the guests, he saw there a man which had not on a wedding-garment: and he saith unto him, Friend, how camest thou in hither not having a wedding-garment? And he was speechless. Then the king said to the servants, Bind him hand and foot, and cast him out into the outer darkness; there shall be weeping and gnashing of teeth. For many are called, but few are chosen." (Matt. xxii.11-14)

What do you suppose this lack of a wedding-garment means? In the ancient language of parables, which still appears in dreams, a garment is used in the sense of what clothes the mind. The meaning of a garment is psychological when it is used in parables. Do you not think that a person may have wrong attitude to this Work and yet appear to belong to it? A person might wish to have no real, inner conjunction with the Work, but only wish to make use of it for his own purposes. A wedding has to do with conjunctions, and not having a wedding-garment would mean not having any emotional desire to unite with the Work inwardly. Such an 'I' can very well enter into the early formation of the Deputy Steward. It would not be so acceptable to the Master—that is, to Real I—who stands above Deputy Steward. It would be, so to speak, a liar. It would perhaps be like the chatterer in *The Pilgrim's Progress*, which Bunyan describes as being told "in the similitude of a dream". This figure is called Ignorance. Bunyan implies that what he is ignorant of is knowledge of himself. He chatters up to the last moment of the mystical journey of Christian and then vanishes into Hell.

One can do the same thing from a pure or an impure motive. You can take up something in order to shew off or from the love of it. A person can take up this Work, not from any love of it and all it implies and can lead to, but for entirely different reasons. Now in this connection I am going to speak of the Neutralizing Force of the Work. You know that the Work teaches that Essence, with which we are born, cannot of itself develop beyond a certain point and has to become surrounded by Personality which is something acquired from and necessary for life. The result is that Essence remains undeveloped. This internal situation which must be established first of all before anything else can take place is expressed by saying that Personality is then *active*, Essence passive, and Life is *neutralizing*. This is the first Triad. The second Triad is made by the influence of the Work and results in Essence becoming *active*, Personality *passive*, and the Work *neutralizing*. One can call the first Triad first education and the second Triad the second education. This second education is not necessary for life, but it is essential to self-development in the meaning of the Work-teaching.

What is the nature of the Neutralizing Force of the Work, which has the power to *reverse* the first Triad and make Personality passive and Essence active? Let us take two statements made by Christ on this subject. On one occasion Christ asked His disciples:

"What was it that ye disputed among yourselves by the way? But they held their peace: for by the way they had disputed among themselves who should be the greatest. And he sat down, and called the twelve, and saith unto them, If any man desire to be first, the same shall be last of all, and servant of all." (Mark xx.33-35)

On another occasion He said to them:

"Ye know that the princes of the Gentiles exercise dominion over them, and they that are great exercise authority over them. But it shall not be so among you: but whosoever will be great among you, let him be your minister; and whosoever will be chief among you, let him be your servant." (Matt. xx.25-27)

In these two passages, life-values are reversed. The self-love is, so to speak, knocked out. In life, the self-love seeks to be first in everything. Christ says it must be last. In another place we will speak further about the nature of the Third Force of the Work.

*Amwell, 8.11.52*

## NOTE ON TRIADS

The Work teaches that every manifestation has three forces in it. Nothing is made, nothing created, by one force or two, but by three. This trinity of forces is made up of Active, Passive and Neutralizing Forces. The smallest thing, such as an atom, has three forces in it. The Active Force is the initiating force, the Passive is the force of resistance, and the Neutralizing Force is the connecting force or relating force between them. If there were no Neutralizing or connecting force, Active and Passive Forces would stand in opposition to one another and nothing could happen. Now if the connecting force alters, the other two forces alter. We have to think of Neutralizing Force as something capable of tilting the balance between Active and Passive Force in such a way that active can become passive, and passive become active. If you think of a triad as being like a plank supported near its middle on a stand or fulcrum so that one end is up and the other down, then if the fulcrum is moved a little towards the down-side, the end that is up will go down, and vice versa, as would a see-saw. In other words, there can be a reversal of sign by altering the Third Force. Now this Work teaches that as adults we consist of two distinct parts called Essence and Personality. Personality is active and Essence is passive. We are born, however, with Essence alone which grows only to a small extent. In our earliest years we can think of the mother forming part of an obscure triad in connection with our Essence. The Essence is Active Force and the mother is Neutralizing Force. At that age life presents itself to the child as wonder. It is told in fairy-stories, many of which contain Esoteric Teaching. We can conceive that these lay a foundation in the Essence of what can become Magnetic Centre later in life. I mean, that the natural wonder of Essence and the memory of fairy-stories may connect later with the Work-triad through which Essence becomes active again and begins to grow. Looking at it in this way, the Mother-triad and the Work-triad may be related. But between them the Life-triad must necessarily intervene for many years. We must remember that from the Work point of view the Essence is the growing point of the real man or woman. If the Mother-triad persists too long it becomes harmful. The child will shun life. The Life-triad will be delayed and its stages not properly formed at the right times. The Life-triad, which comes after the Mother-triad, gradually forms the Personality through which life is met. The Personality is distinct from the Essence and surrounds it as a protection like the husk of a seed. Essence ceases to grow and becomes passive. Personality grows instead. The Personality is not the real person, but it must necessarily be formed. The Neutralizing Force is now no longer the mother, but life itself. Personality becomes Active, Essence becomes Passive, and Life acts as Third or Neutralizing Force. This is the Life-triad. It must be well-formed before the Work-triad can begin—if it ever does. If it does, the Personality acts as food for the growth of Essence.

I remind you of all this because we forget to ponder the meanings of these very important initial truths of the Work. The slow formation of Personality, which should be as rich as possible in experience and knowledge, is what can be called the first education. If a man has not this triad formed in him sufficiently owing to a narrow unintelligent life, his ultimate further development, which is his second education, will be difficult. He will have to educate himself in many directions. One should know and experience all one can before trying to form the next triad, which results from a second education, and is not formed by, or necessary for, life. It is against life. The Work, and all that it teaches, belongs to the second education; the object of this second education is to *reverse* the triad formed by life so that eventually the Personality becomes passive, and the Essence, becoming active, once more grows, feeding on some of the energies that have gone into Personality. This process is very gradual. If a man begins to work on himself, let us say with regard to separating himself from his negative emotions, he begins to draw energy out of certain parts of the Personality. If the man has some genuine affection for the Work and some genuine belief in it, this energy will move in the direction of the Essence. If not, it will return to Personality. Only what is genuine can nourish Essence. Pseudo work, pretended work, will simply increase the power of Personality, especially that part called False Personality. You must not think, please, that a dramatic moment comes in which your Essence suddenly becomes active and your Personality passive. It is a gradual process of waking up from sleep through knowledge of the Work, acknowledgement of it, understanding it, willing it, and finally doing it. I am speaking to those who greatly desire to awaken from the sleep of life. During this process, which fluctuates to and fro, a man experiences a gradual alteration in the way he thinks. This new thinking is called *metanoia*, or change of mind, which is a word constantly used in the Gospels and wrongly translated as repentance. This change in the way of thinking belongs to the beginning of the second education, and is a sign that the Neutralizing Force of life, that previously held in its grip Personality as active, and Essence as passive, is beginning to be *partially* replaced by another quality of Neutralizing Force. If you are in this situation you can be described as being partly in the Work. If there is no change in your thinking, and you continue to think only from life, you are not in the Work. Observe this in yourself. Unless this part of you that has begun to think in a new way is kept awake by effort, you will return to your former state. If you do not take the Work itself seriously and never think interiorly about it, only many strong efforts will lead to recovery. You must come face to face with yourself. A good deal of mercy seems to be shewn here, however, but maybe a door inside you will be shut finally. This door ultimately communicates with Higher Centres. You must remember here a phrase once used in the Work—"No effort—no work: no work—no awakening: no awakening—death"—when, in fact, one becomes one of the world's crowded dead who walk the streets amongst the few quick. The quick are those whose minds have awakened, and who have begun to think interiorly for themselves.

It might be asked whether the whole of the Personality has to be somehow done away with. This is quite a wrong idea. Everything useless and spurious in the Personality has to be done away with, and especially that part called the False Personality which is founded on the self-love, and is linked with Imaginary 'I' and makes the attainment of Real I impossible. Much false knowledge must go. Now in recent talks it has been often mentioned how in the outer part of the Emotional Centre, the part turned towards life through the senses, self-love reigns. What is called Love of God and Love of Neighbour in the Gospels cannot exist where the self-love is dominant. The self-love cannot love what is higher than itself. Self-love loves the self and what it possesses, so that it includes children, homes, property, money, position, and all the rest of it. As long as the self-love is dominant, the triad in which life is Third Force cannot be reversed. The concealed object of the Gospels is to reverse the Life-triad and so bring about the development of Essence. We are told we must become as little children. We might expect to find many hints as to what the nature of the new Neutralizing Force is that is not life. I remind you once more that Gurdjieff's definition of this Work was *Esoteric Christianity*. He meant the inner meaning of the sayings and parables of Christ as distinct from the various dogmas of different churches and denominations that have been established in the world. In my experience it is only the Work that reveals them. Now since the self-love characterizes the formation of the Life-triad, we might expect that some of its ramifications would be mentioned in the Gospels as being things to work against in oneself for this development that life does not give us. By the way, you must all understand that the Work will never become *your* Neutralizing Force unless you *work*. For some reason that is not quite plain to me, people do not seem to understand this yet. They forget to connect the Work with themselves, or do not wish to. I repeat that the Work can never become your Neutralizing Force unless *you* work. Listening to what the Work teaches will not change you at all.

In the last paper two examples were given that gave a hint of the nature of the Neutralizing Force that makes Personality passive and Essence active. I will quote one of these examples again. Christ asked His disciples:

> "What was it that ye disputed among yourselves by the way? But they held their peace: for by the way they had disputed among themselves who should be the greatest. And he sat down, and called the twelve, and saith unto them, If any man desire to be first, the same shall be last of all, and servant of all." (Mark ix.33-35)

You know that the self-love always desires to be first. A man who has a good opinion of himself likes to have his own way and does not like to be under anyone else. If he has to be under anyone he becomes envious and difficult. This is the normal situation in life. To seek to be first, to seek to be the greatest, the most highly placed, is regarded as normal ambition. All this is based on the self-love which dominates our life-relations. Life as Third Force in the Life-triad seems, psychologically, to be mainly the self-love. One can then write the Life-triad as Personality Active, Essence Passive and Self-Love Neutralizing Force. From this we can see that the Third or Neutralizing Force of the Work-triad cannot be self-love.

Now I will turn to the Sermon on the Mount. Amongst other things, it says:

"Blessed are the poor in spirit" (those who do not identify)

"Blessed are the meek" (those who are not resentful)

"Blessed are they that hunger and thirst after righteousness (not self-righteousness)

I have written about these elsewhere. What I want you to understand is that there is something being said here about what the Work calls the formation of the Work-triad by means of which Personality is made passive. By means of what the Work opens our eyes to, we see what all these and other statements in the Gospels, which seem so difficult to understand, mean. They are not an end in themselves. They are not about just "being good". They are *instructions* about how to make Personality passive enough so that Essence can grow and Real I or Master can enter. For the Master cannot enter the Personality. Once Real I enters, the Work-goal is reached. The means and methods of reaching it can then be laid aside. I will speak more fully of this in future papers.

*Amwell, 15.11.52*

### SELF-REMEMBERING AND THE WORK-TRIAD

In the last paper the three possible phases of Essence as active and then passive and finally as active again were spoken of. The third phase requires a Neutralizing Force other than Life. I said that if we want to understand what this Neutralizing Force is like, we can find it described in the Gospels as well as in the Work. The study of the Work helps us to understand what Christ was talking about in the Gospels and vice versa. The two are extremely closely connected. The Work is the inner meaning of Christ's sayings and parables, and Christ's sayings and parables are what the Work teaches. Understand that I am not speaking of all the machinery of ritual and dogma subsequently built up by different churches. Now both the teaching of Christ and the teaching of the Work are about the Third or Neutralizing Force, which renders Personality passive and Essence active. They are descriptions and instructions concerning it. I will quote the last page of the previous paper:

"Now I will turn to the SERMON ON THE MOUNT. Amongst other things it says:
    "Blessed are the poor in spirit—(those who do not identify)
    "Blessed are the meek—(those who are not resentful)
    "Blessed are they that hunger and thirst after righteousness (not self-righteousness)

"I have written about these elsewhere. What I want you to understand is that there is something being said here about what the Work calls the formation of the Work-Triad by means of which Personality is made passive. By means of what the Work opens our eyes to, we see what all these and other statements in the Gospels, which seem so difficult to understand, mean. They are not an end in themselves. They are not about just 'being good'. They are *instructions* about how to make Personality passive enough so that Essence can grow and Real I or Master can enter. For the Master cannot enter Personality. Once Real I enters, the Work-goal is reached. The means and methods of reaching it can then be laid aside."

Now in answer to those who say they cannot see what this Third Force is like, I can only say that it is like the Work. It is the application of the Work to our lives. If I am then asked what it means to apply the Work to one's life, I will say that it begins with observing what is going on in oneself along certain definite laid-down directions. And if I am asked by older people what these are, I can only marvel. The Work puts many things more clearly than they are expressed in the Gospels. To me it seems that the necessity of self-observation is not put so definitely, emphatically and continually in the Gospels as it is in the Work-instructions. Nor are the directions about what to observe so clear. In saying this I am quite aware that a great deal is said, but it only became clear and alive to me after I had been many years in the Work. Therefore, as I have said before, in my view and experience, the understanding of the Work is necessary for the understanding of the Gospels. This is especially the case, I would say, in realizing that the Gospels are not just about "being good" or looking pious or humble or living in poverty or being poor in spirit. They are instructions about how to make Essence active so that it can grow and make contact at a higher level with Real I. The aim is *contact*—not being *good*.

One mystery about Real I is that it makes contact with what is real but what is real in us *is not developed*. The real man or the real woman is at present only a not-grown Essence, but can become a developed Essence; and this is a unity which becomes I in you and you become it, but not the "you" that is the Imaginary 'I' with its accomplices, the most evil of which is the False Personality. Imaginary 'I' is replaced by Real I. Can you conceive of such a change? Can you believe that this worthless, strutting, pretentious, ignorant, worldly, little fraud called Imaginary 'I', who pretends he is a millionaire and can do anything, can be replaced by someone who really is a millionaire who not only understands the language of Higher Centres but is not remote from even God? G. said: "Behind Real I stands God." He also said: "You think you are millionaires, but only by seeing you are nothing can you become real millionaires." But the mystery of Real I is a mystery, which means that it cannot be explained in any formatory language. An experience cannot be. You can take it simply as *not* being what you call 'I'—as when you exclaim: "Don't you know who I am?"—when you don't know yourself but imagine you do. It is an entirely new feeling and sensation of I. In Self-Remembering we may experience it. It has nothing to do with self-love and the poor feelings of I connected with it—either with the flattered self-love or the injured self-love. Now since we have moments of touching Real I long before our Essence is developed, it must be there already—fully developed as are Higher Centres, though we are not in contact with them. Yet we are told that Essence must develop in us for Real I to come, and that is the goal. When it comes we become it. As G. said: "A man is then truly *Master of himself.*" Consciousness must therefore shift from all inferior lower feelings of I to that of Real I. One can only say that, unless Essence grows sufficiently and Personality is rendered passive enough, our contact with Real I is rare—perhaps once or twice in a lifetime. If Essence develops—that is, if the third Triad is practised for long enough with understanding—it suddenly (I think) could reach a level which is that of Real I and the two become identical—one in the other. Several times Christ speaks of the necessity of keeping awake lest the Master come *suddenly*—"like a thief in the night". It is said in the Gospel of Mark:

"Watch therefore: for ye know not when the Lord of the house cometh, whether at even, or at midnight, or at cockcrowing, or in the morning; lest coming suddenly, he find you sleeping." (Mark xiii.35, 36)

It is apparent that the development of Essence is a return-journey or ascent (like that of the Prodigal Son) since it came down from a high level. I have sometimes wondered if the two sons became one—the one who remained with his father and the one who came down to the world and its life and through remembering his origin ascended again. I think it must be, as I cannot find any explanation of the second son who remained. By *remembering his origin*, the son who descended into life realized he was eating husks and began the ascent. This is similar to the Work-Triad replacing the Life-Triad and a reversal taking place. The Essence now grows up to the level of its origin. This brings me to speak briefly of the necessity of Self-Remembering in the Work-Triad. You have to find various ways of not just being in life—otherwise what you do will go into the Life-Triad. To feel that your origin is not from the earth or your parents or your ancestry is *one*—only one—way of remembering yourself. "Call no man your father on earth" (Matt. xxiii.9). Christ says one must do things in His Name. It is required of you to think and work secretly in the Name of the Work and not for reward. Otherwise it becomes meritorious and so goes into Personality. It is good to perceive internally the truth of something the Work teaches and do it because you see its truth and not because you are told to or want to be first. You should often remember that all your life exists and everything you have thought, felt, said and done is there, in a higher dimension, hidden from the senses. You have to face your life from the Work point of view. It helps you to remember yourself if you realize that your life is a circle and what you do consciously now changes both the past and the future, and what you do mechanically changes nothing. Instead of wishing to find fault, wish to understand. Try reversing the blame *really* and see the same fault in yourself. Every time you remember something in the Work in regard to what you are identifying with and negative about at the moment is a form of Self-Remembering. It lifts you a little above your life-induced moods which you so easily believe in. Every time you say: "This is not I," when brooding and negative and grousing, adds a little to awakening. To remember *early* in the morning that you are doing this Work and to notice your mood and thought and not identify with them can change the whole day. Try to take the events the day hands out to you as just exactly what you are given to work on. There are hundreds of ways of remembering yourself—that is, of preventing yourself from falling flat in the mud of life. All these different ways of daily Self-Remembering which put us in the presence of the Work set in motion octaves that, when we live mechanically, and asleep in life, do not proceed. New hydrogens—that is, energies—are produced.

Re 24 and Mi 12 are produced. Also Fa 24 and Sol 12. Notice clearly how without the often given shocks of Self-Remembering the human machine only produces La 24 and Si 12. Now La 24 alone cannot awaken the whole Emotional Centre. It supplies the self-love division. But the three substances 24 supply the Emotional Centre in all its three main divisions. That is, while La 24 supplies the outer division, Fa 24 supplies the middle and Re 24 the inner. Now if you take three men, they are the same in so far as they are men, but their potentialities may be different. Without additional substances—the same in density but different in potentiality—Essence cannot grow. This is why Self-Remembering, so that we can feel the presence of the Work, is necessary for the Work-Triad. Without Self-Remembering, whatever we do will go into the Life-Triad, and Personality will remain active and Essence passive because we will be working in the name of ourselves.

# THE NECESSITY OF METANOIA FOR REVERSAL

## INTERNAL CONSIDERING

Making internal accounts against others is part of Internal Considering. To make internal accounts against another means that you feel the other owes you. To keep on feeling that another owes you is a sign of a bad relationship to the other person. It is one form of Identifying. Every kind of Internal Considering springs from Identifying. At present we are studying the practical meaning of G.'s definition of the Work. He said it was Esoteric Christianity. We will expect, then, to find something said in the Gospels about what the Work calls *making accounts*. We will not, of course, expect to find the actual term "making accounts" used, but a similar idea. One of the main parables on this subject is as follows:

"Therefore is the kingdom of heaven likened unto a certain king, which would take account of his servants. And when he had begun to reckon, one was brought unto him, which owed him 10,000 talents. But forasmuch as he had not to pay, his lord commanded him to be sold, and his wife, and children, and all that he had, and payment to be made. The servant therefore fell down and worshipped him, saying, Lord, have patience with me and I will pay thee all. Then the lord of that servant was moved with compassion and loosed him, and forgave him the debt. But the same servant went out, and found one of his fellow-servants, which owed him an hundred pence: and he laid hands on him, and took him by the throat, saying, Pay me that thou owest. And his fellow-servant fell down at his feet, and besought him, saying, Have patience with me, and I will pay thee all. And he would not: but went and cast him into prison, till he should pay the debt. So when his fellow-servants saw what was done, they were very sorry, and came and told unto their lord all that was done. Then his lord, after that he had called him, said unto him, O thou wicked servant, I forgave thee all that debt, because thou desiredst me: shouldest not thou also have had compassion on thy fellow-servant, even as I had pity on thee? And his lord was wroth, and delivered him to the tormentors, till he should pay all that was due unto him." (Matthew xviii.23-34)

Now Man, a self-developing organism by creation, does not realize how much he owes by remaining asleep in life. He thinks he is owed. Thinking sensually, he must. This attitude needs to be reversed. It cannot be except by ideas that bring about *metanoia*—that is, change of mind. The man has to be given new ideas to think in a new way. He has to think *esoterically* and not sensually about himself. Sensual thought is external, based on outer appearance, on things as they seem. Esoteric thought is internal and is about the inner meaning and purpose of one's life on this planet. It is not a matter of the senses but of the understanding. The Gospels and the Work speak only about the inner meaning—that is, they speak esoterically. Esoteric means *inner*. According to outer appearances, human beings may easily think that they are owed: according to inner truth, it is they who owe. This is a reversal of thinking. It is a new way of thinking. It is indeed *metanoia*. All the ideas contained in the teaching both of the Gospels and the Work can slowly make us think in a new way. That is, if we think. They can bring about *reversals* of thinking. The similar esoteric ideas in the Gospels and in the Work are to give us minds *beyond* our ordinary minds. Essence can then grow. But unless we *receive* and *assimilate* these teachings, nothing can happen. People will continue to think in the same way. No reversing ideas will enter them. Now if *you* think in the same way, *you* will remain as before. It is said that as a man thinks, so he is. Many, however, will not think in a new way. They remind one of a shuttered house with unopened newspapers, bread and bottles of milk, piled up in the porch. They take in nothing. There is, perhaps, no one alive in the house to take in anything.

Now when a man in the Work begins to realize how much he owes by his life of sleep and yet can have it cancelled, he ceases to preoccupy himself daily with what he believes others owe him. He no longer regards himself as he did when immersed in his self-love. All Internal Considering arises from the self-regard. The more the self-regard, the more the Internal Considering. When a man makes accounts against others, he is identified and loses force. He makes a sore place in himself. To lead a life of Internal Considering is to consider only yourself and how people treat you. It leaves out how you treat people. The idea and practice of putting yourself in the position of the other reverses the direction of thought. It needs conscious effort. All the Work-ideas reverse things. They require conscious efforts to apply them. These must be renewed continually over the years until they lead to change of thinking that is real. The vision of life and yourself is then different. Amongst many other things, you will understand the meaning of the parable of the man who owed millions.

*Amwell, 6.12.52*

## RIGHT ATTITUDE TO LIFE

As regards attitude to life, it is much the best to think that the experiences we have are necessary for us. Otherwise we will be continually making accounts and complaining that things are not fair. Taking up this point of view about our experiences gives more meaning to ourselves. This is the only way to get something from every experience. It is the only answer as to why we may have so many unpleasant experiences. Now in order to keep up this point of view towards our experiences we must remember and be awake. We must be awake to the conscious view that the experience belongs to us *because our being needs it in order to develop*. We then see that the material for our development lies in our experiences. But without this consciously taken view we cannot see this because we are asleep. We think that these experiences should not come to us and that they have no possible meaning for us. But they are exactly the material that we have to work on. It is by means of these experiences that we develop at the expense of our imagination. The imaginary person has to go. But people do not understand this. Everywhere you see people not understanding what they have to do in this respect. Everywhere you see two imaginary people living together, each in their own world and making nothing of their experiences. Of course, this view alters the standpoint towards life very much, and makes one's day-dreams of secondary importance. The business of living is not according to either one's desires or one's day-dreams, or what one expects to get from life. To take life-experiences as material for work on oneself is a *reversal* of the usual way of taking them. Once you pity yourself, or identify in some other way, this reversal is again reversed and one is back in the ordinary way of taking life. You are no longer doing the Work. Now in all this it is your weak spot—that is, where you are most vulnerable—that prevents you from using these experiences instead of letting them use you. Of course, if you never observe yourself, you will never be able to see your weak spot. There may be more than one. These weak spots have to be strengthened and can only be strengthened by means of the Work. You have to face some experiences. I mean, that you cannot avoid all experiences that are unpleasant, because if you have the money and opportunity to do so there will be no development. You will probably grow more and more narrow and selfish, which always seems to happen when there is no development.

Now the taste of working is quite definite. When you are taking the experiences of life more consciously, it is a right arrangement of things in you that gives you a certain inner taste. Life is not driving you. But when you identify, and therefore fall asleep, this inner taste vanishes and in place of it you have what I have called before the taste of life, which by comparison is very tasteless. The taste of life is always the same, whatever your particular forms of excitement are. I should say that after a time you should be able to see this for yourself. Now, whenever you work you bring about a reversal of some kind. You have the taste of working. If you do not bring about any reversal, it is not work. It tastes different. For example, to imagine one is working, when one is not really, does not bring about any reversal. People often imagine that they are observing when they are not. This is not working, and has none of the clean astringent taste of working. Imagination reverses nothing. What you do in imagination leads to no kind of development.

Now there is a general diagram connected with the Four Bodies of Man in which it is shewn that Man *as he is* is driven from one end by life. As long as a man remains asleep and is mechanical, he is driven by one end of this machine. He is, therefore, properly called a machine; but if a man begins to develop himself interiorly by working he begins to be driven from the other end—from the side of his Will. If I will from the Work to work on an experience that I find myself in, it will not drive me. I will not be able to change the experience, but I will be able to change the way I take it. Knowing this, my attitude towards the experience will be right. Of course, if every unpleasant experience makes you negative, your machine will be driven by life and you will remain exactly what you are supposed not to remain in this world since we were created not to be driven by life. We were created not to be machines, but at the same time we can be machines and serve Nature, and most people remain machines all their lives.

A developing man begins to be worked in part from the Will side, instead of from the life side of his machinery. He begins to make his machinery work at times in a certain way which is the reverse of the way in which life makes it work.

*Amwell, 13.12.52*

## ON PLACING THE FEELING OF I

As you become more conscious of the quality of your life up to now, you may wonder how you could have put your feeling of I into some things as you did. How was it that you identified yourself with them in that way? You see with a growing clearness that if you had not placed your feeling of I where you did, you would have avoided some of the things you did not avoid. It started, one can see, with this putting of I into something. You reflect—now seeing it more clearly—and say: "Why did I put my feeling of I into that?" You say it like this because you are becoming more conscious and see better. You do *not* say: "Why did I do that?" as people usually say. You say it in a different way because you have begun to understand something that once upon a time you did not understand. Whatever it was that you did, you did it because you put the feeling of I into it. If you had been awake you would not have let the feeling of I go in that direction. You would not have done what you did. You realize that at that time of sleep you saw no connection between the feeling of I and what you did. You were not properly aware of the feeling of I. You may have been aware of what you did, especially after you did it. But you did not realize that you did it because you let the feeling of I pass into it. We let the feeling of I pass into all sorts of things and do not realize what we are doing. It is like signing one's name on cheque after cheque without noticing whom they are made out to. Our carelessness in this respect is incredible. We throw the feeling of I about in all directions instead of guarding it. It is the same with thoughts apart from actions. A thought that someone is lying comes into my mind. I put the feeling of I into it. So I then believe it is true. I have signed the cheque. Now the thought may come to me. That is one thing. But to put the feeling of I into it is quite another thing and the results are quite different. If you are always putting the feeling of I into doubtful and unpleasing thoughts you will become surrounded and hedged in by them and they will all claim to be your own mental children. Everyone suffers, though too often unaware, from putting the feeling of I into thoughts that are clearly not true. Negative emotions give rise to lies always. You should not put the feeling of I into them. If you do not, they will pass on and disappear. The same applies to sensations. If you put the feeling of I into a sensation, it will intensify it. When the Work speaks about separation, it means drawing out the feeling of I. Again it is the same with any particular event or experience. One can identify, take it entirely personally and put the feeling of I into it.

Try to read a book and watch a film or a match without putting the feeling of I into it. If you are always putting the feeling of I into this, that and the other, you will never be able to remember yourself. To remember yourself you must draw the feeling of I out of things, business, objects, ornaments, thoughts, moods, appetites, the vanities of life and other tricks devised to keep you asleep. The feeling of I is something very precious. It is "spirit" but it is entangled in coarse matter. Consider what we put it into.

*Amwell, 20.12.52*

## ON DOING THE WORK

It can be said with sufficient truth that if we really *knew* why we were doing this Work, we would *really* be doing this Work. None of us can say why we are doing this Work, however, although we may say we are doing the Work. The reason is that we do not really know what the Work is in its application to ourselves. What *is* the Work? Here follow a great number of answers—as when O. asked us this question many years ago. Some will use one phrase and some another. They will say: "The Work is a method of awakening", or "It is self-observation", or "It is raising the level of being". Others will say :"It is developing Essence", or "It is seeing inner contradictions". Some may say: "It is increasing consciousness", which is nearer the mark—but what do they mean by their words? These are all phrases—necessary, but not understood. Now practically the Work is not to get something we have not but to get rid of something we have, so as to make room. That we can theoretically understand. But what is it you need to get rid of? Frankly, you do not know. That is the difficulty. It is not clear to you. It wavers. You are too busy to think. So you do not understand in a practical way that the Work at this stage is not to get something you have not, but to get rid of something that you have. I do not mean to *conceal* and still like it, so as to curry favour. I mean to see and get rid of it actually and pray that it may be so. If you do not see your special task—which is the reason you are here on this planet and which is never the same as the next person's—you do not yet know what you have to work on, and if you do not *really* know what you have to work on, you do not properly know why you are doing the Work. Has each of you any distinct idea what you have to work on? As was said at the beginning of this paper, if we really knew *why* we were doing this Work, we would really be doing this Work. The Work, when not specifically applied, comes to resemble nothing but a museum full of a number of things. People wander about in it, now looking at a case labelled "Higher Centres"—which appears to be quite empty—and then looking at a tall wire construction consisting of circles labelled "Ray of Creation", which they view with great disfavour. A figure of a man standing upright and labelled "Man Awake" they compare with themselves, pointing out that they, too, are standing upright. A large glass case of filth and snakes labelled "Negative Emotions", they all proclaim is disgusting and should never be exposed to the public gaze. A beautiful mirror in a frame of fine gold which, when they look into it, makes them appear utterly ridiculous, is regarded as a great joke. Amid laughter you hear exclamations of "How absurd", "How impossibly untrue", "How really impertinent". The mirror is labelled "Self-Observation". At various locations and distances many other cases are being peered at, usually with disapproval.

Let us leave this museum which is only accessible to those who never apply one single element of the Work to themselves, but think of it only as an address where meetings are held. For those who do apply the Work, there is no museum. In much the same way people look on the Church. They regard it as a building down the road that they must attend at a certain time. So many do not grasp that both this Work and the Church are not *things* but *forces* that can regenerate them—provided they attempt actually to *live what they teach*. I am speaking of the living invisible Work and the living invisible Church. They are identical in that they make possible conjunction with forces coming from a higher level. (I am not speaking of the dead Church visible.) This conjunction is what renders it possible for us to be exposed year after year and perhaps even life after life to new influences. These new influences, comparable to vibrations of far higher frequencies than those of the light of the physical Sun, gradually alter our being. They ultimately bring about that definite *transformation* of a mechanical man into a Conscious Man of which the Work speaks in numerous ways. In the Gospels it is called a man being *re-born*. In this connection Christ says a man must be born *from above*. As he is, born from below from his earthly parents, he cannot enter the Kingdom of Heaven, whatever his parentage. "Except a man be born from above, he cannot enter the Kingdom of God" (John iii.3). These higher influences which we are speaking of come "from above". Acting on a man or woman for long enough, they effect a transmutation. Yes—but not unless there is a practical response to them. For example, if you do not apply the Work to your life nothing will happen. The last thing we do is to *apply the Work* practically to the recurring experiences of our life. This shews that we do not know *why* we are doing the Work. On one side is the stream of our daily experiences, on the other, all that the Work teaches us to do. We make no connection between them. So we never grasp what it is we have to work on. It follows that we never know what the Work is. One can say one has faith. Yes—but works are necessary too. If you have faith in one kind of life and live another, what are you? Nothing is more wonderful than to be given a vision of how different one's life is from the Work. This is a sign of increasing consciousness. But it is only a force "from above" that can do this for you—and only if you are willing. One word in conclusion: the conjunction of mankind with a higher level can be broken. Mankind would then have no chance. Christ came at such a critical time. He set things in order and re-established the connection—for a time. Christmas commemorates this setting of things in right order for mankind.

*Amwell, Christmas 1952*

### CONTINUATION ON FEELING OF I

The feeling of I can be squandered in infinite ways. How infinite are the ways of squandering the feeling of I can only be comprehended through self-observation. Do not confuse observation with self-observation. You will not know anything about how you yourself squander the feeling of I, however much you may be a person of good observation. Do not think that a person of good observation is therefore a person of good self-observation. Observation looks only at the world outside you. Self-observation looks in, at the world inside you. The one regards things visible, the other things invisible. You stand between these two worlds, visible and invisible. By the way, have you ever thought of yourself like this? Your relationship to both these worlds, between which you stand, is equally important. Have you noticed that as well? You may have a good relationship to the world outside you and a bad relationship to the world within you. In that case you will be unhappy. Your body may be well, but your soul will be sick. We can call the *soul* in a general way the function of relationship to the *inner* world and the seat of the inner senses. The power of self-observation is an inner sense, rarely used. Through the *body* and its senses we are related to the outer world. We put the feeling of I into what belongs to the world without and into what belongs to the world within. We squander this so very precious thing in both directions. We are unaware of what we are doing. For example, we think and feel and even say: "I am a good person." If you do this, you put the feeling of I into being a good person. Now the two are quite distinct. The feeling of I is not the same as the feeling you are a good person. The feeling that you are a good person may exist in you without your putting the feeling of I into it. If you put the feeling of I into the feeling that you are a good person, you cause two quite distinct things to be conjoined in a most unholy and vicious union. I had almost said a blasphemous one. You are mixing that which originates from far above with what originates from far below. This is called *whoring* in the Scriptures. Putting it as briefly as possible but in a formulation having the greatest density of meaning, *you are not remembering yourself*. You are committing a *sin*—and you should know by now that the real meaning of sin is *missing the mark*.• By putting the feeling of I into the feeling that you are a good person, you are missing the mark and therefore sinning against the Work itself which is constantly telling us that we have to remember we should *remember ourselves*. From all this you can perhaps glimpse why *vanity* among other things is always attacked in this Work, owing to its poisonous and paralysing effect on Self-Remembering. Now if you think, or feel, or even say that you are a bad person and put the feeling of I into the feeling that you are a bad person, you are causing a conjunction between two distinct things. You are doing the same as a person who puts the feeling of I into the feeling of being a good person. You are *missing the mark* and for just the same reason. You are not *remembering yourself*. In both cases you are putting the feeling of I into one or into the other of the opposites—*good* and *bad*. You have heard before that we have to draw the feeling of I out of the opposites. That means one attempts to withdraw the feeling of I from the feeling that one is good or the feeling that one is bad. There is a third thing between the opposites called variously Neutralizing Force, Connecting Force, Harmonizing Force, Relating Force, Reconciling Force, or simply *Third Force*. To become conscious in Third Force is mercy and release. But it will remain impossible if you secretly feel how excellent you are or how blameworthy you are. At the level of the earth it is possible to make contacts with Third Force as Personality is made passive. I mean, there is a relating, connecting, ordering and harmonizing force —in short, Third Force—at this level. At the *lowest* level of creation— represented to the bodily senses as the Moon and to the Soul as torment —*there is no Third Force*—no "Holy Spirit". Here the opposites are widest apart. They are completely separated. There is no relating force.

The most inconceivable extremes of heat and the most inconceivable extremes of cold exist with nothing in between. Nothing harmonizing, nothing of mind, nothing ordered, nothing with meaning, nothing with beauty, nothing of intelligence, nothing of love can exist there. Only horror, meaninglessness, ugliness, shapelessness, mindless cruelty, destruction, dissonance, and mad discord exist. This is HELL. I point this out purposely, because Hell is creeping into everything in this terrible century—even into art, poetry and music, which used to connect us with GREATER MIND. There in no Third Force in them. Everything is disconnected, unrelated. This is the briefest, most comprehensive formulation—absence of Third Force.

*Amwell, 3.1.53*

## ON CHANGING ESSENCE

If you do not know why you are doing this Work, it remains unconnected with you. If it continues to remain unconnected with you, it will not influence you or your life. If it does not influence you or your life, you will remain unchanged. As long as you remain unchanged, the level of your being will remain the same. If your level of being remains the same, your Essence will not develop. If your Essence remains the same, it will always attract the same life. That is, if your life recurs it will attract the same events, the same Personality and the same False Personality. But if the Work brings about a growth of your Essence, your life will not be the same. This is because a development of Essence means that it will *not* attract the same life in recurrence. It is as well to make an effort to understand what is being said here. People think that, if there be recurrence, they will meet the Work again when, say, they are forty, the age at which they met it for the first time. They think this because they do not understand that a growth of Essence means an *eternal* change and not a *temporal* change. Here the literal sensual mind completely fails in comprehension. You should therefore use another instrument—namely, the intuitive, psychological mind, which can work outside succession and definite dates in time. You do not have to argue that because you met the Work when you were exactly forty, then if your life recurs you will meet it again when you are exactly forty. That is sensual thinking. You are leaving out the strange properties of Essence, which is deathless and so not in time as is the body and the Personality, which are acquired in time. Any change in Essence is outside time. Although a change in Essence may have taken place *at a certain time* in your life, it no longer is limited to that time. It has taken place in what is vertical to and above time. The body is in time but the Essence is not so. The Essence may

1657

once more form a body and Personality in time, in the limited dimensions that involve beginning and end, and birth and death, but if Essence has been changed—that is, developed—it will not form the same body and Personality. It also will not attract the same life as it did before it was changed. It cannot. It plays a new tune. Now if you do not observe anything that needs alteration in yourself, you will not change Essence. To break through self-complacency and self-excuse, however, is not easy. People who hear the Work do not see anything seriously wrong in themselves, even when they consider themselves in the light of what the Work teaches, which they very rarely do. They do not connect the Work with themselves. *There is no connecting force*—no Third Force. As was said, if you do not know why you are doing this Work, it remains unconnected with you. How else could it be? I might give you lectures for years about a journey to the East and explain what difficulties you will meet with and what it is best to do, but if you have no real desire and intention to take that journey but intend to stay at home, there will be no connecting force. This is how things are with many. They do not *jump* to catch hold of the rope above their heads. They see no reason to do so. If they did, there would be a connecting force. But there is a gap between the end of the rope and themselves. They remain on the ground. Only the sharp realization that there is something they must change in themselves will make them jump and connect them.

Now the idea that unless I change or try to change something in myself now, it will recur, may wake me up to my situation. Things are not going to get better in time. I may then catch a glimpse of the precipice and look up and see the rope above me. This thing in me, that of course I must have *observed*, will increase when my life recurs. Realizing that my special task is to change it, I will be able to see why I should do the Work and what I have to rid myself of. In this way, breaking through self-complacency, I can connect myself and the Work, perceiving I need it badly. Once I do so, I will begin to *understand* the Work as living and not merely know it as dead words because I know something about *what I have to work on in myself*. Only when you know what you have to work on, will you know why you are doing this Work. Then you really are doing the Work and it will respond to your inner needs. Remember always that only the Work can develop Essence. Life cannot do so. What you do for life-reasons only increases Personality. What you do for Work-reasons—and be careful here for so many try to do this Work for life-reasons and so deceive themselves—develops Essence. What you do for reward, for appearance, for convention, for merit, for self-interest, *will not influence* the eternal Essence. Another quality of effort, another thinking, and emotions of another kind, are required.

## WORK ON ESSENCE

When you begin to know what it is you have to work on, you should not tell everyone. There is a great deal said about inner silence in the New Testament. For example, we are told that we must not let the left hand know what the right hand does. ("But when thou doest alms, let not thy left hand know what thy right hand doeth" Matt. vi.3.) In this Work we have to move consciousness more and more internally. Many things have been said about the external parts of centres, and internal parts of centres that communicate with Higher Centres. The external parts of centres communicate with the external senses and the external world. You do not wish to become more external but to become more internal. If, therefore, you wish to become more conscious of what lies internally in yourself, you do not wish the small 'I's that live in the external divisions of centres to try to express what it is that you are working on—what it is you have gradually discovered you must work on—because there is something almost sacred in this discovery. It is more in the nature of a revelation granted you when you can stand it than than a so-called logical process of formatory 'I's. What can the small 'I's in formatory centre know about the whole of us? How can the formatory centre, which is Third Force blind and therefore merciless, dictate to us what we should do? It can only say that we are bad or we are good. It works in opposites. Your heart knows much more about you than your head does. I fancy that the Emotional Centre in its interior part knows a great deal about what our Chief Feature is, and all the connections with it that we have to work on. It cannot be expressed in a word. A novel or a play might express it.

Truth lies *between* the opposites. Therefore, it is impossible to express it formatorily. Language uses either one opposite or the other opposite, but we do not know that there is another language which lies between the opposites, spoken by Higher Centres: one that we can by training listen to a little, but not put into formatory words—one, indeed, that often clothes itself in dream-allegories or parables. I do not, therefore, think that one should try to put into words what one feels one should work on. Moreover it is not possible to give a sincere observation about oneself in public, as I think most of you will agree. Of course, one can play the rôle of being sincere and frank and never hiding anything from anybody. Then, of course, you are simply showing off so as to gain the esteem of others. Most of what we do is for this reason. Now asking questions in the group is not the same as making these so-called sincere observations about oneself. Asking questions belongs to that side of the Work called *Work on Knowledge*. Observing oneself belongs to that side called *Work on Being*. The idea of self-observation is to make one more widely conscious of oneself and what lies in oneself, in one's being. It is a difficult and intermittent thing to do in the present moment. It is easier to notice yourself in retrospect, both immediate and remote. You thus get a new memory of yourself—a Work Memory. This gradually shews you that you are not what you thought. It alters your ideas of yourself. If you try to speak about your observations to others, it brings them forward to the external parts of centres, and your Work Memory is not formed in the right place. It cannot be formed in the external parts of centres. Of course, you must be aware of a very simple trap that lies here. It is something like this: a person says to himself that he must not talk about his intimate self-observations, so he will keep silent about them and tell no one—the result being that the person ceases to observe himself at all. This is the case when you only do things for reasons belonging to external life and have no interior life that has any reality or seriousness to you.

Our observations and our desires concerning what we wish to be changed in us must move inwards towards Higher Centres. Only then do we receive help. It is written in Matthew vi that if prayer and alms-giving are kept secret "thy Father which seeth in secret shall recompense thee." This is what I meant in the previous paper when it was said that if we do things for life-reasons it cannot develop Essence, but if we do things for Work-reasons it can. If you pray so as to be seen of men nothing will happen, but if you pray in secret you will be heard and rewarded—in secret. This is the psychological idea. It refers to the place we act from in ourselves. For what reason are you doing the Work? From what place do you act—if you act at all? That question has been asked before. As was said, if one has begun to see something that one must really change, some too flagrant contradiction, then one is in a position to do the Work for a definite reason—for a Work-reason. Many traps, however, lie here as well. You may see something about yourself that you consider must be changed and you may be right, but you try to change it for life-reasons—such as for the sake of your reputation and appearance. You are not doing it for the sake of your belief in the Work and your wish to live the Work. So the Work will not help you. Your effort will not help in the development of your Essence. It originated from the outside. You can see I am talking about something that I would rather not try to put into words. There is a passage which runs like this:

"Hypocrites! who cleanse the outside of the cup and within are full of extortion and injustice. Cleanse first the inside so that the outside may also be clean." (Matt. xxiii.25, 26)

Do you imagine trying to change something for the sake of appearances is cleansing the inside? This cleansing of what lies inside—that is, internal to outward appearances—is to cleanse and develop Essence itself. This has to come first. That is the important point. It is not life-reasons that will bring this internal cleansing about. Your Personality may appear beautiful. Externally you may appear to be deeply religious and most pious and moral, but it is what you are internally that matters. Internally, you may think that religion, and all that kind of thing, is poppycock. You may appear kindly and sincerely concerned about other people, but internally you may not care tuppence about them. You may seem most earnest about the Work, and inwardly think it is silly rubbish.

Now, are you going to tell me that you are often distressed by the complete contradictions that exist in you between your outer behaviour and your inner thoughts and feelings? You are not. Why? Because you do not observe yourselves. Without self-observation we are rarely disturbed solely about ourselves. People do not therefore work on what they specifically should. They do not see, for example, specific and dangerous contradictions existing in them. We all see motes but not beams. This is owing to the action of buffers. Buffers prevent us from seeing ourselves. They prevent us from seeing contradictions in our behaviour. So we seem to be satisfied with ourselves. At least, we are not dissatisfied about something specific. Moreover, these busybodies, the self-justifying 'I's, get to work if there is any trace of feeling that we are behaving in a contradictory way and may actually be in the wrong. To endeavour to make our behaviour more uniform and calm will not meet the case. That would be an external matter. We are told we have first to cleanse this inside part of us—this part which is at present undeveloped, irresponsible, naughty, and so often contradictory to what we pretend to be outwardly in Personality, and we cannot do it for life reasons. Certainly, we cannot do it from anything belonging to False Personality, which does things "to be seen of men". *There is, however, a trace of Real I in us, we are told.* If we did anything from this trace of Real I, we would not be doing it from False Personality, or Imaginary 'I'. Nor would we be doing it for life reasons. We would be acting from Work reasons (which may go right against life reasons). But it takes a long time before we become conscious of the differences in the qualities of the feelings of I. Also, to make effort for the sake of nothing tangible, or visible, or profitable, in life, or obviously praiseworthy, seems strange to many. It seems strange to the Personality. Yet if we could make effort from *the right feeling of I* we would be rewarded—in secret. How rewarded? Essence would grow. A growth of Essence means a development above time—a supra-temporal change—something that does not end with death. But if we make effort from the wrong place and the wrong feeling of I, we can get no response of this kind. The Essence is the eternal part. If ungrown, it recurs again and again. It *seeks perfection.* But life-efforts will not perfect it. It remains imperfect. To seek perfection in something without ambition entering in, or praise or any similar life-motive, would develop Essence. "The young man asked Christ: 'Master, what good thing shall I do that I may have eternal life?' and Christ answered him: 'If thou wouldest be perfect, go, sell that thou hast, and give to the poor, and thou shalt have treasure in heaven: and come, follow me.' " (Matt. xix.16, 21)

## AIM AND IMAGINARY 'I'

The Work explains to us that we must have an AIM. It says that without an AIM we cannot *do* the Work. We can listen to it, attend meetings, sit looking at the diagrams on the board, but this will not be the same as *doing* the Work. And unless we *do* the Work we will never *understand* what it is all about. This peculiar relationship to ourselves, that we call I, however, and conceive to be really and truly *us*, does not permit us to have personal aim in the Work. Personal aim implies some aim you have about yourself. It is about changing yourself—about changing something you have observed in yourself. But the existence of Imaginary 'I', which is the Work formulation for this peculiar relationship we have to ourselves that we call I, prevents us from having any intelligent aim about ourselves. It acts as a powerful hypnotic. Owing to it we appear to be real persons, real men and women, unified and definite, with names, careers and positions, the same to-day as yesterday—solid and unshakable, undeniable facts. This is due to our fatal habit of sensual thinking with regard to everything. It would be a good experience for us to look in the glass and see no one there at all. But because we think sensually of ourselves, we say: "That's me," confidently to the image in the mirror. This keeps Imaginary 'I' in high fettle. It nourishes internal considering and negative states and endless other things contributing to human misery that would never affect us *once we realized that this 'I' does not exist save in imagination.* It is, in fact, composed of imagination. We are all told to work on imagination. Imaginary 'I', composed of imagination, hypnotizes us into believing we are one—*unity*. This prevents us from seeing ourselves. Not seeing ourselves prevents us from having a Work-aim. So we drift along in Imaginary 'I'. We have, of course, various life-aims, but these are not the same as Work-aims. You may have an aim to pass an examination or to buy a house or to get promotion or to change your circumstances in some way. Everyone has aims of this kind. They are life-aims. Aims of this kind are not Work-aims. Life-aims need life-efforts. But Work-aims need Work-efforts. Work-efforts are different from life-efforts. They are in a different direction. They are not in the direction of changing your circumstances but in the direction of changing yourself. But as long as Imaginary 'I' reigns undisturbed in you, you will not discover this direction of changing yourself.

By way of commentary let me give a brief allegory to illustrate the action that Imaginary 'I' has upon us. Suppose a man invites you to see his house. You gather it is a substantial building. Passing through a high obscuring wall, you find confused masses of materials, scattered about in heaps without any order, some just rubbish and some useful. There is no house. The man, however, who remains outside the high, obscuring wall seems unaware of this and continues to speak as if he possessed a house. But it exists only in his imagination. It is *imagination* that makes these heaps of material into a house. Now we know that if we *imagine* we have something, it will prevent us from observing that we have not. Imagination will act like that high obscuring wall that prevents the man from realizing what lies beyond. This is the action of Imaginary 'I' on us. *It prevents us from seeing anything wrong with us.* It prevents us from observing our true state in the light of the Work. It prevents us from seeing *anything* that we seriously have to work on in ourselves. So it prevents us from having any intelligent, apposite, personal Work-aim, and therefore prevents us from making Work-effort appropriate to our inner state. It does not prevent us from making outward life-effort. But it prevents us from finding *anything* inward to which we unmistakably should apply the Work. It prevents, in quite a simple but subtle way, any application of the Work-ideas to ourselves. Imaginary 'I' retains its full power until you begin faintly to realize that when you say "I this" and "I that", the word 'I' is possibly of not nearly so much importance as you think. When you begin to realize this faintly you will be allowed to begin to observe yourself and eventually find something in yourself that can become a personal, intelligent aim to work on. Remember you must find and see indisputably *for yourself* what you have to work on. Otherwise you will neither believe it internally in your heart nor perceive the truth of it internally in your mind. That will mean that any so-called Work-effort you make will be entirely externally done for the sake of appearances or of finding favour, and will only strengthen what is false and imaginary in you. For a man to be told, for example, to work on habitual lying, will be useless. Only by observing in himself, alone, in secret inwardly and in silence, that he lies, can he work effectively on these lying 'I's in himself. His aim will be appropriate and real. But such a man will have already faced up to the stripping off already of Imaginary 'I'.

*Amwell, 24.1.53*

### NOTES ON MAKING PERSONALITY PASSIVE

#### PAPER I

If the question is asked: "What does it mean to make Personality passive?" the first answer is that by yourself you cannot make it passive. Help is necessary. But you must connect yourself with that help and be willing to submit to its operation and follow its directions. Let me repeat that again. You—whoever you may be—cannot by yourself make your Personality passive. You are helpless without help. You cannot do it by yourself. And let me add, unless you eventually realize this, you will not get any help. If you think that you, in your own wisdom, intelligence and power, can make your Personality passive if you wish to do so, you have a greatly mistaken idea of yourself and of what you will be up against. And again, if you imagine, in the privacy of that secret heart of yours that is continually scrutinized by Higher Centres, that there is nothing in you that need be made passive and therefore that there is nothing seriously wrong with you that should be got rid of or rendered passive, inactive, then you will certainly never be given any help. Why on earth should you be? Your Imaginary 'I' envelops you like a robe of phantasy and prevents you from seeing your own unhappy weaknesses and painful defects. Do not mistake it for a robe of glory. Enveloped by this robe of phantasy which is your Imaginary 'I', you can only fail to observe yourself. It will act like a mist through which everything in you is seen very obscurely. So you will not observe in any distinct and real way what lies in Personality. Personality will therefore continue to remain active. But if you could make some of the things belonging to Personality *conscious* to yourself by observing them standing in a growing sharpness to the insight and not obscurely as through a mist, those elements would become less and less active as the directed light of consciousness fell more and more fully on them. Yes, we have heard all this many times already. I know we have. But have *you* taken it in yet? Have you *understood* or tried to understand what the Work means when it says it is not primarily based on Faith or Hope or Love, but on *Consciousness*? Do you understand with your own understanding that it seeks to increase our consciousness —and why? It seeks to increase our consciousness—of ourselves first of all, and slowly and gradually our consciousness of others—so that among many other results we see them in us and ourselves in them—a thing that destroys conceit, smugness, pride, vanity and all despisings and contempt, to mention a few of the devils in us that murder others daily in spirit. That is why the Work begins on its practical side—the side of *doing* it—with self-observation. Self-observation means seeing oneself as one is and not as one imagines—a vast task, but expected of us, since we are expressly created to undergo a transformation or re-birth, which an active Personality prevents. Certainly that part of Personality called Imaginary 'I' will do its best to prevent anything like this from happening. It will continue whispering to you: "I and none other", while the truth is that there is no single I and plenty of others. But the power of Imaginary 'I' is enormous. People simply do not believe that they have not got an unchangeable, ever-present, permanent Real I *that controls them.* Let me repeat that: I say that *people simply do not believe that they have not got an unchangeable, ever-present, permanent Real I in control.* So this powerful illusion—this sleep-trick worked by Imaginary 'I'—stands in the way of any of those revealing moments of real self-observation *which would destroy the illusion.* Thus it continues to stand like a mist between the Work itself and its powers, and ourselves and our hidden nothingness. So nothing strikes home to startle and shake us. It prevents us from obtaining the help we need. Why?

Because, although we hear the Work often, we do not really apply it internally to ourselves as a result of the unmistakable evidence of our own self-observation. So it does not connect with us. If it did, we would receive, little by little, as we can stand it, the waiting help necessary to make Personality passive so that the miracle of re-birth can begin to take place.

Now we know that Personality remains active *as long as Life is the Neutralizing Force.* We are all mechanically connected with Life and its demands. We also know that the Work teaches that *another Neutralizing Force* is needed to make Personality passive. This is the Work itself. We are not mechanically connected with the Work. No one can mechanically do the Work. It requires a daily *conscious* effort. We talk about it perhaps but *we do not do it.* It is only by conscious efforts that we can be connected with the Third Force of the Work. It is extraordinary to observe how one does not do the Work. I ask each of you —do you know what you are working on? We *do* life, of course— but not the Work. But only through *doing* the Work can Personality be made passive, for this is the only way *to connect with the Third Force of the Work.* So you will see how absurd a man is if he thinks he can make his Personality passive by himself in his own way while Life is obviously his Neutralizing Force. It simply cannot be done. Only the Work can do it. So hearing the Work is not enough. You have got to *do* it. Christ said: "Whoso heareth these words of mine, and doeth them not, shall be likened unto a foolish man, which built his house upon the sand" (Matt. vii.26). The Work says the same. The sand is the Personality.

Now one sign that a person's Neutralizing Force is still wholly Life is when there is no change in the thinking. The Work says definitely that it is to make us *think in a new way.* It must do so for anything to happen. It can do so—if we receive it with enough willingness and genuine efforts at understanding it. But it is possible to listen to its teachings year in and year out and still think just as you always did. That is, you still think conventionally—as others of your ilk—imitating what you heard these others say, which you have accepted without challenge, still clinging to the same mental attitudes and prejudices, however harmful to you, and still using the same conventional, borrowed phrases about yourself and about people and things. Of course, this is not thinking. It is merely making a mechanical series of noises. The Work demands the actual use of your own Mental Centre—within the first year, I fancy. Otherwise I notice it tends to make little or no impression on the mind later on. It should strike you early—and then later on again, and so on. Not penetrating inwards to the inner divisions of the Mental Centre as a shock to thought, it remains external as words, without much—or even any—connecting meaning. So nothing is assembled, nothing is joined up. No connections are seen clearly. It then cannot change the former thinking. The Work is poured into the old attitudes and perishes. *You cannot superimpose the ideas of the Work on your former mental attitudes and habits of thinking.*

Some of you have never begun to think *from the Work about Life*, but still think from Life about the Work. That is, you still think in the old way. You do not think in any new way. So the Work cannot enter you. Finally, if you do not think in a new way—that is, *from* the Work—you will never think in a new way about yourself—a thing of the greatest importance to self-change.

*Amwell, 31.1.53*

## ON MAKING PERSONALITY PASSIVE

### Paper II

The idea that Personality has to be made passive throughout life, and little by little, before inner development can reach any perfection, is one of the *Great Ideas* taught by the Work. Now unless your mind catches some of the Great Ideas of the Work you will not ever really comprehend what it is all about. It is not much good catching at little things and giving them no background. That will not expand the mind. You will remain in small details and little formatory arguments. The early Church Father, Origen, (3rd century A.D.), quotes a saying of Christ: "Seek the great things, and the little things shall be added to you: seek the heavenly things, and the earthly things shall be added to you." For us the heavenly things are the great things of the Work.

Let us examine once more the idea concerning Personality. The Work teaches that *Life does not develop us wholly*, but only in part. Life brings about the development of Personality and this is very necessary as a first stage. But the further stage of development, latently possible in Man (who by creation is a *self*-developing organism), is not brought about by Life. Two points come in here:

(1) This further stage of development can only be brought about by making Personality passive;

(2) Only the Work can do this. That is, a man in Life and of Life and knowing only Life and its aims and viewpoints cannot make his Personality passive. This is formulated by the Work in terms of another great idea—namely, that *Man can be under two quite different Neutralizing Forces*. As long as he is wholly under the Neutralizing Force of Life and its aims and viewpoints, Personality *must* remain active. But if a man *receives* the Work and its aims and viewpoints, a new Neutralizing Force begins to act on him through which Personality little by little is made passive. This new Neutralizing Force does not come from the direction of Life.

Now all that has just been said must be grasped clearly by each one of you. Your own Mental Centre must be employed by each one of yc , so that the meaning of this part of the Work really enters in and feeds the centre and begins to set up a new way of thinking, both about the situation of yourself and of others on this earth. This is to think *from the Work* about Life, and it has got to be done. I assure you all that unless the ideas of the Work are received into your individual minds and begin to enter definitely into your own individual thinking, the Neutralizing Force of the Work will not make contact with you. Your mind will remain shut to it. No change in thinking will take place. So you will not receive help and in consequence the Personality will remain as active as ever.

We understand, then, that Life itself is the supreme force that keeps Personality active. Now a force must act on something to produce an effect. Let us try to see, therefore, what this force acts upon in ourselves. To find an answer we must turn to what the Work teaches on this subject. We cannot expect to get an answer from Life, since Life itself has made the Personality in us and its force keeps it active. I will make a selection of some of the things in us which, as the Work points out, keep the Personality active:

(1) Imaginary 'I'.

(2) False Personality.

(3) Conventional, mechanical attitudes and beliefs, all you have taken for granted, your customary habits of thought (which are not thought), your mechanical judgments (which are not judgments), your one-sided points of view (whether for or against), your various un-perceived prejudices. (Much more could be said here. What is mentioned especially keeps Personality active.).

(4) Sensual Thinking—and all the fallacies that arise from the senses and thinking only from their evidence.

These factors in us upon which the force of Life acts so as to keep Personality active will be enough for the time being. They are by no means all, as a detailed study of the Work shews. In the previous paper (Paper I in the series "On Making Personality Passive") some of the effects of Imaginary 'I' were described. We will now consider False Personality. People ask if these are not the same. They are the same only in so far as they are both composed of imagination. They both cause people to attribute to themselves what they do not possess. Imaginary 'I' causes people to imagine they have a real, permanent, unchanging I and so prevents self-observation. False Personality causes people to imagine they have all sorts of qualities and virtues which they have not. It is the False Personality that gives itself airs and minces around and assumes poses. It is an actor—a hypocrite. The worst of it is that it deceives its owner so easily. A man or woman comes to believe in these poses and virtues and superiorities manufactured in the work-shops of False Personality. This is a pity, if they are extensive, for awakening will then be all the more painful or indeed impossible. All that the False Personality causes us to attribute to ourselves has to be stripped off, skin after skin, in the long stage of awakening. Similarly,

Imaginary 'I' has to be stripped off so that we can discern clearly the mob of 'I's of every kind that stand concealed behind it as by a mist and realize we are not a unity. *Both Imaginary 'I' and False Personality are Lies.* They trade only in lies. Nothing of truth can connect itself with either of them. But their lies are readily believed and seized hold of. People love to imagine they have special gifts and unusual value. Consider how people lie and how they excuse themselves through lies from facing any unpleasant truth. But please begin with observing yourself. Notice how you lie to keep the False Personality going. Always remember what was said in the parable of the mote and the beam: "Thou hypocrite, *first of all* get rid of the beam in thine own eye." In the Work one must begin self-change with oneself always. In Life one never does. It is the other person's fault. You will agree that to walk through Life with a *beam* in one's eye could not be taken as a sign that one's Personality has been made passive through consciousness. The parable says:

"Why gaze at the splinter in your brother's eye when you do not deeply and thoughtfully perceive the plank in your own eye? Hypocrite, remove from within the plank from your own eye *first of all* . . ." (Matt. vii.3, 5)

The removal from within of the plank in one's own sight of oneself is only possible through an increasing consciousness obtained by long, uncritical self-observation. Reflect on the meaning of *hypocrite*, as used here. Compare it with the meaning of *False Personality* in the Work. Are they not the same? To become conscious of the hypocrite in oneself would seem to be the same as becoming conscious of one's False Personality.

*Amwell, 7.2.53*

## ON MAKING PERSONALITY PASSIVE

### PAPER III

Our bodies all move from yesterday to to-day together. Part of us is in the common movement in Time and part not. The part in Time can be seen: the part that is not cannot be seen. For instance, you cannot see Personality or Essence any more than you can see thought. When the part in Time, which is the body, is separated from the part not in Time, it ceases to work, its organization breaks up and it becomes functionless. It dies and is buried and people say: "So and so is dead. I *saw* him buried." The greatest confusion in spiritual matters arises from this kind of thinking which naïvely believes that the whole of a person is visible. This is pure undiluted sensual thinking which is one of the things that keep Personality active. It thinks a person is his visible body and that there is nothing else to him. Now the fate of the invisible Personality after the lifetime of the body ends is not the same as that of the invisible Essence. We are told that the Personality, formed and acted upon by life, is destructible and disintegrates. The Essence, however, returns to its Star, being the deathless power of growth in us, which we neglect. We prefer an increase of the Personality, which our self-love and the world easily supply. We are also told that the Personality, if hardened, disintegrates slowly. Many things harden it. Implacable hate, insatiable love of power, intractable vanity and great pride do so. It retains consciousness the more one has put the feeling of I into it, and so identified with it. If the Personality has been made passive, consciousness necessarily passes from it into the side of Essence and Real I. Personality can then rapidly break up. Ouspensky often spoke of the danger of crystallizations in the Personality. He mentioned that in simple folk the Personality has no hard places and breaks up with little suffering. On the other hand, the richer the Personality formed round Essence the more there is for Essence to use for its growth— provided a man works on himself to make Personality more and more passive. If he does nothing in that respect he lives and dies as a seed that comes to nothing. As a difficult complex experiment he has failed. Man is created a complex experiment since he is made for this life and another life while in this life. This brings me to the mystery of Essence and the existence of esoteric teaching in the world. Why does esoteric teaching exist? The answer is that it exists because life cannot make Essence grow. Life makes Personality develop but not Essence. Here is the problem; and here lies the source of some apparent paradox in the Work—as when it is said it is better to have little Personality and best to have a rich one. Two different things are being spoken of. A man is duplex. He is under two sets of influences called *A* and *B*. *A* influences arise in life and the Personality is related to them. *B* influences have another source. They are sown into life by the Conscious Circle of Humanity—that is, by *C* influences. They are changed into *B* influences chiefly owing to sensual and formatory thinking. If a man absorbs only *A* influences, his Personality is kept active. His Essence cannot grow. If owing to Magnetic Centre, which is that in us which can distinguish the difference between *A* and *B* influences, the man begins to absorb *B* influences, then he may come in contact, varying in degree, with *C* influences. *B* influences, such as the Gospels and this Work, concern themselves with the growth of Essence. If a man is taught what they mean and what they are telling him to do, Essence *may* begin to grow. But it does so only at the expense of Personality. You cannot retain your full-blown Personality and develop Essence at the same time. That is an idle dream, springing from vanity. Personality must say with John the Baptist: "I must diminish for Essence to increase." That is the supreme idea behind esoteric teaching. "Except ye turn and become as little children, ye shall in no wise enter the Kingdom of Heaven" (Matt. xviii.3). A great deal has to be stripped off Personality in order to reach the little child. Because Essence cannot develop through *A* influences, *B* influences *must* exist. If it could, there would only be *A* influences. Man would not then be the difficult, complex and paradoxical experiment that he is created to be. He would not be a self-developing organism. *Life*, mechanical Life, would complete him.

*Amwell, 14.2.53*

## SELF-OBSERVATION AND RELATIONSHIP

When you say you like a person it does not mean you do like the whole person. There are sides you do not like. But you like some sides enough to put the sides you do not like into the background. Occasionally this arrangement of like and dislike alters and the sides you do not like come into the foreground and for the time being you do not like the person. In our human relationship this is a pretty constant situation. If you do not work on yourself and the phases of dislike are allowed to make you think and feel negative and you take pleasure in identifying with them, the relationship may be made a miserable thing. Once you identify and become badly negative with a person, you have spoiled something. It is your fault. You have not worked on yourself. You never thought you had to, perhaps, and were silly enough to imagine that relationship just happened by itself. Now no relationship happens by itself. It needs conscious work *on either side*. If one person works, and the other does not, it means hard work—or it becomes impossible. He, working on himself, refuses to quarrel. She is furious because she cannot make him negative—or vice versa. If neither side works, then they serve one of the purposes of Organic Life, which is to feed the Moon. Their bear-garden quarrels, their mutual dislikes, criticisms or hatreds —the whole infernal brood of negative emotions and thoughts—set up vibrations of a certain "wave-length" that are transmitted and used by the Moon which is beneath us in the descending order of Creation. Nothing at a higher level wishes food of such a filthy kind. You must realize that most people are very often, if not usually, in a negative state —including yourself—and manufacture this bad quality of psychological food. We live in a Universe in which everything is made use of and everything is useful for something. It is like an economically well-run farm. Nothing is wasted. If we make evil use of our psychic energies, the products are used for something else. Our negative emotions, nastily enjoyed, but useless to us, are used as dung is in a farm. Consider the vast quantity of them being produced every moment all over the world. A little imagination like this helps you to grasp the terrible significance of this part of the Work-teaching—that says the human world is governed not by sex, as some think, but by negative emotions. To a being on the Moon, having an organ of sight that responds not to the vibrations from the Sun but to vibrations of negative emotions, the Earth must look as if it were covered in flames.

Now to return to this question of liking some sides of a person and disliking other sides. We do not see another person through *his* Imaginary 'I'. He takes himself as *one* person—as a unity. His Imaginary 'I' causes him to think so. But you see him differently. You see him as made up of many different sides which are often quite contradictory. He does not. He says: "Don't you like me?"—as if he were only one person. If you answered that you like some sides of him (or her) it would come as a shock. To what is it a shock? Why, to his Imaginary 'I', which is not perceived by him—nor is it perceived by you. It is not perceived by him, because he does not observe that he is not one but many. It is not perceived by you, for you see him as many and not as one. So is the life-game played. But if he begins to *observe himself* and slowly realizes—and how slowly—that he is not one 'I' but many 'I's wrapped up in a cellophane wrapper labelled 'I', he begins to be a different person. He has begun to work on himself. He sees through the fatuous and vain illusion of Imaginary 'I'. He begins to see himself as you do. And if you now say to him that you like some sides of him but not other sides, he (or she) will not be mortally offended or hurt. He (or she) will become much stronger and not nearly so vulnerable and upset. Now two people, reaching this stage of increase of conscious-ness and so of inner development, will be able to make a relationship which would have been impossible before. Both of them can be con-scious of negative sides that they must separate from, not identify with, not enjoy, not put the feeling of I into. Such people, knowing this, and doing it, and so standing, as it were, in the entrance porch of the Work, are so different from people asleep in life, that it can scarcely be believed. Now for those who cannot begin to observe themselves and in con-sequence cannot take in the Work, this paper may be of use. They can see others as having many sides, some of which they like and some of which they dislike. They will no doubt admit this. But they do not see the same thing in themselves, because they are spellbound by Imagin-ary 'I' which makes them believe they are one and not many. They do not believe they have different sides—which means different 'I's in them—and so cannot get on in the Work. There may be another reason for their blindness apart from Imaginary 'I'. It may be as well that they do not see themselves as others see them. It may be that their conceit could not face it. But it is usually a matter of Imaginary 'I' that blocks the way to self-observation.

Now whenever you see a side of somebody which you dislike, try to define it as clearly as you can. Then try to find the same thing in yourself by observation of yourself. This *may* help those who find it impossible to observe themselves unaided. People do not do this in

Life. People in the Work are supposed to do it. Later on, they must do so.

*Amwell, 21.2.53*

## OUTER AND INNER

Since some papers on inner and outer parts of centres are to follow, I would like to preface them with a general note on the psychological meaning of *inner* and *outer*. I hope some of you will be able to follow what is said in this note and gain a distinct idea of what it indicates. I say this because if you cannot gain any conception of your own of what is being spoken about, it will make it impossible to understand the papers that will follow. I advise you to stop internal considering and listen mentally to the meaning behind the words and ask yourselves if you have understood anything and if not, to ask questions, and in this way make a personal effort to understand. This helps you and everyone else. Never think that the meeting has nothing to do with you personally or that you have no responsibility in regard to it and can sit back and take no part. Such a view shews a bad attitude to the Work.

First of all there is an outer and inner sense to things, which are quite different. This may seem extraordinary, but it is true. The same thing seen outwardly is quite different when seen inwardly. Yet it is the same thing. Owing to this being the case, a great deal of confusion and argument arises. For the sake of simplicity let us divide the mind into an *outer mind* and an *inner mind*. The same thing viewed by the outer mind becomes quite different when viewed with the inner mind. If there are two men, one of whom is viewing a thing with his outer mind, and the other viewing it with his inner mind, they will get totally different impressions of it. It will seem that they are viewing two quite different and unrelated things. Yet they are viewing the same thing, but with two *different minds*. One is viewing it with his outer mind, and the other is viewing it with his inner mind. When anyone having only an outer mind reads some phrase in Scripture to the effect that God in his anger casts a man down into hell, it appears to mean literally what it says. To the inner mind the meaning is inverted, since God cannot be angry and the apparent meaning is transformed into its inner sense, which is that a man by anger casts himself down to a lower level of being. Again, all parables have an outer and inner meaning. Now it will be evident that since the two minds, outer and inner, view the same thing in such completely different ways, they cannot be continuous, but must be discontinuous. By this is meant that one cannot merge gradually into the other. They must be as distinct and separate from one another as are the two rooms in a house, one of which is on the ground floor and the other on the floor above. This discontinuity of the two minds shews that their functions are different. That is, they have uses that are different. The outer mind is used for the world without. It is turned towards life and its affairs through the senses. It can be clever or stupid, or well or poorly developed. It should be developed as widely as possible. Its knowledge is of the kind you can buy anywhere and at any time. The use of the inner mind is more difficult to define. In the majority of people it is not used at all. It is not opened up, like an unoccupied room, whose door has never been opened. You cannot pass freely from the outer mind into the inner mind, for they are not on the same floor. Some people assume they can. When they meet the Work and are told that a *change of mind* is first needed (*metanoia*), they use the same mind as before, year after year, and so get stuck or sticky. As I indicated, the inner mind is comparable to a room *upstairs* on the first floor, while the outer mind is on the *ground floor*. Without possessing any sense of scale, such people do not comprehend this "higher" and "lower" *in them*. I will remind you that scale signifies ladder (scala) and a ladder is for going up or down and its rungs are discontinuous. If they were not, it would not be a ladder, but a plank. To go up one rung, one must leave the ground floor. You must leave your ordinary outer sensual mind, with its ways of thinking and of viewing things. This some find impossible. Yet it is possible, *if you let go*. What? I have no idea what it is in your case. You must discover it for yourself. You should look in the direction of what seems incredible to you—I mean, about yourself.

Now the inner mind when opened up and dusted and aired can receive and entertain guests—or let in, say, thoughts and insights—that affect the outer mind and eventually control it. This is how things should be. This is right order. When the outer mind rules us, it is wrong order. Wrong order makes us unhappy. The inner, being much higher in dignity and excellence—that is, in scale of being—should control the lower. When, however, we exalt the lower and endow it with false dignity and excellence, that certainly is something ridiculous and painful. Yet people do; and fail to get upstairs. Something, therefore, must happen first—to get upstairs. Now the lower or outer mind cannot open the higher or inner mind. Please understand and register here that *outer* is *lower*, and *inner* is *higher*. Outer divisions of centres are lower and inner divisions are higher in scale. Also what is higher is "cleverer" than what is lower; the higher can see and comprehend the lower, but the lower cannot comprehend the higher. This is the same as saying that what is inner can observe and comprehend what is outer: but what is outer *cannot* observe or comprehend what is inner. It follows that the outer or lower mind cannot open the inner or higher mind. That is, sensual thinking cannot open the inner mind. As long as you are thinking sensually, you are on the ground floor of your own being. You have to start thinking in a new way to get upstairs. The first object of the Work is to make you think in a new way—to change your mind. As I said recently, you cannot do this if you persist in thinking about the Work *from life*—that is, with your outer mind. You must begin by thinking about life *from the Work*. When you *receive* the Work inwardly, it begins to open the inner mind, for it is designed to do so. You then begin to see life from what the Work says about it. You see it quite differently from the way you did when you viewed it from your outer mind. This is because you are beginning to view it from your inner mind, which the Work is opening. This illustrates how the same thing, viewed from the outer mind, becomes quite different when viewed from the inner mind. It is the same thing but viewed by two quite different and discontinuous minds, placed on different levels—*in yourself*. Do not think that you can casually get hold of this Work by adding some knowledge of it to your outer mind. It will never take root there. You cannot sow wheat in Piccadilly. Only the right quality of *valuation* of it will make it fall in the right soil in you where it can grow—and that is, the inner mind. And by valuation I do not mean valuing it in terms of life-values, such as eminence or ruling or power or distinction or fame or position or opulence or luxury or possession. These are the driving forces of life. They belong to the outer mind.

*Amwell, 28.2.53*

### NEGATIVE EMOTIONS

When you are very negative towards a person, every unpleasant experience flows towards his image in your mind. Even an unpleasant character in the novel you are reading becomes him. Sometimes you cannot get him out of your head. He is with you when you go to sleep and is there when you wake. He or she becomes like the devil. What does this shew? It shews that you put yourself under the power of a person when you become negative with him or her. The person has power over you. This person makes as it were an actual depression in you, and everything drains towards it. It becomes a marsh which can spoil your mind. It is very dangerous. Eventually this marshland in you must be drained—a big engineering job. Yet does it not seem to you that by feeling negative and perhaps hating another person, *you* have the power and not the other person? Is it an illusion? In one sense, no, because all negative emotions lead down to physical violence ultimately and people feel they can hurt or kill one another. In another sense, yes, because by letting yourself become negative you gave the person power over you without his necessarily knowing anything about it. It would appear then that we do *ourselves* a grave injury by becoming negative with another person. Notice it is always a *person*, actual or imagined, that makes us negative, and never a *thing*.

Negative emotions easily attract us. People get to enjoy them. There is a story that an Angel visited this earth. For a long time he thought everyone was mad. He could not understand what they were enjoying. After a time the Angel got infected also. He began to enjoy negative emotions and became mad like the rest. A messenger was sent down to inform him that he had failed in his test. He had forgotten something and now he must remain on earth until he had disentangled himself from all his negative emotions, and that made him more mad than ever. This is an allegory of our own situation on this planet. It also illustrates one aspect of negativeness, which is its power not only of persisting but of adding to itself like a spreading fire. You can feel negative towards the whole world. To change the image, negativeness submerges you like a flood. If you have not made an ark within you, you can be spiritually drowned. If you follow the directions of the Work, however, you can make an ark that becomes increasingly seaworthy by experience. It is built in three parts. Noah was directed to make an ark of *three* storeys. I have never seen one in toy-shops that has three storeys. The Work says that Man is a three-storey house but that it is all in disorder. It is certainly often flooded with negative states, intellectual as well as emotional. Negative thinking with negative emotion is destructively dangerous. Did anyone ever clearly tell us what being negative is and how evil and dangerous it is? Weeping or being sad and soulful-looking used to be regarded as a sign of spiritual development. There are lots of very fine paintings of such negative emotions. They have been much admired. Nowadays there are lots of ugly and distorted paintings. They are much admired and equally negative. Each period has its fashionable negative states. People love their negative emotions. They will not let go of them easily. Is it strange that there does not seem at first sight to be much in life that can replace them? Other emotions become dull, compared with the curious delights of being negative, such as planning revenges. Also, being gloomy or bad-tempered, or self-pitying and bemoaning, or tart and stinging, or maliciously vexing, are so easy. Have you reflected on this? They go on by themselves. Has it ever occurred to you that there must be something in negative emotions comparable to a fascinating drug? A drug gets a hold on a person. It cannot be shaken off without great difficulty. Does a negative emotion give some similar kind of solace as does a drug? Could the world really do without its negative emotions? I do not think so myself. But in the Work we have to learn to do so. One thing that helps us is to learn to express them less unpleasantly or violently. That requires a little conscious attention. Ouspensky said that by mechanically expressing our negative emotions we increase them. But we can study how to express them a little more consciously. This modifies their harming power. Of course I do not mean you should express them with a sweet, deadly smile or anything like that. It has been said before that negative emotions and not sex govern the world. They destroy sex. Do not regard yourself as exceptional and being free from negative states. Are you never sulky? Are you never jealous or envious? Have you no grievances? Does nothing ever rankle? It is always worth while observing and tracing the subtle action of negative emotions in you. They are the source of so many things you do which you think you are doing for some other reason. All negative emotions seek expression in hurting someone, sooner or later.

Because negative emotions spoil everyone's life so much, it is just as intelligent to study them as any other human disease is studied. Data must be collected. There are typical physical illnesses and typical psychological illnesses. As regards negative emotions there are *three lines of study*. All three are necessary to disentangle us from their coils. The first line is to study negative emotions in yourself. You can only do this by means of self-observation. You have both to *observe* and *remember*. You must build up a Work-memory. But to do so, you must be willing to admit that you have negative emotions. Now people do not quite admit it. It is not hypocrisy. They even say they do not really quite know what negative emotions are, and yet it is not hypocrisy— it is because they do not make themselves fully conscious of their negative states—and won't. Some thin tough veil has to be stripped away here. Do you ever hear any one flatly saying without venom: "I am negative"? No—they say: "I am fed up", or "I am upset", or similar phrases as "I am vexed" or "I am furious". But the fact is that they are negative. Now the case is like this: when you do not admit something in yourself to the full light of consciousness but veil it, it retains its secret power over you, however you seem to struggle. Do you know that if even a violent and angry person begins to see clearly and becomes more and more fully conscious of his violence and anger and eventually makes no further attempt at justifying himself or finding excuses for himself, he will gradually become different? *This is done for him.* For such is the action of the light of consciousness when we turn it on ourselves—which we almost never do. We are asked by the Work to turn a ray of this light into our inner darkness. Do we? We prefer darkness to light. This means we prefer negative states which are states of darkness. Now to observe oneself honestly is the remedy—provided it is not accompanied by a nice picture, taken by a firm called *Self-Love*—of yourself honestly observing yourself. This is the kind of thing that happens, does it not? We always seem to be doing something else as well as what we are doing. There seems always to be some picture there.

I will speak of the second and third lines of the study of negative emotions some other time. I will only mention here that the second line is studying negative emotions in those connected with you, and the third line is studying the action of negative emotions in the world. Since the Work teaches that negative emotions govern the world, if we study the world from this idea, we shall be thinking about life from the viewpoint of the Work. This is quite a simple example, but I do not expect many will see what is meant. All the same, it is really necessary to think about life from the ideas of the Work.

*Amwell, 7.3.53*

## THINKING FROM THE WORK ABOUT LIFE AND FORMING WORK ATTITUDES

One reason why people get hold of the meaning of the Work so slowly is that they continue to think about the Work *from Life* instead of thinking about Life from the Work. As some find it difficult to understand what is meant in saying this, I will try to give some explanations in this commentary. Many of the ideas that the Work presents to you are strange when first heard. For example, the idea that Man is asleep sounds strange. What you have been told and seen in Life is that a man is either asleep in bed or awake and up and doing. As long as you think from what you have been taught and what you have seen in Life, this Work idea will appear untrue and indeed quite absurd. For how, thinking from Life, can it be said that *Man is asleep?* Certainly he is asleep sometimes. He has to be. But at other times he is wide-awake. Look at all these people hurrying along the street or jumping on to buses and streaming into tube stations—are you going to tell me that they are asleep? Their eyes are open. If you address them, they will answer you. Some of them are reading newspapers. How can a man asleep read a newspaper? So you think it is nonsense to say Man is asleep. Exactly. It *is* non-sense. It is not a matter of the senses. It is not a matter of the sensual thinking derived from the evidence of the senses. In spite of all you say, the Work is right. *Man is asleep.* Your difficulty lies in the fact that you do not understand what the Work means by being asleep. With your sensual thinking, you take it literally, as meaning actual physical sleep. This is one example of what I mean by "thinking of the Work from Life". From the points of view laid down in you from your experience of Life, the idea that Man is asleep is not acceptable to your mind. Therefore when you try to get hold of the Work teaching that Man is asleep you are trying to superimpose an idea on a level of thinking that flatly contradicts it. The Work idea is then not capable of being assimilated by your mind. You are pouring new wine into old bottles. This mistake was pointed out some two thousand years ago. It is not surprising, therefore, that the Work tells us emphatically that its object, first of all, is to make us *think in a new way.* It is a most mistaken technique to keep trying to pour new thinking on to old thinking. But as long as you cling to your former ways of thinking, to your former opinions and attitudes, you will continue to think of the ideas of the Work from your ideas of Life.

You will remain unable to see Life from the ideas of the Work. You will constantly forget what the Work teaches because you are being stupid enough to try to understand them in terms of Life ideas. In this way you are constantly destroying them, and so you will not get hold of the Work. But if you receive the Work in a place that is special through your evaluation it will build itself and organize itself in you. Then you will be able to see Life from the Work. You will *see* inwardly what the Work means when it says *Man is asleep*. You will *see* that everything happens in the only way it can happen *because Man is asleep*, and you will also see that you have been asleep all your life. You will *see* why the waking state of Man is called by the Work the "so-called Waking State"—a state which G. describes as an evil one in which Man can do infinite harm to Man. You can *see* that Man does not *remember himself* in this state and for that reason is asleep in his spirit. You will understand and see in the light of truth that Man is asleep just because he does not *remember himself*: and that you are asleep for the same reason. You will understand that if humanity reached the third level of consciousness called in the Work Self-Remembering, Self-Consciousness and Self-Awareness, everything on earth would be different. Men would not make the speeches they do, would not write the books they do, not speak as they do, not behave to one another as they do, and not hate, cheat, ruin and kill one another as they do. You will see and understand that Man does not *remember* himself but forgets himself because he identifies with everything and everybody. He does not observe himself so he is not conscious of what is in himself or of his contradictory states. Because he is self-complacent he does not realize he is in any danger and so is not *aware* of himself as he would be if he knew he was in an alien country and no longer believed that the pageant of material life alone led to any real goal. And all this insight and truth and much else will come about because you are thinking from the Work about Life and not the other way round. Now unless you begin to think in a new way, unless you undergo *metanoia*—which does not mean repentance, but change of thinking—you will not form any Work attitudes in yourself. You will retain your habitual attitudes that Life has built in you. An attitude begins with a thought. That is, it starts in the *Mental* Centre. If you keep thinking in the same way, a crystallization takes place and an attitude is formed. You then think and speak from the attitude, only you are not aware that you do so. You believe that you are thinking for yourself. People full of crystallized attitudes are very tedious. They are not the quick but the *dead*. To the simple-minded they often seem towers of strength—because they always say the same things. Now Life attitudes will not help a man in the Work. The ideas of the Work striking against Life attitudes will arouse antagonistic reactions of all kinds. Their own existence is threatened. Everything in your psychology fights for its life—that is why self-change is so difficult. Now as long as you do not *think in a new way*, you cannot form new attitudes, because an attitude begins with a thought. If you do not think often about the Work and its age-old significance, if you inwardly think little of it, if you are incapable of comprehending that it is esoteric Christianity because, as G. said, it is based on the inner meaning of the parables and words of Christ, then no Work attitude can be formed within you. You will continue to be imprisoned by your Life attitudes and your Personality will remain active. After listening to but not hearing the Work for years you will remain just the same. The Work will not accept you because you will not receive it. But if you do receive it, another history begins for you. You will begin to *hear* and *see* the Work—that is, become conscious of its truths. That will indicate that the formation of Work attitudes has begun. These are not formed in the same part of the mind as Life attitudes. They are formed in a more interior division of the Intellectual Centre, nearer to Higher Centres. They can therefore weaken Life attitudes and do away with them, for what is interior has greater power than what is exterior. You can understand that if a man never thinks deeply and for himself about the teaching and significance of the Work, his thoughts will not fall on the deeper, interior division of the Intellectual Centre. If he thinks only superficially of the Work, it will fall among the Life attitudes in the external mind and come to nothing in that man. It will fall on stony ground and wither. Remember this, then: an attitude begins in the mind of Intellectual Centre. It begins with thinking. Eventually it influences the mind of Emotional Centre; but the point is that it begins in the Intellectual Centre. When you truly begin to look at Life *through* one or other of the Work ideas you see Life in another way, and begin to *think* in a new way. This may begin a Work attitude in the mind. But it will be a young thing among heavy, pompous old men and women within you, so you must remember to love, encourage and defend it. Otherwise this small, very precious, new thing—of which you may dream—will perish, as it has done in so many so often. When a Work attitude is formed it transmits the endless meanings of the Work. A Life attitude blocks them. Work attitudes are like windows: Life attitudes are like walls.

*Amwell, 14.3.53*

## COMMENTARY ON END, CAUSE AND EFFECT

According to the formulation given by the Work, three forces enter into every manifestation. One force cannot produce a manifestation. Two forces cannot. Three forces only, in the relation of active, passive and connecting forces to one another, can do so. Three active forces, or three passive forces, or three connecting or neutralizing ones, cannot produce a manifestation. What I mean is that the three forces that *create* the manifestation must bear to one another the relationship of active, passive and connecting. It is this question of *relationship* that is interesting. The same force can be active in one triad, passive to another, and neutralizing in a third triad, according to how it is related to the other two forces. The formulation may seem clear enough. We do not, however, understand it clearly. Even if we meditate often on its meaning, it remains mysterious for, in fact, it passes upward into the mystery of the primal Trinity Itself, which no man has ever comprehended with his sensual mind or contacted with his limited senses. Nevertheless there are records existing of those who have beheld something of its infinite meaning for a moment but only when the suprasensual mind has been suddenly opened. This we call the *inner* mind of which we have been speaking recently. The "third-force-blind" outer or formatory mind is obviously a useless instrument for this purpose. I will say here, however, that, in place of plodding along with *that* mind laboriously, hoping to get hold of the Trinity by its means, it is better first to acknowledge that we are in the presence of something immensely far above us, and then, with this emotion, attempt to grasp what we can at our level. There are many *preliminary* ideas bearing on the mystery of three forces that we can to a small extent realize and for which approximate examples can be found.

I will begin with this question: why is it that two equal men, apparently doing the same thing, can reach such different results? The answer is that their *ends* are different. Let us say that the end of one is *power* and the end of the other is *use*. In addition let us suppose that they will employ the same means to *effect* their ends. That is to say, they will go to the same University and listen to the same teachers and study the same books. Notice that three things are involved—*end, means* and *effect*. Now these three things interpenetrate one another. One is in the other. The end penetrates the effect and the means penetrates the effect and the effect is related to the end. Concerning the interpenetration of the three aspects of the supreme Trinity, John records many of the deeper sayings of Christ. His Gospel is of a totally different quality from the others, and people do not read it because it is not so much a narrative of facts as of *relationship* on the highest level. Read with the wrong attitude it may seem negative and even reiterative. Actually it is the most powerful Gospel of all. From it you can see for yourself, when you are ready for it, why John was the disciple whom Christ loved. It speaks about the Second Conscious Shock which, by the way, has nothing to do with physical love. It speaks about the relationship of Christ to God and to His disciples. We are not going to discuss it. To return to the case of the two men we are imagining. The quality of their ends is dissimilar. In one the love of rule, the love of power, the love of high position, etc., form the end he is aiming at. This interpenetrates the means he employs and the attainment of the aim, which is the result or effect. The end is in the effect and is in the means. Yet all three are different, but so conjoined and interpenetrating that they form a single oneness or unity. This man becomes an archbishop: his love of rule is now satisfied. In the case of the other man, his primary end is to be of use. Employing the same means as the other, he becomes a priest in a poor district where no doubt he is much loved. I am not being sentimental. Now the results are so different because the primary ends were so different, though the means were the same. This example is trivial, but it faces each of you with the question of why you do the Work. What is your reason? What is your end? Are you just trying to be first? Is your end supernatural powers? Has envy got to do with it? Is your end to renew your youth—not, I would say, a very delightful end? Your aim or end, of course, changes as you understand more of the Work. Since it involves your death, it is bound to do so. I speak psychologically. At first you want more of this and that, and heaps more of it. Later you want less and less of this and that. It all turns the other way round—or should do so. You want to get rid of things you observe in yourself. You want to sell lots of things you thought fine, and buy *one* thing. To be in possession of Real I would be wonderful. Of course, if you are working from the influence of a wrong end, like the archbishop we imagined who aimed at ruling, you, privately, from yourself, will not be wanting to buy anything at all, or indeed get rid of anything without an audience. An audience is not the right end. Even so, it is possible to work from the wrong place for a long time and then be enlightened and see what you are doing and acknowledge it in secret to yourself and everything is then put in the right place for you. Then, your work depends on no one else but yourself and you have inner strength instead of weakness. When this stage is reached—and it can be—you cannot be robbed. This is one meaning of laying up treasure in the wrong place and in the right place. The wrong and the right places are in you. A wrong end means a wrong place. The Work laid up in the wrong place in you can be broken into or stolen. The verse about this is as follows:

> "Lay not up for yourselves treasures upon earth, where moth and rust doth corrupt, and where thieves break through and steal: but lay up for yourselves treasures in heaven, where neither moth nor rust doth corrupt, and where thieves do not break through nor steal." (Matt. vi.19,20)

Perhaps some of you have little idea as yet how difficult it is to do anything in the Work from an absolutely pure motive and to avoid doing a thing "to be seen of men".

As regards the meaning of earth and heaven in the above saying, the expression is often used for what is at a lower level and what is at a higher level. We know already that lower and higher correspond to external and internal. The lower is external to the higher which is internal to it. To lay up treasure in heaven therefore means to understand the Work with your inner mind because such understanding cannot be taken from you and depends on nothing external such as encouragement or praise. But we have seen this when approaching the matter from other angles in previous papers.

*Amwell, 21.3.53*

## COMMENTARY ON DOING THE WORK

People get held up in the Work because they do not apply to themselves what it teaches them to do. It is necessary both to hear *and do*. In this commentary I will speak of some points that bear on this matter of *not doing* the Work. I will omit the whole question of *hearing* the Work, save to say that it means to hear with the mind, and to add that a negative attitude makes this impossible. I expect people at least to be willing to receive the Work. The first thing that people do not *do* is to observe themselves. One of our unused *inner* senses is the faculty of self-observation. We have to train ourselves to use this internal camera. If used, it eventually presents us with full-length portraits of ourselves entirely different from what we should ever have expected. The *sensual* mind is based on the evidence of the *external* senses. If you make use of this inner sense—this inner camera—of self-observation, you begin to open a mind above the level of the sensual mind. In the Work it is a wise man who begins to think above the sensual level, and a foolish one who will not. What you learn from self-observation obviously is not sensual, but beyond the outer senses. Actually, it begins the supra-sensual mind in you. The inner camera, however, is not easy to use. You stand too close to it at first. The next point that I call attention to in this commentary concerns *identifying* with everything going on in yourself—every thought, feeling, sensation, mood, attitude, phantasy. You say 'I' to everything and observe nothing. Everything is you. This is a state of complete sleep. It is like thinking the crowd in the street is you. The next point is that when you do observe something you try to change it right away. This is not what the Work teaches. What it says is that you must practise inner separation—a process of disjoining yourself from yourself.

As I said, people notice something in themselves and immediately think they have to change it, but they find that they cannot. I will give an example. At one of the sub-groups someone said that she had observed herself acting from an attitude, but had not the knowledge and the power to change herself. Of course she cannot change it. An attitude is a very difficult thing both to observe and change. What she has to do is to try to draw the feeling of I out of this action from attitude every time it occurs, and remember herself, so as to absorb the energy. She must separate internally from it. Instead of that she is trying to change the attitude, whereas she should draw force out of it by not identifying with it. She is saying 'I' to it instead of saying: "This is not I. I am not this attitude" or "Although this attitude is in me, I am not it." Or something like that. This drawing of force out of something that one observes is one of the important practices of the Work. To think that you can change something directly without inner separation means that you are trying to change it from the level of your ordinary 'I's; but you will never change anything from this level any more than you can lift a plank you are standing on. Observing I is on a different level from other 'I's since it is connected ultimately with Real I. Sometimes it is unusually difficult to separate. This is especially the case when we do not really wish to separate, as in the case of some negative emotions, which we secretly enjoy. You cannot separate from something in yourself that you are clinging to all the time and do not wish to let go of. People deceive themselves very easily here.

The next point that I will mention in this commentary is that you all justify yourselves very easily. To justify oneself means to take the view that you are right and maintain it. People even justify their negative states and discard the witness of inner taste. One way is to deny you are negative. People do not admit they are wrong. Do you know why? Well, try to observe and thus get to know the reason. This knowledge takes time—indeed, years, and is not good for conceit and self-worship. To digress for a moment: the injunction written on the Temple of Delphi in Ancient Greece was KNOW THYSELF. This shews at once that it was an Esoteric School. An ordinary life-school is about knowledge in general: an Esoteric School is about self-knowledge. This means many things. We have to know about ourselves and what is hidden in us that is evil, and what possibilities have been prepared for us from Creation. In this Work, for instance, we have to know from self-observation that we are asleep and in what sense. We have also to know that we can awaken from sleep, and how to. If you get to know through self-observation why you always justify yourself, and why you will not face the stark truth that you are wrong, you will know a lot about yourself. Begin by stopping self-justifying. Can you? This kind of knowledge—that is, self-knowledge—changes you. It is part of awakening. Awakening is not quite pleasant. One suffers and also is so very glad. You feel you are at last doing what you wanted, but had forgotten. Now, in connection with self-knowledge, I return again to self-observation. *Self-knowledge begins with self-observation.* If you cannot observe a thing in yourself you can have no knowledge of it. If you have no knowledge of it, you are identified with it. You cannot draw force out of something in yourself if you do not know by observation that it exists in you. Do you grasp this clearly? Others may and do have knowledge of it. But you haven't. It is not included in your meagre erroneous conscious inventory of yourself. Do you realize that your own consciousness of yourself is not by any means the same as the consciousness of yourself possessed by another person. I am afraid the two would not tally. As you are, you could not bear to become conscious of what others are conscious of in you. It would be far too strong medicine—even if only one friend was concerned.

Now we come to the next point. Why does *relationship* scarcely exist in the mechanical world and habit and compromise take its place? Why are two people potentially such an explosive mixture? They would not be so explosive if they had some reciprocal degree of self-knowledge through the practice of self-observation. Why? Because it leads—say, in my case—to seeing myself in the other and the other in myself. You cannot hurl violent and bitter remarks at one another, when each of you is hurling them at yourself. This opens the real, inner heart, because it goes deeper than and beyond the closed self-willed, self-loving, exclusive heart. What can you feel so exclusive and precious in you when you clearly begin to see yourself in others and others in yourself? It is a revelation—at the expense of self-idolatry and self-conceit. Notice it is a true and real expansion of consciousness to see yourself in your neighbour and your neighbour in yourself. You can then understand that the development and extension of this *conscious relationship* would lead to that *compassion* for the world that, we are told, characterized the great teachers of humanity in the past. The word is used of Christ. It would not be a sentimental *act* but a permanent *state* of insight with a new feeling of I. If I observe my neighbour in myself and if I observe myself in my neighbour, do you think I can feel superior to him? Consider the complete change that would take place in the Emotional Centre if this mutual criss-cross, double and inter-penetrating consciousness of seeing what is without in your neighbour and within in yourself together were born in you. Contrast this with the shut-in state of the undeveloped and mechanical Emotional Centre where only the various forms of self-love and self-interest reign. I remind you here that one of the emphatic objects of this Work is to *awaken the Emotional Centre.* Have you ever meditated on what this might mean and passed in review the average quality of your everyday emotional states? What is an awakened Emotional Centre? At least, it cannot mean enjoying still more violent moods and negative emotions. Are you satisfied with such emotions? If not, then what about ceasing to attribute them to another person, and beginning to attribute them to yourself and finding the causes in yourself? The Work strongly advises us to *do* this. Yes, I repeat, *do* it. We are talking about *doing* the Work. It says that we must become responsible for our negative emotions and ultimately realize that it is always our own fault if we are negative.

But the point here is that if we sufficiently clearly saw ourselves in our neighbour and our neighbour in ourselves—consciously and not sentimentally—if we had something of this magical, interpenetrating reciprocal consciousness that the whole world needs as well as ourselves, the Emotional Centre would be purified from its negative part. The neighbour makes us negative. It would then be not only unnecessary to draw out the feelings of I from negative states aroused by our neighbours

1684

but our feeling of I could completely change. Now this change in the feeling of I would foreshadow the coming of Real I. With your present, exclusive, narrow, feeling of I, in which you try in vain to balance yourself and keep falling down and breaking your crown, you could not bear the approach of Real I, which would seem to deprive you of your very existence. But as you know, this Work is to prepare lower centres—from which our ordinary feeling of I arises—for the reception of Higher Centres, to which Real I is related.

*Amwell, 28.3.53*

## THE SECRETARY AND THE THREE BOSSES

In speaking of "the three centres", the Intellectual, the Emotional, and the Instinctive-Moving Centre are meant. These three centres occupy the three-storey house with which Man is compared. On the top floor is the Intellectual Centre, on the middle floor the Emotional Centre, and on the bottom floor is the Instinctive-Moving Centre. Although the Instinctive Centre and the Moving Centre are sometimes spoken of as distinct, they are so closely related to one another that sometimes they are taken as one centre called Instinctive-Moving Centre. Sensation and movement are interlocked. If you had no sensation in your legs you could not walk. At the same time, you can have sensation without movement. These three centres were called by G. "the three bosses". In speaking of them he remarked that they do not understand each other's language. It is as if one boss speaks Greek, another Italian, and the third Turkish. These three centres, he said, are connected with a secretary who rings them up as occasion arises, but unfortunately she does not understand much of the messages she receives and usually rings up the wrong boss, and makes a great many mistakes. The last time I saw G. draw this diagram, which he did long after midnight, in a freezing theatre, with the stump of a candle on the back of a Persian rug, he put the secretary just outside the three-storey house. The three centres were not drawn as full circles, but as segments of circles. Three lines connected the secretary with them. What, then, can we do, you might ask, if such conditions exist in us? Can we possibly replace this secretary who does not think for herself, who looks things up in stereotyped books of reference and who often rings up the wrong boss for the job in hand? Now this question has never been answered briefly so far as I know, and cannot be. It is necessary to make a commentary about the matter. I will begin in this way: Ordinarily we do not know anything about our centres and are really unaware we have them. In spite of the long established neurological findings of levels and the comparative localization of function in the brain, people in general understand nothing of centres. They usually dislike the idea. The illusion of Imaginary 'I', and the deception that they are conscious masters of themselves, make the laying-bare of their underlying machinery distasteful to them. They do not seek new thoughts, new emotions or anything new. The Work tells us we must observe our centres, and it tells us this very early. It helps to break us up. Almost at the beginning of his teaching in London, O. reiterated the importance of observing our centres and what they were doing. As long as you do not observe them, you will not be aware either of them or of the wrong work of the single secretary who rings them up. Why should not you ring up your centres instead of this stupid secretary, who gives them wrong orders and does not quite understand any situation in life, and looks things up in antiquated reference books? What hinders us? The answer is lack of consciousness—and habits. You have ingrained habits of thinking, ingrained attitudes, ingrained ways of reacting, stereotyped conventional feelings, and so on. All this must have something to do with the secretary who is so stupid. Now, when you act from acquired attitudes are you not acting stupidly? You are prejudiced, which means judging beforehand. So you are not acting from your understanding at the moment. If that is the case, you will get more stupid and prejudiced as you get older, because whenever you act in a stereotyped way from attitude in some particular situation you are failing to use your understanding—and that means death. Do you really believe that your mechanical attitudes *are* your understanding? They are what prevent you from intelligent understanding. They make you mentally rigid, whereas you should become more and more flexible in this Work. Have you noticed also that people with strong ingrained attitudes usually have very rigid, stiff postures, as if on parade? From this you can see how certain parts of the centres become covered by a network of attitudes, associations and habits, which connect them up wrongly. You have habits of thinking, habits of feeling, habits of moving, habits of sensation. This network overlying the centres is the telephone system used by the secretary when she receives incoming impressions. It must be evident to anyone that a centre itself will not be able to work flexibly and intelligently as a whole in its own field of activity as long as a network of habitual, mechanical reactions overlies the part usually employed. The shock of living should really make us desire to have our centres working better. However, people do not see that their centres work mechanically until they are told that they have centres and begin to observe them in the light of this Work.

Notice that G. drew only segments or parts of centres in the diagram mentioned. These he called the mechanical parts of centres. He strove to open up unused parts of centres by new thinking and new movements and posture to begin with. When impressions fall on these used, mechanical, wrongly-connected parts of centres *nothing happens*. I mean that no new food of impressions is taken in and assimilated. The old telephone system operates. The old responses, the old reactions, are obtained. This is represented in the diagram of the three foods as impressions 48 entering the top storey and meeting with a block. Energy 48 is not transformed. The block is caused by the old ways of taking things—the old ways of thinking and feeling, the old postures, etc. Now 48 is not yet *in* the machine any more than is 768 as such. A lamb chop in your stomach is not yet you. It has not begun to be "digested". So G. put the "secretary" *outside* the three-storey house. Now Observing I should replace this hypothetical and stupid secretary. By observing centres while they are at work, you can become conscious of what they are mechanically doing. Consciousness *begins* to replace the secretary. Consciousness is a *connector*. Whatever it may be in itself it connects us with things as does light on a dark night. Your machine is unconsciously connected up in all sorts of wrong ways. You are not conscious of it. As G. put it, our machines are dirty and need cleaning and re-connecting. To become conscious of wrong connections is to connect them with your consciousness. It is a *new* connecting that can change some things fairly easily, others not. Suppose you stop being violently angry whenever the post is late. Suppose you *observe*. Suppose you break this wrong connection consciously. It is not difficult once you observe it enough. This Work is about increasing consciousness, about becoming more conscious to ourselves of ourselves, and of what lies in us. The light of consciousness *cures* many wrong things. You can see why. Through increased consciousness we become aware where previously we were not aware—that is, of what we were unconscious. By observing your Emotional Centre in this Work, for example, you become aware of the number of negative emotions, great and small, which proceed from it, which you had not known before were in existence in you. It should make you less critical of your neighbour. You see, in short, that you have been going about in a state of sleep as regards the activities of your own Emotional Centre, which simply made bad chemistry and poisoned you every day without hindrance. You merely thought your neighbour was a so-and-so. Similarly, observe your Intellectual Centre. No doubt you will be astonished at what thoughts you find going on unchecked. In both cases you are making *connections through consciousness* and so weakening the power of old connections. For by the light of consciousness you are enabled to see some of the wrong work that has been going on. This wrong work is due to the network of old habits and wrong associations lying over the surface of the external parts of centres that prevent impressions being assimilated.

Now, have any of you really observed your three centres at work uncritically? It is more interesting than going to the cinema, O. said. I will give you a slight example: In the early morning I am lying half asleep. When one is half asleep one can observe more easily because the secretary is asleep. I observe that my Intellectual Centre begins by itself to make a plan about what is to be done after I get up. This plan forms itself slowly and dimly, attracting and repelling different vague ideas. (If I give it full attention, I will be fully awake.) It has to do with making some special corrections in something that I have written. I continue to observe. It begins to work at how to make these corrections. The centre is working by itself as it should. People call this subconscious activity. While this is going on I observe that my Instinctive Centre is apparently not taking any part in the plan, nor is my Emotional Centre. These two centres seem quiescent as far as I can observe. I then notice a novel lying on my bed-table which I had just begun the previous evening, and which I had found interesting. Just then I observe that I am very comfortable in bed as if someone actually said so to me. It looks a raw, miserable morning. It then becomes apparent to me that the Instinctive-Moving Centre is saying it does not wish to make the effort of getting up. It prefers to remain comfortable. Also, I notice that the Emotional Centre now wants to continue reading this interesting novel and is not interested in the intellectual plan to correct my manuscripts, any more than the Instinctive-Moving Centre wishes to leave the warm sensation of the bed, and make the movements necessary to getting up. In the end I stay in bed and read the novel. Two centres were against one. The Emotional and the Instinctive-Moving Centres were against the Intellectual Centre. The result is a foregone conclusion. If the Emotional Centre had not been attracted by the novel it might have become interested in the special corrections that the Intellectual Centre was going to make. The Instinctive-Moving Centre would then have had to yield to the combined forces of the Intellectual and Emotional Centres. One interesting thing in all that is that I notice that my Intellectual Centre, as things turned out, began to justify my staying in bed by saying that since I had had relapsing influenza it was probably just as well not to do any work.

*Usual Diagram*

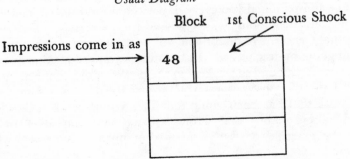

The idea is that impressions fall on old "places" (associations, attitudes, habits). This is the *Block*. They are not transformed unless "1st Conscious Shock" is given where Block is. (*Anything* that makes us more conscious belongs to 1st Conscious Shock, e.g. if we *observe* how we are re-acting.)

On the occasion mentioned in the paper G. drew the matter thus:

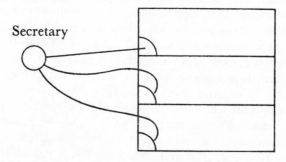

Secretary

This means that an impression coming in was transmitted to the same "place" automatically.

This is the Block or mechanical telephone system that makes us take everything in the *same* way. It lies in external parts of centres. The Block is simply this mechanical system of connections. G. was merely shewing how it was connected with the mechanical part of all three centres.

*Amwell, Easter, 4.4.53*

## OBSERVATION OF MOODS

We speak to-day of moods and the observation of them. When you are able to use Observing I properly, you then have a point of consciousness that is independent of your moods. This point of consciousness is above your moods. It observes them from above. It does not become submerged in them. If you observe the mood going on in you, you are not it. You are not *identified* with it. It marks a definite step in the Work when you reach this stage. I must point out that if you do not practise self-observation, you will never reach this stage. Nor will you ever understand why the Work insists on your observing yourself. I will also add a word of advice. Do not imitate people who quibble about self-observation or who never grasp that they themselves actually have to observe themselves. Now the process of self-observation is like gradually prying apart two surfaces of wood that have stuck fast together. At first it seems impossible. You cannot find the right tool to insert between them. For some time you cannot see where to insert it. The two pieces of wood seem one indissoluble piece. I use this rough image to illustrate how your consciousness and your mood are fused together and seem one and the same thing. They seem indissoluble. This is an error. They can be separated little by little. Consciousness can be gradually drawn out of the mood. By practice you can observe your mood more and more distinctly as something objective to you. By practice you can look at your moods as you look at a pond. A pond is an object of sense. It is objective to you. You do not take a pond as yourself. But as long as you are fast asleep in life, as long as you are the mechanical slave of yourself, you will take everything that happens within you as being you. This means that your relationship to the inner world of yourself is as undeveloped, as infantile and imbecile, as your relationship to the external world would be if you thought a pond or a tree or an elephant was you. Now a mood is something that belongs to your *inner* world. You cannot see it walking on the pavement beside you. It is useless looking in that direction, even though your nurse told you it was a black dog. But you can observe it *in yourself* instead. Do you realize that we live in *two* worlds, outer and inner? This Work is all about our relationship to the inner world. We begin to study it by means of developing Observing I, which is turned inwards. It is called an inner sense.

By employing Observing I over the years, we become educated enough to be aware of a great psychological country lying *within* us, invisible to the outer senses, but visible to inner sense. This country, slowly revealed, has its towns and villages, roads and pathways, hills and valleys. Many people live in it, known and unknown. In dreams we find ourselves in this country. Actually, it is this inner country that we see and walk about in, in dreams, and not the external world. It has good places, and places of great danger inhabited by evil people, just as has the country our external senses open on to. As long as you are totally asleep to yourself, as you are if you never observe yourself, you stumble about blindly in this inner country, not understanding that it exists and not realizing where you are going. All our happiness depends on where we are in this country and also all our unhappiness. It is where we are inside, not outside, that matters. Now a particular *mood* is a particular *place* in this inner country, where you may often stay for a long time. But even when you have become educated internally to a considerable extent and know some of the features of this inner country and some of its good and bad places and inhabitants, you may not be able to observe a slow, gradual thing like a mood. Like everything else that has to do with the pendulums of mechanical emotions, moods are in opposites, and you pass from one mood to an opposite mood. Full observation is to observe *both* the opposites, both ends of the pendulum swing. But a mood is a slow thing, not like a sharp, quick, vivid emotion. All the same, a mood is an emotional state and corresponds to a place in your inner world. People frequently deny that they are in a mood. They may have been in a sullen mood for days and yet deny it quite sincerely. This is partly because moods are so difficult to observe. It is difficult to focus the camera of Observing I on them. Yet it is most important to observe them because a mood, like a fog, may persist and drain force subtly from you, shewing a brief, excited opposite phase and then settling down again. Sometimes a quiet, unpleasant mood is represented in a dream as a fog in which you are groping your way. Now if you *can* observe a mood you are not wholly in it. Your consciousness is then partly going up into Observing I but the rest of your consciousness still remains fastened to the mood, that is, it remains *identified* with it. So you both are the mood and are not. This marks the beginning of separation. If you do not go to sleep too long, the separation will become wider until your consciousness can look down from above upon the mood which used to envelop it completely. It will now seem like a belt of fog in a distant valley far below you. You will wonder why you used to go so often to that valley and stand in that fog. Apparently you thought it necessary. The more your consciousness passes up to the level of Observing I, the more will you wonder why you ever wandered into the places you did.

*Amwell, 11.4.53*

## NOTES ON LOWER AND HIGHER CENTRES

### On Balancing a Centre

The Work teaches that there are two Higher Centres *in* us, termed Higher Emotional Centre and Higher Intellectual Centre. These are distinct from the lower Emotional and Intellectual Centres. The two Higher Centres are fully developed and constantly working, but we do not *hear* them. *Their vibrations are too fine.* The lower centres, unless developed, are not *tuned* in to them. That is to say, we cannot hear the messages that come through them from higher levels of consciousness. Now we know that it is a principle in the Work-teaching that what is at a higher level perceives and comprehends what is at a lower level, but that what is at a lower level cannot perceive or comprehend what is at a higher level. We see the same thing in visible life, which reflects the invisible things of higher meanings. A stupid person cannot comprehend an intelligent person. The lower does not comprehend the higher. A monkey cannot comprehend a man. In the same way, we could not understand an awakened, Conscious Man, a Man No. 7. He would be quite different from us. The disciples could not understand Christ (who was "No. 8 Man"). We suppose a Conscious Man to be some sort of greater and more impressive ordinary man. We cannot at first easily realize that he is *another kind* of man—a completely NEW MAN. Later on, as we build ourselves up to the level of Deputy Steward, we begin to catch glimpses of what this means and may possibly see some connection with the words:

"The wind blows where it lists, and you hear its voice but do not know whence it comes and whither it goes; so is every one that is born of the spirit." (John iii.8)

We can understand that to be "born of the Spirit" has to do with being born of another Neutralizing Force than Life. Now a Conscious Man can "hear" Higher Centres, and so can follow their unusual intimations and directions. He will not be predictable as is the life of a mechanical man. As G. said: "He is no longer a machine, so mechanics will not explain him. He has instead a *psychology*." His lower centres are both "purified" and "balanced" so that they are now tuned in to the fine vibrations coming from the Higher Emotional Centre (which works with Hydrogen 12, a very fine energy-matter) and the vibrations of the Higher Intellectual Centre (which works with Hydrogen 6, a still finer energy-matter). This means, among many other things, that the *inner divisions* of the Intellectual and Emotional Centres are fully opened up in such a man. But as long as a man uses only the *outer* divisions of his ordinary centres (wherein only sensual thinking and self-emotions reside), he is tuned in to the World. He then cannot "hear" his Higher Centres, though they are constantly working. Even if he could, he would be "blind" to their meaning.

If we begin to speak again of Balanced Man—that is, No. 4 Man—we must now extend our conception of what the Work means by this term *balance* beyond what has been given previously. Let us consider a single centre. If a man only uses the *external* division of a centre, the one turned towards Life through the medium of the senses, *that centre is not balanced*. It is obviously not balanced. The single part of it, however, that is being used, will make judgments and decisions about important matters, just as if it were *the whole centre*. For example, the external division of the Emotional Centre, where the powerful emotion of self-love rules by itself, will deliver emotional decisions about people and situations which would be quite different if the whole Centre were working. This is absurd, and accounts for a great deal of the amazing absurdities and violences of our customary emotional life. In the same way, the external or *formatory* division of the Intellectual Centre comes to conclusions about great questions, as, say, the nature of the Universe, that are entirely based on the limited logic of *Yes OR No* and on sensual thinking—that is, on thought based solely on the evidence of the external senses. This again is absurd. But it accounts for a great many of the mindless absurdities of modern interpretations. The point is that the *whole centre* should work and not a small outer part of it all by itself. If only a small part of a centre is used, its judgments and conclusions are bound to be invariably *wrong* except in trivial matters. We are then using *unbalanced centres*. You will see that I am speaking in a special way. But if the Work begins to open up the inner divisions of centres (as it can if *you work*) which communicate, not with the visible world and its meanings, but with the meanings transmitted by the higher levels that belong to Higher Centres, the centre itself becomes increasingly *balanced*. Otherwise a man is open on one side and shut on the other. Thus he is unbalanced, psychologically speaking. Now how can one begin to open the other side, the one turned towards meanings streaming down continually from Higher Centres, to which we are deaf? Only by *work on oneself*. (Have you, by the way, done a stroke of work on yourself to-day—or this week—either on the line of Knowledge or the line of Being?) When men or women do any work on themselves—inwardly (so as not to shew off) and intelligently, which is seeing what they have been or are up to in relation to what the Work teaches—then *it is recorded*. You are doing something special. You are not working for a life-reason, but a Work-reason. You are using momentarily the Neutralizing Force of the Work and not that of Life. You are diminishing Personality a shade. That is why it is special and that is why it is recorded. It is recorded in *inner* divisions of centres and thus begins to open them up. Higher Centres—which are in us—*know us* and understand us, for the higher level perceives and understands the lower. That is why every genuine Work-effort is recorded in a special place—that is, in inner divisions of centres. We need not fear it has not been noticed. We are fully known and transparent to those at a higher level who communicate through Higher Centres. We do not know ourselves but we imagine we do. We are deaf and blind and so need to be cured. Paul said, speaking of his end: "Now we know in part, but then shall I know fully, even as also I have been fully known" (I Cor. xiii.12). Why do some of you grope in darkness, after so many years, still not understanding what work on yourselves means? What is wrong with you? Can you observe *nothing* in yourselves that is patently contradicting the Work-teaching?

*Amwell, 18.4.53*

## SOME REFLECTIONS ON SELF-OBSERVATION

When you are ill the Personality is not so active, or should not be. Unless you are crystallized in negative states you have a chance to observe yourself from a certain angle. Different voices talk in you. You can actually hear them. These are different 'I's, out of a job for the time being and idling about in the city of yourself. If you are very ill, these cease and the city is quiet. This is when the Instinctive Centre is drawing on every source of energy for its own use, as in war. A sign that you are recovering may be that amusing 'I's re-appear and you hear them talking. A humorous view of oneself seems medicine of a high order used by the Instinctive Centre. As regards symptoms and sympathy many things can be noticed. Many 'I's desire sympathy while others do not like it. Certainly the desire for sympathy lurks behind a symptom. This may not be apparent until a show of sympathy is expected and not given. Then some 'I's, as it were waiting to feel aggrieved, become negative and indignant among themselves. This may keep the symptom going. Symptoms and sympathy can stand in a complicated relationship to each other. To be told you are lucky you are not worse has a mixed effect on different 'I's. Also, to one's childish 'I's a symptom is like a feather in one's cap. One does not wish to give up one's suffering—I mean certain 'I's do not wish to. Sometimes the observation of a symptom may shorten its duration if it is done impersonally—that is, from Observing I. But not so if it is self-pitying from neighbouring 'I's for then a swarm of minor symptoms may enter consciousness, all chattering away. It is then necessary to practice inner *STOP* decisively. With the increasing light that comes from impersonal self-observation it is extraordinary to see how much of what we say and do springs from unappeased resentments, recent and old, and how little we know it. Taken back in Time in illness we see them all standing out like figures caught in a searchlight. This leads me to the following reflection: One sees that resentments are bound to rankle as long as we lead the half-life of man asleep. Mechanically we are only one-sided. We do not see the other person *in* ourselves and ourselves in the other person and cancel out our resentments by this method to which I so often call your attention. We see the other person but not ourselves *simultaneously*, which is only a half of the whole matter and renders so much of life insoluble. In this Work we have to find and fit the missing half on. Then the rankling points are sheathed. It is like fitting the two edges of a cracked plate. The jutting out bits fit exactly into the opposite bits. In this you are helped eventually—as you are in everything in the Work—once you truly begin from your own understanding to work at seeing yourself and the other person simultaneously, as it were one person—you in him, and he in you. This takes many periods of work and integrity both in observation and remembering, together with periods of relaxing and amusement. Now let me say here that this to and fro movement, contraction and expansion, systole and diastole, is necessary for all sides of our work. A heart always in contraction (systole) would be useless. Moreover a *valve* is needed to prevent what flows in from flowing back again. If you work and then always get negative you have no one-way valve. Your psychological heart is without a valve and so is useless. It needs a valve that opens and shuts, that lets in and prevents letting out. Without a valve, what you gain is taken away from you in the inevitable swing of the opposites, so that in your moments of relaxation and pleasure you must be careful to be awake. Of what use to work and then let it go in a flare-up or depression? Something more resolute and intelligent is required of everyone in this Work.

Now without self-observation no change of self is possible. We hate to observe ourselves. Consider how you never do it. Amongst other things only the *Light* of increasing consciousness shed by self-observation and Work Memory can cure us of the strange illness of being a half of what we really are  Otherwise the other half of us remains in the darkness permanently. This strange unnoticed illness, however, serves the purposes of Organic Life or Nature—the sensitive living film that covers the earth and demands to be replenished relentlessly—because we then seek the other half of ourselves in the opposite sex. This means that the side of us which is not in our consciousness, and so in darkness, is seen as if outside us as a person quite different from us, often mysterious and fascinating, although actually ordinary. This acts either in one or the other way. The woman feels fascinated by the man, or the man by the woman, but not mutually it would seem. Mutual attraction is not fascination. Fascination is based on illusion. When the man becomes increasingly conscious of the woman in *himself* he cannot fall in love. He cannot be fascinated but he can be attracted. It is the same with the woman. I suppose the word "infatuation" can be substituted for "fascination", but whichever word you use the meaning is a powerful enchantment. We know from previous studies of the Work that when we are identified we cannot see a thing right—as it really is. There are degrees of identification. We can be less or more identified. In the Fourth State of Consciousness, called Objective Consciousness, we see things as they really are. That, of course, includes ourselves. We would see ourselves and others as we and they really are. The state of being "in love" would be unknown since it characterizes half-people. As long as a man is "in love" relationship is impossible.

Now Personality is the function of relationship to the external world. It is what relates you to things. If you have a weak, untrained Personality, your relationship to the external world is a weak one, and you are probably a nuisance to others. This is the same as saying that your function of relationship to the external world is weak. We will now touch briefly on the meaning of soul. The soul is the function of relationship to Higher Centres. The soul should be turned inwards, but ordinarily it is turned outwards towards some object or person in the world of the senses and remains undeveloped. This should not be. For example, a man should not get his soul entangled in a woman. People will say he is under the power of the woman, but he is really under the power of his own soul. You must understand that the world of the senses and the external world are the same. The Personality gives us no relationship to Higher Centres, or to our inner world. It is turned outwards to external life. This Work seeks to develop a relationship to what lies hidden in us. The development of Observing I begins to turn the soul away from the senses, as does also all work against mechanicalness. It turns it inwards. The undeveloped soul does not wish in the least to perform its proper function. It wants to go on looking out of the window. Intractable things, like naughty children, need patience. The soul acting in the self-love *possesses* us. That totally misunderstood saying "In your patience possess ye your souls" (Luke xxi.19) properly translated is: "It is by patience that you will secure possession of your souls." When the soul turns round it finds its proper place and begins to exercise its proper functions inwardly, which have to do with the reception of meaning from Higher Centres. The Person-

1695

ality cannot receive messages from Higher Centres, and if it did, could not understand them because the language of Higher Centres has nothing of Time and Space in it, and is, therefore, not logical as we understand logic. It is not formatory. But the soul can receive messages and new meanings. In the case of a man the soul is female. In the case of a woman it is male. A superficial shallow person's soul is not developed. All sorts of traps and pitfalls centre on these simple facts. One thing, at least, can be understood here, and that is that a man successful in external life cannot proceed straight on in the same way to developing a relationship to Higher Centres. Nor can a woman. With the man or the woman a new start has to be made—and in fact a reversal—and quite new ideas taken in and thought about, and quite new kinds of efforts made. But one of the great difficulties is to wrest the soul away from being identified with the things of life. When it is so identified it is the point of greatest *intensity* entering into the identification and makes it difficult to break. When, through self-observation, which is observation of one's inner world, and other work, the soul is partly turned round away from the things of external life and its appetites and its commerce with inferior 'I's, it may begin to pick up meaning coming from higher levels and develop. If it remains glued to the senses as, say, to a person, this will not happen. It will be unable to change its direction. The person then lives and dies and misses the mark. He has not completed himself. But if a man or a woman becomes related both to the external and internal worlds aright they are not half men or half women any longer. They are *completed*. They are whole men and whole women. When the rich young man asked how he could attain eternal life Christ said: "If thou wouldst become *complete* sell what thou hast and follow me" (Matt. xix.21). Do you imagine this merely means that he had to walk about trailing in the dust after Christ? No, it meant he had to undergo a completely new development, in a new direction, inwardly, making passive all he had got so far by counting it of no value. He seems to have had a good opinion of himself.

*Amwell, 25.4.53*

## THE MIDDLE DIVISIONS OF CENTRES

In a previous paper it was emphasized that a centre is divided into three divisions, external, middle and internal. I said that I would not speak about the middle division for the time being. The middle division is intermediary between the outer and the inner divisions, and can, so to speak, look both ways. It is the part that you reason with and where you form your conclusions about things. The outer division, as has been said, is under the sway of the senses and is the seat of the sensual mind. If the middle division inclines towards the outer division it re-enforces it and the man reasons and thinks wholly sensually. If, however, the middle division inclines towards the inner division the man can also think psychologically or spiritually. Adopting for the moment an older formulation of these three divisions, the outer division can be called natural, the middle rational, and the inner division spiritual, corresponding to three degrees of Man, namely natural man, rational man, and spiritual man. Now, in matters spiritual, the sensual mind is of no use save to deny them and there have always been various things said or commanded about the danger of mixing spiritual matters, which require psychological understanding, with matters of the outer senses which open only on to the external world. For example, there is the third Commandment: "Thou shalt not make unto thee a graven image, nor the likeness of any form that is in heaven above . . ." (Exodus xx.4). One meaning of this Commandment is that the conception of "God" must not be sensual, based on an object. "God" is not to be thought of as an object apparent to the senses. We really have to understand here that "God", or put in Work terms, the Absolute, is not a created thing, for what is created needs a creator. "God" or the Absolute is uncreate; that is, not in Space and Time where visible creation exists. In this connection Christ expressly said, "God is a spirit: and they that worship him must worship him in spirit and in truth" (John iv.24). He is not an object of the senses living somewhere in Space, moment by moment. The soul which is the function of relationship to your inner world and whose destination is to be turned away from the senses towards another order of truth called "God" must not be turned outwards to things seen, but inwards to realities that are invisible and cannot be touched, but can be fully experienced as inflows of new meaning at intervals—that is to say, turned towards the two Higher Centres as the Work indicates. Those Higher Centres open into higher Cosmoses one of which is the Sun-Cosmos. When the Work says that we have to prepare our lower centres, which open on to lower Cosmoses, for the reception of Higher Centres, one thing necessary is the opening of the inner divisions, and this is impossible if we remain sensually minded.

Now, a man who uses his middle division only for reasoning and arguing from the senses, from the evidence of things seen,—that is, from percepts—and draws conclusions or concepts from the manifold illusions of the senses—the simplest of which is that the Sun goes round the earth, or that man is nothing but his physical visible body— necessarily experiences great difficulty in believing that any other realities can exist that are not apparent to his five external senses, aided or unaided. As often as not, indeed, he will make a joke of the whole idea, or secretly ridicule it. Many do this even without realizing it. This attitude will entirely prevent the opening up of the inner divisions of centres which is the object of all esoteric teaching, including this Work, and makes the difference between a mere two-legged animal and a Man.

A man is only a Man through his understanding, and unless the inner divisions of his lower centres are open he understands nothing aright. This difficulty of believing always goes with an inability to reach the level of psychological thinking, which is above logical and materialistic thinking, and is necessarily accompanied by an insistence on material facts and literalness in dealing, for example, with the Scriptures or any other esoteric writings. Therefore, the idea of hidden or esoteric meaning in Holy Writ is not given any credence. That is why Christ said to the lawyers, "Woe unto you, lawyers! for ye have taken away the key of knowledge: ye entered not in yourselves, and them that were entering in ye hindered" (Luke xi.52). Psychological understanding is the key taken away, leaving only literal understanding. No one, however, can understand a parable literally. Consider the parable of the ten virgins who had ten lamps and only five had oil in them. Do you imagine this is to be taken literally and that actual virgins and actual lamps and oil, as sense-objects are meant? No. What is meant, is that a person having a properly formed knowledge of this Work, which is the inner meaning of Christ's teaching, and never *doing it* will not be permitted to enter the Conscious Circle of Humanity and the door will be shut against him. The psychological meaning is totally distinct from the sensual meaning. Esoteric teaching cannot be understood with the sensual mind, and can only give wrong results if the attempt is made. Spiritual or psychological understanding is quite different from sensual literal understanding. But with the man who insists on material facts and literal meaning as being the only kind of truth—and no doubt tells his housekeeper to see that the lamps are kept filled—the result is that the inner divisions of centres are never opened up and cannot be. They remain shut, and the whole psychology of the man is tilted steeply towards the world of the senses, and to sensual evidence. However, if some of the ideas of the Work penetrate as far as the inner divisions of centres owing to the man not reasoning sensually and literally about them—such as "Man is not actually asleep surely"—the whole attitude changes and the *truth* of the ideas begins to be realized as a personal inner experience. This is due to the work of the inner divisions which connect things in a new way, and is quite different from the connections made by the external divisions. Such a person is *awakening*. He has now granted to him some degree of inner perception of truth and, as I just said, this comes from the working of the inner division of centres. He is no longer tied down by the sensual mind to literalness and to fact, as being the only form of reality. He no longer argues formatorily as to whether a thing is true or not true, for he has begun to see truth for himself. He no longer looks uneasily around to ascertain if others believe in a statement made by the Work, and if they appear to do so, hastens to subscribe to it himself, always anxious to follow the fashion. No, his behaviour is quite different. His strength is now in himself individually and is not dependent on audience. But such is not the case with the man who suffers from the uneasiness of never being able to see the truth for himself and watches others to see what they think. Such a person gets his truth from other people and does not see the truth for himself, although he may profess to do so. He reads books without being able to see whether they contain truth or not. With such a person the truth is not *in him*, but a thin varnish laid on him. Now what is not really in you is taken away at the death of the body. Only what you have seen the truth of for yourself, through inner perception, and have acknowledged, is yours and remains with you always. This may seem harsh, but if you come to think of it, how otherwise can it be? How can you expect to live in a finer state of matter where everything secret in your life is made manifest, falsely varnished? You will be laughed at. It is indeed a tragic thing to observe a man who has no inner perception of truth as yet awakened in himself, and who cannot really comprehend in his sensual understanding what the Work is talking about. He is perhaps nervous or may be sullen, or simply rigid and tight-lipped. He takes nothing far into himself, having nothing inward to take it in with, for he has never himself faced truth or really desired it, but has always followed the opinion of others in order to be, as he believes, on the safe side. Whatever the acquiescence he may seem to give, and even wishes to give, the Work rests merely on the surface of a deeper denial of it. All this we have often spoken of before. You must understand that the sensual mind will always deny this Work because it is a matter of psychological understanding and not a matter of sensual fact. The Work, which seeks to open the inner or higher levels of a man's being, which are situated in the inner divisions of centres, is not allowed to—often owing to something akin to cowardice. In the case of women this is not so apparent as they are not as a rule mentally hide-bound and, therefore, not cowardly thinkers. It is useless for people in this Work to be afraid to think in a new way because the Work cannot otherwise influence them. They are bound to remain sensually-minded people for whom the life of the world is sufficient, and in whom the inner divisions of centres must always remain shut. Created self-developing beings they live and die—*shut*. The meanings by which they live will then consist mainly in what is found in the lower compartments of the three-storey house of man—namely, in sex, in movement, and in comfort and eating and drinking. G. taught that this triad of centres, with the meanings derived from them, supplies the stimulations required to keep the major part of sleeping humanity fairly satisfied. He compared it with living in the basement.

You will see from what has been said that a great deal depends, therefore, on how a man reasons—that is, on how he uses the middle or rational division of his lower centres. He can reason to the effect that everything in the Universe is meaningless and happened accidentally *somehow*, and that a long time ago there was nothing, and then there was something, *somehow* or other, and then an atom appeared *somehow* and then billions and billions of atoms appeared, and eventually worlds appeared *somehow*, and life appeared *somehow*, and finally man appeared *somehow*. A great many people nowadays seem to reason in this extraordinary way, and so make it impossible for the inner divisions of centres to awaken. This must lead to a general decline in understanding, and even in the simplest forms of intelligence. So I ask you—how do you reason? What is your view of the Universe? How do you think? Does the meaning that is latent in the Ray of Creation seem incredible to you? Do higher levels of being seem fantastic, or at least very doubtful? Have you decided for yourself, and from truth perceived in yourself, that there are higher degrees of being and consciousness—even Divine being and consciousness—or do you suppose that you have already reached them, and that there is nothing higher than yourself? No greater mistake can be made than to think that your own individual view of the Universe makes no difference to you and does not matter in the least. It matters a great deal, for what you think and how you reason about the Universe and the meaning of your existence in it, either *shuts* or *opens* the most important divisions of the Intellectual and Emotional Centres. Ideas are very powerful. One idea can shut and another idea open the inner mind and heart. Certain ideas can make the difference between a natural man and a possible spiritual man. They can make the difference between a mechanical man, a man driven by external life as by a belt like a machine, and a man capable of becoming less and less mechanical and more and more conscious and eventually having a real psychology and becoming, in short, a real Man possessing a Real I and therefore unity of being.

*Amwell, 2.5.53*

## THE CONJUNCTION OF THE OUTER
## AND INNER DIVISIONS OF CENTRES

In the previous paper on the three divisions of a centre—namely, into outer, middle and inner divisions—some of the uses of the middle division were mentioned. I will briefly recapitulate what was said. The middle division *reasons* and can reason in two directions. In one direction it can reason about life as seen, from the evidence of the senses—that is, from appearances. In that case, the ground of its reason lies in the five senses. That is to say, it reasons from the external division which is turned outwards to external life. By external life I mean the life you see, hear, smell, taste and touch—the life of the world and its manifold affairs, the life of appearances and of things and people as they seem to the senses. All this, sometimes called the phenomenal world, makes up what people usually regard as *reality*. Do you also think that there can be no other reality than what is evident to your five limited senses? If you do, then your thinking is *sensual* and you have only a *sensual mind.* I am repeating all this because the question has to be faced by everyone and a definite conclusion come to—not a grudging conclusion accompanied by a shrug of the shoulders, but a thoughtful, individual one. For if you regard reality as confined to sense, the middle division will always look to the external division for truth, and will reason from it, and never turn to the internal division and discover another reality and order of truth beyond sense. You will then be a *dead man* (or woman) from the Work point of view, however clever and efficient you are. In this connection let me add here that we are surrounded by a descending scale of electro-magnetic vibrations, starting from cosmic rays, about which our senses tell us nothing, save of one small octave for which we have a sense-organ and which we call *light.* Are you going to say that some of the lower octaves of these electro-magnetic vibrations, travelling at 186,000 miles a second and passing imperceptibly through the room at this moment, that can be transformed into audible sound-vibrations by your radio, do not exist? Can you then take your five senses as the criterion of reality? I repeat, can you? for some of you will not face this issue and shuffle about un-easily in your minds and keep your feet on the earth. I will not refer to the invisibility of thought and consciousness.

We now pass on to what might be called the greatest problem of esoteric teaching—namely, the opening up of the inner divisions of centres and forming a conjunction of them with the outer divisions by means of a strong middle division which can look in both directions and comprehend lower level truth and higher level truth without regarding them as contradic-tions. Only through such a conjunction can the outer division with its sensual thinking and sensual truth, called facts, be controlled and take its right place in the scheme of Man's possible development. For the inner division, turned towards vibrations coming from Higher Centres, which are openings into higher levels in the *Ray of Creation,* is *at a higher level* than the outer division turned to the five senses which open on to the world, and only what is at a higher level can control what is at a lower level. You cannot control the sensual, Natural Man in you save by means of the developed, non-sensual, Spiritual Man. The middle division, which is the Rational or reasoning division, stands between the Natural or Outer and the Spiritual or Inner, and can connect them. As I said before, I am using these terms taken from an older system on purpose, in place of the Work terms, Moving (or Mechanical), Emotional and Intellectual.

The three divisions of a centre can be compared to three men living in three rooms in you. These men are of different heights. The first lives in the external division, which is the outer room, and he should be the shortest, the second in the middle division which is the middle room, and the third in the inmost division which is the inmost room—he should be the tallest. If the man living in the middle room sides solely with the outer man, you have no relationship with the inner man. Also, since the three rooms are not on the same floor but above one another, if the middle man sides only with the external man, he always looks downwards. On the other hand, if he sides with the inmost man, he looks upwards, or rather he tries to—and despises the things of sense. If the middle man believes he must do *either* one *or* the other, he is weak. If this is the case with you, then you have a weak middle. If the middle man is strong, however, he does not confuse scientific with psychological truth. He sees each in its own scale and does not bring them into collision as opposites. He can look both down towards the senses and the mind of the senses and its meanings and truths, and also upwards to the supra-sensual mind, which receives meaning and truth of another order from the Higher Centres that are continually working in us, but which we cannot "hear". From these considerations it becomes apparent that the extreme scientist, who believes only in the truths of Science, and the extreme religionist, who regards Science as the work of the devil, are both wrong. Each has a weak middle. Each looks only in one direction. Each despises the other. Each is one-sided. Gurdjieff once said that one of the objects of this Work is to unite the Science of the West with the Wisdom of the East. Hitherto the East has known no scientific development and the West no wisdom.

Now this Work is not based on sensual thinking. It is not turned in that direction. It is not about things you can perceive with your five senses. You cannot weigh and measure it or examine it with a magnifying glass or a microscope. The direction is inwards, towards the inner parts of centres. The order of truths it teaches are not of the same order as scientific truth. It is not about facts of the senses. It has to do with facts of your being and with bringing these facts into the light of consciousness, which leads to Change of Being. Scientific knowledge does not change a man's being. A man of poor, mean, nasty being, or of definitely evil being, such as a man who wishes only to get power at all costs over others, and in whom the love of rule is the chief love, can gain scientific knowledge and use it for destruction and it will not change his being a jot. But Self-Observation, Self-Remembering, Non-Identifying and Non-Considering can change a man's being if they are practised—together with other things that we study in this Work.

## THE OPENING
## OF THE INNER DIVISION OF A CENTRE

Unless the inner division of a centre is opened, a person is governed by the external division. This is the same as saying that unless the supra-sensual mind is opened a person is governed by the sensual mind. Further, if you are a thinker and reason from the evidence of the senses only, and believe that sensual reality is the whole of reality, the middle division will reinforce the sensual mind and you will form conclusions about Man and the Universe that cannot admit either that human life on earth, or the stupendous Galaxies of Suns extended through space, have any meaning at all. This negative reasoning will have the effect of closing the inner divisions of centres. As the inner divisions are the highest and most important divisions of the lower centres in a man and when opened make the man a Man as distinguished from an animal, negative reasoning and the forming of negative conclusions are methods of self-destruction. With those who have Magnetic Centre self-destruction of this kind is not likely, but there is always the danger of *imagination* proving equally destructive by leading them astray sometimes into incredibly foolish beliefs. Foolish beliefs do not open the door leading to the inner divisions of centres. Foolish beliefs just as much as disbelief keep the door shut. My impression is that people long steeped in imaginary beliefs cannot begin any real work on themselves but wander from one system of imagination to another. In this Work, we are sternly told to struggle against imagination and its illusions. Here I will add in parenthesis that you must often observe whether you are only working in imagination and not on imagination.

Now in considering what is necessary to open the inner divisions, it is evident that a sensualist, believing fundamentally in his depths that only what the senses reveal is real, will have the disease of disbelief standing in the way of his further development into a MAN. This seems as difficult to cure as foolish imaginary belief. We are not told how Christ cured the blind man whom He led out of the City of Bethsaida. We know only that Bethsaida represents disbelief, as stated in Matthew xi, verse 21.

"Woe unto thee, Bethsaida! for if the mighty works, which were done in you, had been done in Tyre and Sidon, they would have repented long ago in sackcloth and ashes."

The account of the cure is as follows:

"And he cometh to Bethsaida: and they bring a blind man unto him, and besought him to touch him. And he took the blind man by the hand, and led him out of the town; and when he had spit on his eyes, and put his hands upon him, he asked him if he saw aught. And he looked up and said, I see men as trees walking. After that he put his hands again upon his eyes, and made him look up: and he was restored, and saw every man clearly." (Mark viii.22-25)

The blind man represents the man suffering from the disease of spiritual blindness. This is the illness of the sensual man. The first step in his cure is to lead him out of his disbelief, but we are not told how Christ did this. It is simply said that "he took the blind man by the hand and led him out of the town". Once he had been led out of the disbelief of his sensual mind, his "eyes" were given something coming directly from Christ. In the language of parable the eyes represent the understanding. To lift the eyes is to lift the level of understanding. This had to be done twice before he saw spiritual—that is, non-sensual —truth clearly:

"When he [Christ] had spit on his eyes, and put his hands upon him, he asked him if he saw aught. And he looked up, and said, I see men as trees walking."

He gains partial sight. Notice here that a tree draws its life from the Sun above it as well as from the Earth below it.

"After that he put his hands again upon his eyes, and made him look up: and he was restored and saw every man clearly."

He now sees, not men as trees, but men. Now the truth of sensual man is derived from what is below him, from the evidence of the senses, not from ideas. His thinking is from things and is therefore passive, determined by appearances, and so in opposites. But to think spiritually is to think, not passively from the evidence of the senses, but from ideas that must be understood with effort, and therefore it is active. Spiritual truths are therefore symbolized by men, not women. The awakening of *male thinking*, which the Work can bring about *if you think from the spermatic ideas* it teaches—such as that Man can reach a higher level of consciousness—means that you have begun to gain access to the inner divisions of centres, which are turned to Higher Centres where no opposites exist.

Now if you fundamentally disbelieve this Work and the ideas in the Gospels, but do not observe you do, you will be indignant with those who seem to disbelieve it. This is simply due to seeing what is really *in you* as if it were outside you in others. This is a common enough occurrence. It is necessary therefore to bring your own disbelief into your consciousness so that you can face it yourself. It is better to do this because otherwise you will not be able to see the truth of anything the Work teaches for yourself, because you will be denying it inwardly all the time. But if you face your disbelief sincerely, you will be helped, if there is any willingness to believe. This brings us to another thing that is needed in order to open the inner divisions—namely, the inner acknowledgement of what is wrong with you from the Work point of view. The Work speaks of several things that it is necessary to avoid and of three main things that it is necessary to do. The object is to attain a definite goal which cannot otherwise be attained. If you neither attempt to avoid what the Work indicates nor do what it tells you to do, you naturally miss this goal. Does this strike you as astonishing? Now it is evident to anyone who has reflected on the Gospels that Christ gave directions about something quite definite. Most of the people who listened to Him had only outer or sensual thinking and so could not understand His meaning. They are well-drawn types of grim, sensual thinkers belonging just as much, if not more, to the present time as to the past. In speaking of the internal mind and how to open it so as to enter the Kingdom of Heaven, Christ repeatedly explained that a man, externally good and pious, but internally quite otherwise, cannot possibly experience this stage of development. He misses the mark. It is the state of his internal and invisible life that matters. What does he *really* think and feel? Now a man in the Work has to come to the realization for himself how and when he is missing the mark—as clearly and practically as a motorist who discovers he is going in the wrong direction. For example, to let in without resistance and add fuel to and enjoy one's negative emotions is to miss the mark that the Work has in view. It is to *sin* against the Work because the Work teaches that negative emotions prevent awakening. Otherwise it would not be a sin. It is only a sin in relation to what the goal or mark is. Sin in the Greek means to miss the mark. Now if a man cannot or will not interiorly acknowledge how or when he sins against what the Work tells him not to do or to do, he does not value it. He does not take it seriously. It carries no weight with him. But if he refrains or if he tries to *do* for the sake of the Work—from a feeling for the Work—from a genuine private secret desire to seek and obey the Work without shewing off—then he will find the door to the inner divisions begins to open and new meanings begin to enter. These new meanings gradually control and set in order the sensual or external man. The internal division is then in conjunction with the external division. The inner man contacts the outer man.

## APPLYING THE WORK TO YOURSELF

I will begin by repeating once more that if you continue to think of the Work-teaching from life-standpoints and from the way you have always thought about life, it will not penetrate your mind. This means the Work will not be able to change your mind. It will not change your habitual ways of thinking, your habits of thought. But if you seriously think about life from the ideas that the Work teaches, your mind will change, and the first stage of your regeneration will begin—called metanoia, or change of mind, or change of thinking, or new thinking. In the Gospels it is wrongly translated always as "repentance"—as "Repent ye", where it should be "Change your ways of thinking, change your minds, think in a new way". Now the sensual mind, based on appearances, is not the soil for the Work-ideas to grow in. It will indeed stifle the Work—as it continues to do in so many people who have listened for a long time and take nothing in. They never start with a Work-idea and think from it. For example, they do not take the Work-idea: *Your Being attracts your life* and think from it. They continue to see life as something apart from themselves that often treats them badly. They even make internal accounts against "God", actually thinking that "God" likes to be spiteful or mean or difficult and spoil everything for them. They are simply seeing qualities in their Being, to which they are blind, projected, like a magic-lantern slide, on to their conception of "God". What they see in front of them is really behind them. It is in them. So others are to blame—or "God" or luck. If they really thought that their Being attracted their life, they would turn round, away from their senses and look "behind them" and see what things in them caused their unhappy experiences. But do you imagine they will do this? No, they will not: because although they have heard again and again that one's Being attracts one's life, they do not believe it, and if you do not believe a thing you do not think it, because you think what you believe and refuse to think what you do not believe. That is, they do not, in this case, *change their minds* in respect of the particular teaching that their Being attracts their lives. They continue to think as before, never seeing that the fault is in them. And so, in the same way, none of the Work-ideas has any effect on their minds because they disbelieve them—or, if you like, they do not believe them. For if they believed them, they would begin to think *from* the Work-ideas and their minds would change and they would look at their Being and begin to see in themselves the cause of why this thing or that always went wrong. As they became gradually more conscious of what was in them and saw what was their own fault, their Being would begin to change and then their life would not attract the same unhappiness or disasters. All this would follow when this Work-idea was taken in in the *mind* and allowed to work its power on it to alter it.

Now here, for instance, is a person who seems always to be in a muddle, who rushes about in a perpetual hurry, looks worried and is usually complaining of unhappiness. Let us suppose the person has listened for years to the Work. What is wrong? None of the ideas has penetrated the mind. The mind is as it always was. It thinks as it always did. As a result, no Work-effort is made, or can be made. The application of the Work-ideas to oneself is never done—perhaps never dreamed of. The idea that one must connect the Work with oneself is listened to, time after time, the words are recognized, but nothing is done and the ideas of the Work and their meaning for them are not thought about. Now you are all taught that there are three lines of Work—work on oneself, work with others, and work that assists the Work. All are necessary. As regards the first line, work on oneself, there are two branches—work on the knowledge of the Work and work on one's Being. In proportion as you apply your Knowledge of the Work to your Being, through the link of self-observation without justifying, you gain in Understanding, the most powerful and valuable thing you can make. But how is this possible if you never think with your own mind about the knowledge the Work teaches and so begin to change your ways of thinking? Yet people remain surprised when told that of course they must think about the Work-ideas for themselves— yes, and think a great deal and eventually never cease to think in this new way. You must use your *mind* in this Work. The Work begins with the mind. You cannot work on the line of Knowledge of the Work unless you use your mind actively. And you cannot change your Being save through applying this Knowledge to it. You must see in your mind—in your gradually forming new Work-mind—what you have to work on in your Being. What, by the way, are you working on? There is no use in blind work or stupid effort or meaning to work to-morrow. Intelligent work is based on something you observe to-day, now, in yourself, something that the Knowledge of the Work teaches you that you must work on. For example, do you observe, to-day, *now*, that you are wasting much nervous energy on internal considering? Well, then, here is something to work on *now* by taking the feeling of I out of it. I will give some extracts from a recent letter which may help some of you who do not seem to use the Work practically.

The writer, whom I do not know, first acknowledges the help that the Commentaries have given her in moments of difficulty. Often she has opened one of them and found a solution to her own particular problem. She then describes an experience that she had after being in a bad mood all day—a mood which she had often in the past wished to change but could not. On this occasion, reading the Commentary on the Mind, she realized that what she was reading directly applied to her difficulty. She writes as follows:

"I had come to the Commentary on the Mind, and realized it was the very subject I was struggling with, and on page 548 I began to see the answer to what has defeated me almost since I can remember. Reading the words in the 2nd paragraph, 'But if I start with the mind', before reading further I wrote down why, and how, I minded the particular problem that had spoilt the day. As I wrote, I experienced an astonishing sense of freedom—it was literally a release from my bad state which was startling in its instantaneous effect. I suddenly *saw* I *could* stand aside from these moods; that they were not, and need not be, *Me*, as I have always been accustomed to think, and so to fear and dread them. Picking up the book, I found this expressed in the following sentences concerning trying to observe how and why. Further on, on page 549, the words 'Just to say, "I must not mind"'. . . . echo what I have always found, namely, that they were useless! But never until that moment had I been able to find *how* not to mind."

You will notice that she used the Work intelligently and connected her state with what it teaches and obtained immediate help as a response. I will quote part of what is written on page 548 as she seems to have meant to do herself in the letter. The subject on this page is *mechanicalness* in each of the centres. I mention *habits* of thinking and habits of feeling—habits which people do not notice as being habits and therefore mechanical but take as necessary and right ways of thinking and feeling—in fact, the only possible ways. I wish some of you could see this for yourselves and realize in a dazzling moment of insight how much you unnecessarily and uselessly suffer owing to *mechanical* dead habits of thought and feeling and that you need not suffer if you let the living Work into your minds. Can't you get rid of that hopeless, puzzled look? The Commentary goes on as follows:

"The Work starts with the mind as do the Gospels. It starts with changing the mind, with seeing things differently, with new teaching, new ideas. Unless this begins to take place, unless we begin to see, mentally, ourselves and life in a new way, we cannot expect to work on the other centres except in a purely unintelligent way. I may sit all day on my haunches; I may refuse food; I may subject myself to the greatest physical torments as a Fakir—but the result will be quite useless because it is not linked up with my understanding, and so will lead to no inner development. But if I start with my mind and observe, let us say, how I mind things, in what way I mind things, and ask myself why I mind things in this way, and think of the Work, I will begin to have some insight into the thing I have always taken for granted as being indisputably myself and always right, which I call my mind. I will begin to see that my mind, such as it is, with this little heap of stones in it, is a funny, limited thing and something that I cannot possibly say is always right. In fact, I will begin to see that my mind is possibly wrong and all my ideas may be wrong and that, in a sense, I have to get rid of this form of my mind, of this small way of thinking about everything, and so of this way of minding. Can you imagine someone coming to you at a moment when you are minding something very much and saying: 'Do you not see that the reason why you mind this so much is because there is something wrong with your mind, and that you are wrongly minding and you should try to change your mind and think in a quite new way about this thing you are stupidly minding so much?' No doubt you would be very cross. Now try to look more deeply into this question of why you mind things and catch a glimpse that it is because there is something in your mind that makes you mind in this way, something in your thoughts, which only come from your minds, such as they are, for as long as your minds are formed in this way they will always produce the same kinds of thoughts. I mean, try to see that you must mind things, because of the heap of stones that you take as the only mind you can have." (Vol. II, page 548.)

*Amwell, Whitsun, 23.5.53*

## THE PRISON OF NEGATIVE EMOTIONS

In esoteric teaching we are always told that we are in prison. No one sees the prison. To the sensual mind a prison must have walls and bolts and bars. The prison we are in has none. It is chiefly made of *states*. In the Work we study them. All wrong emotions keep us in prison. There are many degrees of negative emotions just as there are degrees of Hell. The change from non-negative to negative emotions is as definite as a chemical change from alkaline to acid. We get to know this eventually when we realize we are in prison. Negative emotions seem far cleverer than non-negative emotions. They seem more fertile, more interesting, more ingenious. This is because they lie. Like all liars they try to persuade you. The object of negative emotions is not only to destroy truth but to harm. All evil seeks to harm. It is extraordinarily easy to harm. We do not easily know how to do good to others but we easily know how to hurt them. There is a distinct pleasure in harming. Consider the pleasure of scandal. At the root of negative emotions lies violence. There are degrees of negative emotions —both continuous and discontinuous degrees. A particular negative state may increase or diminish; or it may deepen and become dangerous. A discipline is needed in regard to negative emotions. It must begin with self-observation. You must know and acknowledge when you are negative. People will not do this. A discipline should never become an end in itself. It is a means to an end. The discipline bearing on negative states has as its end the gradual weakening of their power to imprison us. It is part of the general technique of the Work which is about escaping from prison. It is necessary to find and invent every method you can to prevent recurring events from making you negative. It is not a matter of armour but of self-knowledge and coupled with it an adroitness similar to that shewn by the Syro-Phoenician Woman in the answer she gave when she was compared to a dog. She did not get negative.

When she asked Christ to heal her daughter, He said:

"Let the children first be filled: for it is not meet to take the children's bread and to cast it unto the dogs." And she answered and said unto him, Yes, Lord: yet the dogs under the table eat of the children's crumbs. And he said unto her, "For this saying go thy way; the devil is gone out of thy daughter." (Mark vii.27-29)

The Work teaches that negative emotions govern the world. They are extremely infectious. One man can make a thousand negative. One negative person can turn a house into a Hell. This ability to affect others gives the negative person a sense of power. It is an evil power. Negative emotions seem to destroy any sense of humour in people. I read that Grimm's Fairy Tales are being re-written. The Good Fairy is described as a "deviationist". Can you genuinely laugh if you are negative? Not at yourself, at any rate. Perhaps we never really laugh at ourselves, but pretend to. Most of life is pretence and even if we half-know it, we take it seriously. For there is some invisible binding force that gets mixed up with everything we do—like a cord that we should have cut through long ago with a sharp knife. The Work calls the effects of this uncut cord *identifying*. Being identified is the source of negative emotions. Here you are, for example, as pleased as Punch with something that you have just made, mixing yourself with the job and the job with yourself, and then some idiot goes and lights the fire with it. You would have to be very adroit to prevent yourself from becoming negative. But if you had been awake you would have observed how you were identifying while doing the job and that would have helped you not to react so negatively. If you never identified, you would not mix what should not be mixed with what you do, and you would not be negative. If you always remembered yourself, you would never identify, and if you never identified you would never be negative. This simply means that if we lived at the level of the Third State of Consciousness we should never identify and so would never be negative. But Man is asleep. People live in the Second State of Consciousness—the so-called Waking State—and do not know that this is the prison-house in which they unknowingly live, perhaps rather puzzled by what happens, but not seeing the cause of it all. Thinking in this active way about life from what the Work teaches instead of the other way round, you can see that to struggle piecemeal with this or that negative emotion is like trying to deal with a newspaper in a gale of wind. In the atmosphere surrounding the earth above a certain altitude, there are no storms. It is the same with us. If you could reach the altitude of consciousness belonging to the state of Self-Remembering, Self-Consciousness and Self-Awareness, you would be travelling above the inevitable. and natural storms that belong to the lower level of consciousness. To be negative is to sin against the Work. It is to miss the Mark. Do you feel this? You can, and indeed, must, find and invent for yourself ways of circumventing negative emotions. To find something that requires *directed* attention is one way, if you can bring yourself to do it. Another is to remember and recall and go back in time to similar previous occasions—provided you have got a Work-memory based on genuine self-observation and not merely the usual illusory lying memory. Watching the state is always useful—if you can without joining it. Another way is to see what made you negative—if you can. Efforts of this kind make you more conscious and that always helps because it puts you in better parts of centres, in less slummy places in the inner city of yourself. One has to feel that one is wrong if one is negative—really feel it—not because you were told but because you see it for yourself. Without this feeling all you do will be useless and meretricious and artificial. *The true Way Out is Self-Remembering.*

*Amwell, 30.5.53*

## THE NEUTRALIZING FORCE OF THE WORK

It is difficult to find the Neutralizing Force of the Work. A long search for it is inevitable. Everyone having attained sufficient conviction that the Work is something real and that it leads to a goal, has to enter upon this search, alone, for himself or for herself. It can never be communicated in a direct way, any more than can the taste of an apple to anyone who has never tasted one. The long period of search for the Neutralizing Force of the Work begins when you realize that you are *not* working in the right way. This realization is a passing feeling, a momentary taste. It is not a thought. I mean that anyone can *think* he or she is not working in the right way, especially people who make a habit of and enjoy worrying about anything and everything. But I am speaking of an emotion, an inner taste, a swift, emotional insight, and not of a thought. You do not know, but feel you are not doing the Work aright. Observe that I am not saying that you feel *how* to do the Work aright, but that you feel that you are not doing it aright—for a moment. You are not told what is right but only that something is wrong. This is the way of the Work once it has begun to act on you. It does not indicate what you must do, but it may give you a quick feeling of dislike for what you are doing. It checks you—for a moment. It is left for you to find out what you should do. To be told what you *must* do would be like compulsion, and useless, for compulsion does not lead to inner development. To do a thing because of compulsion is very different from doing it from understanding. It is only through understanding, which means *seeing for yourself why a thing is necessary,* that inner development can take place. And eventually, let me say here, you have to see for yourself why the Work is necessary for you. This brings you close to the right attitude to it. Since the Work teaches us that, as long as Life is the sole Neutralizing Force acting on us, the Personality will remain active and Essence passive, it is necessary to seek for another Neutralizing Force. A passive Essence cannot grow. This means that there will be no growth of Essence as your life goes on, beyond the partial growth that took place in early childhood. In that case you live and die unfinished—an experiment in self-development that has failed to complete itself. Of course, if Life did complete us, esoteric teaching would not exist. The Essence becoming more and more thickly surrounded by Personality may even be cut off from it. You are then dead. Personality now rules you, and you will lose the power of thinking for yourself, amongst many other things. Only another and different Neutralizing Force coming from esotericism can alter this situation—and eventually reverse it. This other and different Neutralizing Force in our case is the Work. Its origin is outside Life. This does not mean that immediately you come in contact with the Work, this change or this reversal takes place, as some imagine. Far from it. For years you will still use the Neutralizing Force of Life and think from Life about the Work. You will not think about Life from the Work. That is one of the difficulties. You cannot help working from the Personality for a long time and so your efforts will be from the wrong place in yourself, and from the wrong motives. Without the strength of new thinking from the ideas of the Work, you will be trying to make Personality passive by means of Personality. But after a time you may begin to see that this is so—to some extent—owing to brief feelings that things are not quite right with you. As I said, it is difficult, and needs a long search to find the Neutralizing Force of the Work—the force which eventually makes Personality passive. Meditating on how the Personality with its acquired prejudices, imitated attitudes, buffers and all its mechanical reactions, surrounds Essence like a high fortified circular wall, we may well see it is what chiefly imprisons us. It guards itself. Consider how you retaliate resentfully. It is active—that is, it is in charge of you. The part of us that can grow after Personality is formed sufficiently is now shut in as in a small cottage within this wall—which we take as ourselves. Is it not strange that we have to build up this wall, brick by brick, in the first part of our lives as strongly as possible and then take it down again in the second part and enlarge and build on to the cottage with some of its bricks? Reinforced by the False Personality with its inexhaustible powers of deceiving, the Personality, which is this wall, can very easily take up the Work in such a way as to make a person believe he or she is working from the new Neutralizing Force of the Work. Whereas all the time he or she is working from the old Neutralizing Force of Life. Perhaps he or she desires to excel or be thought to have mysterious powers and so on. But whatever the motive, if people continue to work from the Personality and thus from motives belonging to the Neutralizing Force of Life, the Work cannot take proper root. If they never experience peculiar transient feelings that they are not working aright, they get stuck. They may not know it. They need a shock. One reason for this is that they do not see any truth in the Work for themselves. They speak of the Work from memory but not from the perception of its truth. To see truth acts as a *shock*—which they do not give themselves. This is because the order of Truth taught by the Work can only be understood by the more interior divisions of centres and not by the outer divisions where the sensual mind is lodged. The Work is not sensual truth. The soil of the sensual mind is not suitable for the seeds of the Work to grow in. It can remember the teaching of the Work but not understand it. Now if you never see for yourself and understand the truth of any single one of the ideas taught by the Work, you have *no point in the Work*, as it is called. Within you everything shifts like sand in the desert. There is nothing to hold on to. To have no point in the Work, even after years of contact, and to make no determined attempt to find one, but to continue to listen to your own objections and scepticism is a state of affairs that can never be expected to attract the Neutralizing Force of the Work. The attitude is all wrong. So Personality will remain dominant and you, as an experiment, will fail. Again —to *pretend* to have a point in the Work will do nothing towards lessening the power of the Personality. The truths of this Work can free us from the Personality, but not if you pretend to see them and value them and secretly do not. The attitude is very bad. Again—to try to do the Work, or to teach it, from the 'I's trained for your daily life-work or profession, will certainly not be teaching or doing it from the right place. The attitude is at fault. You will be pouring the Work into old bottles. You will speak from the wrong 'I's. Again—a man ambitious in life cannot switch his ambitious life-'I's straight on to the Work. He cannot, as it were, say: "Come on, boys, we'll get this little job of self-change cleared up in no time." A successful man or woman may feel that as they seem able to "do" in life, they can equally well "do" in the Work. But that feeling cannot be transferred directly on to the Work, save wrongly. It is a feeling typical of the False Personality, which always thinks it can do. But you cannot put self-love and self-esteem *first* in the Work. The Work is not like that. The Work is difficult to woo, and instantly sees anything false in your declaration of love. For the Work to respond and effect its gradual miracle of making Personality passive, and causing Essence to develop, you have to woo it and love its teaching genuinely. You will eventually begin to find the Neutralizing Force of the Work. You will also begin to understand why it was once said that unless you become as little children, you cannot enter the circle of Conscious Humanity—which even a person of highly developed Personality but with undeveloped Essence cannot enter. You will begin to see the reason why he cannot.

*Amwell, 6.6.53*

## OBJECTIVE CONSCIOUSNESS

At the level of consciousness of *Man-asleep* everything is seen subjectively. To see objectively what a thing or person is like is among
other things not to criticize or judge. To be critical of others is only
neutralized by being equally critical of oneself. For when we see that
whatever we criticize is in us, in that respect we pass from a relatively
subjective to an objective state of consciousness. People become mirrors
for us and we become mirrors for them, as G. once said. We are told
elsewhere not to judge lest we shall be judged. Also we are told that
with what measure we mete it shall be measured unto us. This reciprocal
relation between ourselves and the Universe—or others, for other people
are part of the Universe—is clearly given in the Work teaching that
as we change our level of Being we come under fewer laws, and in the
Work-phrase: "Your Being attracts your life." Since people cannot
see their Being, they judge subjectively. That is, they judge or criticize
from what they have been taught is right and proper and from associations. One Work-exercise is to try to see things without associations.
If people had Objective Consciousness they would not judge or criticize
or blame others. All that very considerable unhappy and quarrelsome
part of life would fall away from them for it belongs to the Second
State of Consciousness, which is almost wholly a subjective state. In
it things are not seen as they are. The Fourth State of Consciousness is
wholly objective. At this level everything is seen as it really is. There
are no illusions, and no appearances or pretences are possible. The
invisible, hidden person is clearly manifest as well as the visible outer.
Your inner thoughts and feelings are made transparent as also are all
your secret desires and deeds and schemes and all your life extended
in the Fourth Dimension. If you meditate often on this you will probably conclude that as you are at present you could not endure to exist
among people in the Fourth State of Consciousness, who saw through
you. In fact, you would not know how to live among them. Your polite
conversation and manners and even your charming smile would be
useless. You would feel very awkward especially because in the Second
State of Consciousness people continually lie. They have to. Social
life is based on lying, if you reflect.

Now people may touch the Fourth State, which is Objective Consciousness, before they know the Third State, which is Self-Remembering. If they do, little of what they experience and realize while in the
Fourth State remains in their minds and memories—perhaps only a
phrase or word that seems to have no meaning. This is because they
fall from the Objective Fourth State straight down into the Subjective
Second State, which cannot see anything as it really is. For the sensual
mind is limited by the senses to the surface of things. It sees the outside
of things and is not fit to comprehend what the Fourth State of Con-

sciousness can see. Boehme, trying to describe an experience of Objective Consciousness, wrote: "I can only liken it to a resurrection from the dead." He realized that the prison of the sensual mind is like death. After another experience of the same level of consciousness he says that he seemed to gaze into the very heart of things. His surface consciousness was replaced by a depth of comprehension whereby he saw "the Essence, use and properties of whatever he looked at". He wrote: "In one quarter of an hour I saw and knew more than if I had been many years together at a University. I saw and knew the *Being* of all things." Notice his rate of impressions was greatly increased. He saw in a short time what would have otherwise taken a long time. In the Fourth State of Consciousness he took in more impressions in a quarter of an hour than he would have in many years at a University in the Second State of Consciousness. I must say that I doubt if he would have ever seen what he had seen after a lifetime at a University.

A higher state of Consciousness is not characterized only by an increased rate of perceptions and a deepening of them, which gives greater meaning, but by a "state of bliss"—that is, of a feeling of release. This is because you are no longer in the power of all that belongs to your ordinary level of consciousness. You are released from prison. You have achieved *for a time* the goal of the Work. The state will pass, however, because you have not as yet paid enough to retain it. You pay by applying the Work to yourself. The state momentarily comes as a reward. All positive emotion or "bliss" comes as a reward. Such happiness as belongs to the sensual level is as nothing by comparison. The reward of positive emotion will not, of course, come to anyone who is working only from the self-love. As said, in many recent papers, the self-love and its motives cannot open the supra-sensual or inner parts of centres. Another *quality* of love is needed. Now as regards what was said about the necessity of having the Third State of Consciousness developed in order to retain any experience of the Fourth State, if you remain at the level of the sensual mind you will not be able to develop the Third State of Consciousness because when you try to remember yourself, you will think of your body as being yourself. The literal sensual person regards his visible body only as real. What he cannot see and touch cannot be real. There is no *evidence*, he will say. So, believing himself to be his body, when he attempts to remember himself he will, knowingly or unknowingly, remember his body. This keeps him on the level of the sensual mind in the external divisions of centres.

## MEMORY OF THE WORK AND WORK-MEMORY

In the following Commentary I will speak of Life-memory, Memory of the Work, and Work-Memory. I will also make a brief connection between Work-Memory and that thing spoken of so often in the New Testament, called *Faith*, which is never mentioned in the Old Testament.

★   ★   ★

To begin with memory of the Work as distinct from Work-Memory: when you first hear the Work being taught you, you receive it on the Formatory Centre. The Formatory Centre is the *external* division of the Intellectual Centre. Here memory of the Work is formed. It is that part of the mind that you use when you learn anything at school. The Work has to fall on the Formatory Centre first of all. That is, it has to be learned as any other subject has to be. Some people, on hearing the Work, feel it emotionally, but do not follow it mentally. They do not learn the Work, and the result is they have no proper memory of the Work. Scarcely anything is registered on their Formatory Centre. As often as not it has never occured to them that they have to learn the Work in the same sense as when learning anything else. They think their emotional appreciation is enough. They remain in a muddle all their lives and get everything mixed up simply because they have not got any intellectual groundwork. Sometimes people who are quite capable of learning the Work intellectually for some reason do not attempt to do so. Now, let us suppose a person has reached a good intellectual grasp of the various parts of the Work, but does not feel it emotionally. It then lies merely in his memory, like the talent that was buried in the earth. Given a talent he does not turn it into two. He answers questions in the same way as he would at any examination. The usual reason is that he had not thought about the Work or applied the Work to himself, but merely remembers everything that he has heard about it. Now such a man does not understand the Work. His memory of the Work has not become a Work-Memory; it remains formatory and so lies alongside his memory of life-affairs, of his job and such things. It lies in the external division of the Intellectual Centre. Of such a person you could say: "Yes, he seems to know the Work, but does not seem to understand it." Now as long as the Work lies only in the external division or Formatory Centre he will not see its meaning, but if he begins to apply the Work to himself his memory of the Work will begin to move inwards towards the internal divisions of centres. He then begins to have a personal Work-Memory through experiencing the action of the Work on himself. It no longer lies alongside his memory for things belonging to his Life-memory. When this is the case his memory of the Work is no longer at the same level as, say, his profession. At the same level it cannot grow. This is when the Work "falls by the wayside" as the Parable of the Sower and the Seed indicates. The Seed is the Work, and if it falls alongside the traffic of life-things and remains there, it will not develop. The ideas will not grow in the man, and cannot. If he has a good memory of the Work, he will rattle off answers just in the words as he learns them, and not from a Work-Memory. In fact, he will not be able to answer questions save in a stereotyped, deadening way from memory. Whereas if he answered from his understanding his replies would never be stereotyped, and would conduct force.

Now if a man both thinks about and applies the Work to himself his memory of it changes because it will now become a memory of his experiences. When he has begun to apply the Work to himself he begins to see how it applies to him. The location of his Work-Memory then passes inwards, as was said, and eventually reaches the interior divisions of centres where communication with Higher Centres eventually becomes possible. He receives help from within. He begins then to see the Work and its meaning. He also begins to have what is called a point in the Work. Now, when you understand something you acknowledge it. You can see that a thing is so with the understanding as well as with the senses. Just as you see that an orange is lying on the table with your senses, so you see with your understanding that a thing is true. But the two kinds of "seeing" are on quite different scales. If you could see with your understanding that a thing is true you would acknowledge its truth just as you see with your senses that an orange is on the table and will acknowledge that it is so. If you never see with your understanding that anything the Work teaches is true, you have no belief in the Work and your Work-Memory will be of a curious kind. It will not help you. It will be mainly composed of doubts and denials. You have shut the door by your attitude to the Work. Now if you have opened the door to the Work and have begun to see the truth of some of the things that it teaches about yourself and about the meaning of life, your Work-Memory will be at a far higher level than your formatory memory of it. It will be far higher—that is more interior—because it no longer lies by the wayside mixed up with Life-memory, but has started to grow in good soil. When that is the case, when you remember to remember the Work and summon it to your mind, it will help you. You will feel force flowing into you. You will not have to have *faith* in the Work or try to believe in it. Everything you have understood in it and seen the truth of for yourself, will all be connected together to make a source of energy in you, that has so much strength eventually that, when you summon it, it lifts you right above all the petty things that ordinarily preoccupy you—all your grievances, your negative states, your anxieties and cares, your feelings of loneliness, your self-pity and bitterness, your jealousies, your disappointments, and your disjointed chaotic existence. This is because the Work is all connected together and makes order out of chaos. It is now possible really to remember yourself by getting into your Work-Memory. But if the memory of the Work lies only in the Formatory Centre you will not be able to remember yourself in this way.

Do you grasp that the Work is designed to penetrate to the interior divisions of centres once it is received, and to grow in them, so that gradually you see more and more meaning even in the simplest formulations contained in its teaching? Nevertheless, the Work must fall first of all on the Formatory Centre, and the first memory of it must lie there as clearly as possible. The first difficulty is, then, that people do not learn the Work and never attain a correct formatory memory of it. The second difficulty is that people do not think about or apply the Work to themselves. The third difficulty is that they cannot see, or will not see, *with their understanding*, any truth in it. The result is that it cannot penetrate to more interior parts of centres because it is not accepted. The fourth difficulty is that unless a proper Work-Memory is formed no help is received from it. If you have treated the Work in a cavalier way, it will treat you similarly. Your relation to the Work and its relation to you are reciprocal. A proper Work-Memory is built up over many years. Only what is sincere and genuine can go to its formation. All that you have observed and genuinely seen the truth of and internally acknowledged composes it. It arranges itself—for psychological things of a similar quality collect together at the same level by themselves. It has an existence of its own. When you enter this special memory, you know that it has its own independent existence, and that it is quite different from life-things and life-memories. It is on another level. You see why you must not be held down by life-memories, why you should not identify with them, why you should not put the feeling of I into them, especially into sad or negative and bitter things. You realize that it is this Work-Memory that contains all your past insights, your past self-observation, your past moments of work, and all your experiences *of truth seen and understood for yourself*, and that it is the most precious thing that you have created and possess. This is why the Work teaches that *understanding* is the strongest force we can create. And if you begin to feel the power it conducts, which can lift you above the ills of life, great and small, you are catching a glimpse, I think, of the meaning of the word translated as *Faith*, which is truth seen as being true, and not what you are told is true.

For the Work is *not* religion. It is not a doctrine. It is not a faith that demands a blind obedience and so holds the understanding captive. On the contrary it is a freeing and opening up of the understanding that can now develop, giving you a source of new and increasing meanings and insights as your physical life passes. But this can only take place when you begin to perceive the truth of what it teaches *with your own understanding*. I assure you that this factor is neglected by very many people who imagine they are in the Work.

## THE DEVELOPMENT OF UNDERSTANDING

If nothing of it ever falls on your understanding, this Work that we study here is of no use to you. I mean, it cannot help you. Moreover it cannot help you if externally you believe you believe and inwardly deny it. Its truth has to be seen with your own understanding to become truth for you. Again, if you are told by people you regard as authoritative that the Work is true, although you cannot see with your understanding where it is true, and accept it as being true because you were told it is, you will get nothing from it. Indeed, you will resemble many who believe their religion is true because they have been taught from childhood that it is so. This believing by imitation, by acquired habit and by persuasion, does not develop the *understanding* but blocks it. What we do not understand cannot develop our Essence. Now it is the object of this Work to develop the understanding in a man or a woman. As was said in a previous paper and earlier, a belief by persuasion holds the understanding captive. It prevents it growing in its own way. You are told in so many words: "You must believe. You must not try to understand. You must have faith, not understanding." The result is many beliefs, many faiths, many dogmas, many hatreds, many despisings and many persecutions—and no understanding. Understanding is not sectarian. Understanding conjoins: hatred disjoins. When the Work says that understanding is the most powerful force you can develop, it means just what it says. Now in this respect I cannot see why anyone should say, for example, that surely *will* is the most powerful thing you can develop. Let me ask you this question: Of what *use* is will unless it passes through understanding into action? We are not following the First Way—the Way of the Fakir. Those who enter a Fakir School are ignorant natives. In the Fourth Way, along which this Work begins to lead us, people are supposed, at the start, to be reasonably educated, reasonably responsible, and capable of dealing reasonably with life. It is not for "tramps"—such as those who will not work—or "lunatics"—such as enthusiasts who wish to reform the world. It is not for silly people seeking the elixir of perpetual youth, nor is it for psychopaths. The Fourth Way starts from the level of *Good* Householder. That is, it starts from some degree of good—from some gold. This was emphasized strongly in the early days and needs to be repeated. Moreover when the Work says that understanding is the most powerful thing you can develop, it means that, *beginning with the level of Good Householder*, this is the case. It is not the case with the uneducated native who, following the Fakir-Way, seeks to develop will over his body by maintaining one posture for years. To develop will without developing understanding is not the aim of the Fourth Way. As I said, of what *use* is will without understanding? How are you going to use it? It does not take much insight to see that the results might be evil. Do you think that activity based on a powerful will without a corresponding development of the understanding is something desirable? I have no sympathy with those who believe it is and practise methods to achieve this mindless result.

Now what is *understanding* in the sense in which the word is used in the Work? Is it the same as *knowledge*? No. To know and to understand are two different things. For example, I may *know* everything the Work teaches, with all its ideas, diagrams and practical instructions, written down in the note-books of my memory, but this does not mean that I understand the Work. My knowledge of the Work is not the same as my understanding of it. To many people this may sound strange at first because knowing and understanding are so often taken as meaning the same thing. To take some examples: I may *know* that the Work teaches that Man has fallen asleep and that it is his first task to awaken and through awakening to see what he is really like. This I may know as part of my knowledge of the Work. But I will not understand what awakening is. I will merely know that Man is said to be asleep and that he must awaken, according to this teaching—which, by the way, is called Esoteric Christianity. I will not understand that a man asleep in wrong ideas about himself and filled with the illusions of his False Personality simply cannot change himself until through long and sincere self-observation in the light of the Work he begins to awaken to what he is really like. Nor will I understand that only in this way, through thinking of himself—and of life—in a new light, will he ever get the strength gradually to *die* to what he was. So first he must awaken, then die, and only then he can be re-born. All this is contained, of course, in the Sayings in the Gospels, only they are not arranged in this order.

I may also know, as part of my knowledge of the Work, that Man lives on a lower level of consciousness than is his right by birth, but that being brought up among sleeping people, he fell asleep himself through the terrible hypnotism of imitation. I may know all this—*in my memory*—because I have heard it said on many occasions. But do you imagine for a moment that I *understand* what it means? Of course not. It will be merely words. I may believe them or not; but mere belief will not make me understand.

From all the above you will see that it is only by applying the Work to oneself that any understanding of it is reached. First it is necessary to know the Work, then to apply it to oneself by means of long and uncritical self-observation, in the light of what it teaches. And as a result you will gradually understand the Work. Your understanding will develop. That is, your *knowledge* will gradually pass into *understanding* through applying the Work to your own being, whereby you will see the truth of what it teaches. But if you never can see any truth in the Work with such understanding as you possess, this transformation of knowledge into understanding through applying it to yourself, by means of self-observation, will not take place. In this short paper it remains to be said that a change in the level of your being begins as a result of your gradual observation of it. That is, it is altered by slowly becoming more and more conscious of it—of all that is actually in you as apart from what you *imagine* yourself to be. Consciousness changes being as light alters what is growing in darkness. As your level of being changes, your understanding increases. This is expressed briefly in a diagram relating Knowledge, Being and Understanding. This shews that a man having great Knowledge and poor Being *understands* little.

*Amwell, 27.6.53*

## THE CROWD OF 'I'S IN YOUR BEING

As you know, we take our Being as one and believe we have only one I. This is an illusion, and as long as this illusion lasts it is really impossible to change. There are many other illusions which prevent change of Being. We have spoken recently about how Being must change in order that Understanding can change if we gain knowledge of this Work, but if our Being remains just the same we cannot understand it. It is necessary to apply the Work to one's Being. One sign that a person is not working is that he or she remains just the same year after year.

Now our Being is characterized by multiplicity, by which is meant that we have not one I, but many, many 'I's. Some of these 'I's are very young and have persisted in us unchanged. We have, for example, many childish 'I's that often cause a great deal of trouble. Although our body is of one age we are all ages internally, in our inner environment —that is, in our psyche. Physically we are one age: psychologically we are many different ages. When a person is told to be his or her age, it probably means that the person acts too often from childish 'I's. As I said, some of these 'I's are very young, and are not experienced. It is then necessary to separate from them.

I will just say a word about separation from the different 'I's. Have you ever listened to your 'I's talking in you? Often 'I's carry on a long conversation, but you do not observe it. You think it is you talking to yourself. Because of the illusion that you have only one "you", you cannot do anything about this inner situation to separate from it. To think it is always "you" talking to yourself is to put the feeling of I into what is an 'I' in you, to identify with each of the 'I's that are talking in you. When you believe that it is always "you" talking in yourself and you cannot see that it is different 'I's in you, and that you are making the mistake of putting your feeling of I into each of these different 'I's, it is exactly like thinking that everyone talking in a room full of people is *you* talking. This inability to realize that it is different 'I's speaking in you, and that you are making a great Work-mistake in putting the feeling of I into each of these 'I's, leads to a stalemate situation in you, and makes internal separation from different 'I's impossible. I mean that your Being remains exactly the same because you hold on to it—that is to say, you do not change year after year, but remain just the same, because, by saying I to each 'I', you prevent any change. In other words, you are not applying the Work to yourself. You are not applying what it teaches to yourself. You persist in thinking that you have no 'I's, but that it is always the same *I*. You cannot see that it is different 'I's in you which you insist on putting the feeling of I into, so that you call these different 'I's *YOU*. That is to say, you say: "I think", "I feel", when you should see that it is an 'I' that thinks or feels, and that you can withdraw the feeling of I from it. In fact, by always putting the feeling of I into every 'I' in you, you hold yourself down to being what you always were, and that is the reason why you cannot change—or at least one very big reason.

When you discover that a great many of these 'I's are certainly not you, and especially when you realize that these 'I's are of all different ages, you cannot believe it at first. You are so accustomed to saying I to everything that goes on in you—every voice that speaks in you you regard as I speaking. That is what I mean when I say that you do not listen to your 'I's talking in you, but always think it is *YOU* talking to yourself. That is to say that you are always identified with 'I's that are not you. Now you cease identifying when you withdraw the feeling of I from a thing. If you put the feeling of I into it—whatever it may be—you identify with it, which means that you think it is *YOU*. To identify means to "make it the same". As long as you make the same as yourself the different 'I's in you that constitute the multiplicity of 'I's in your Being, you say to every 'I': "This is I", "This is me". You make yourself the same as these different 'I's. It is necessary to withdraw the feeling of I from them. Then after a time you can say: "This is not I, but *an* 'I' in me that has been a great nuisance over the years and which I now see is not me." When this stage is reached, a great step can be taken forward as regards inner separation. This step can really begin to lead to change of Being.

Have you seen for yourself, psychologically, spiritually, that you would appear like a crowd of people walking along, of every age, and some exceedingly naughty people amongst you, and if you introduced yourself you would include everybody and call each person by your own name? Sometimes a crowd of people appear in dreams, often a very odd crowd—some dressed up, some in rags, and some deformed, and some in better shape, and so on. This is how a dream, in certain cases—when you begin to work—may represent you. This ill-assorted crowd of somewhat queer people represents the multiplicity of your Being, and I can assure you from personal experience on many occasions, that it is a great shock when you realize what this representation of yourself means. But once you have begun to realize that you *are* a multiplicity, and have begun to cease saying I so easily to this crowd, you very rarely have the dream. It comes to assist you in a general way to start. Then it stops. That is because you are beginning to distinguish yourself from the motley procession, this crowd, that you have taken as yourself—as I. In fact, this is one of the times when you may have a glimpse of Real I in the far distance—once you see these 'I's of your personal history are *not* you. But the vision passes. Let me repeat—as long as you think that you are all your different 'I's, you are what is called "identified with yourself". It means that you have no insight into yourself and are not applying the Work to yourself, not believing you are many. It means you have not grasped that you have many 'I's in you, but are still under the sensual illusion that there is only one I, because there is only one Body. As long as you are identified with yourself your Being cannot change.

Now a brief word about the consequences of the different 'I's in us being of different ages. An 'I' may have formed itself early in our life when we were in unusually unhappy circumstances, due perhaps to a parent, brother, sister or governess, and when we felt and thought it was all very unfair. When our circumstances changed as we grew older, we had no reason to feel things were unfair. But this 'I' formed at an earlier time still *persists in us*. Because we do not separate from it, and therefore take it as I, it pops to the surface when any difficulty arises and eagerly controls us and makes us unhappy. In this way are we imprisoned by 'I's that are anachronisms—that is, that do not belong to the present time but to the past. Distinct, calm observation of them as being early 'I's belonging to situations long ended and not valid any more and saying to them: "This is not *I*" or "*I* am not this 'I'", and seeing that even though they spoke some truth once upon a time they do not now do so—in short, separating from them by no longer identifying and so believing them can, after a determined struggle, cause them gradually to wane to shadows. You will feel a miraculous freedom. But if you go asleep to them and once more foolishly let the feeling of I into them again, it is like transfusing them with your blood and they soon revive and with the greatest delight reproduce in posture, expression, intonation, feeling and thought, all the old unhappiness. We all suffer from these early, out-of-date 'I's and always will as long as we believe we have only one I and therefore say I to all the crowd of 'I's of different ages in us. Now please realize that as long as you say: "I wish I were not so worried," you are saying I to your worrying and thus identifying with it. You are not separating from it and starving it. On the contrary you are giving it a transfusion of your blood. For every time you say: "*I* wish *I* were not so worried," you are putting the feeling of I into an 'I'.

## INCOMPLETE AND UNINTELLIGENT
## SELF-OBSERVATION

To work on yourself intelligently is to benefit yourself. It is what you have to do to make your situation better. There is always something to work on but you do not observe it. You look in the wrong direction. You look for big things, for crises, not little daily things. But big things begin from little things. Did you observe that slight but negative feeling that just entered you unchecked and with which you identified straight away? It changed your expression and led to the mood of complaining that you are in now. No, you did not observe it. If you had, your Work-Memory would have checked your going along *that* easy path of associations any further. You should know how it goes by now: first a slight negative feeling of discontent with which you identify and to which you say 'I', then a mood of complaining, then an inrush of feelings and thoughts that everything is unfair—at which even you may be astonished, because you never really observe and acknowledge how many daily inner accounts you make against people who appear to you not to be treating you rightly. These accounts accumulate in the same place in you until that place is full up and explodes. Finally, at the end of this path of associations lies a black temper and then a waste of sadness and depression. Then you recover for a time and are neither depressed nor excited. But after an interval the various stations along this path fill up with energy and all is ready for this chain of states to fire off again in the same order of succession. People do not observe these chains of inner states, one linked to another, or how one state leads associatively to another. They have made no *map* of themselves. Trying to observe one state only they do not see its connection with the previous or with the subsequent one. That is, their observation is incomplete and not intelligent.

The Work says that in the practice of Self-Observation we should notice that things come in pairs. One reason is due to the Law of the Pendulum. A swing in one direction is followed sooner or later by a swing in the opposite direction. For example, one is over-excited and then too depressed. It is useless to observe only one of these two states. It will not stop them. One follows the other and you must draw the feeling of I gradually out of both. Ouspensky frequently pointed out that we did not notice how things come in pairs. He usually would say: "Incomplete observation", when anyone gave a personal observation at a meeting. For years people tend to observe just one thing and perhaps a week later observe another thing. If you do this it is no wonder that you get no map of yourselves—that is, of what lies in you and the paths connecting them in your psychological country within. For example, if you do something that afterwards you feel ashamed of and depreciate yourself about, you may observe what you have done but not observe that the resulting negative phase of feeling ashamed and depreciating yourself can lead round and give strength to your doing whatever it was again. In other words, the doing it and feeling of remorse can form a self reinforcing circle. It is the same with self-justifying or making excuses following bad behaviour. If you could be more conscious and not identify so completely with the remorse or justifying that follows your behaviour, the power of the mechanical cycle might be gradually lessened. Remember to try sometimes to see with your understanding how you are giving energy to what you identify with, and that the only remedy is not to identify. I am no believer in repentance and tears as indications of the turning over a new leaf. As likely as not they will reinforce the active side of the old state. I do not think that vows are of any use either—such as "I will never do that again, I swear it". You will do it again. Such methods of approach are not Work-methods. The uses of observation, not identifying and understanding *are* Work-methods, and they can give permanent results. G. said that once you have really understood for yourself why you must not do something, it is a crime against yourself and against the Work to go on doing it. Some of you must know by now that not to do something because you are told not to is quite different from not doing it because you *understand* why you should not. Pray always, therefore, for understanding. It will be given to you according to your valuation of the Work and according to your realization of your need of the Work and according to your patience with yourself.

Now as regards making more prolonged self-observations so that you can become more conscious of how things are connected in you and in this way begin to make a map of yourself to which you can add. You have heard the phrase "State is place". The idea is that when you are in a particular *state* you are, psychologically, in a certain *place* in yourself. You perhaps know that the surface of the physical brain is divided into different areas or places. One place sees, another hears, another feels on being stimulated, and so on. Consider now the diagram of many 'I's, which is psychological. When you are in a particular 'I' or group of similar 'I's and are identified, they will induce a particular state in you. That is, if they love being bitter and negative, you, being identified and taking them as *you*, will feel bitter and negative. Your *state* will be due to the *place* you are in. That is what it means that "State is Place". There are many dangerous places in the psychological city of yourself. It is necessary to study them by prolonged Self-Observation and try to become increasingly conscious of the roads that lead to them, and why you go down them. This is intelligent observation.

## BRIEF REPETITION OF RECENT TALKS

The more you are identified with yourself, the less can you observe yourself, and the less you observe yourself the less can you apply the teaching of the Work to yourself. The majority of you think that everything that takes place in you is I. How can you withdraw the feeling of I from what you take as I? How can you ever say: "This is not I," when all the time you are convinced that it is? Feeling of I cannot observe the feeling of I. I mean that you cannot observe an 'I' as distinct from yourself as long as you have the feeling that this 'I' is yourself. It is quite true that it is difficult to observe yourself, but that does not release you from the necessity to observe yourself. What so many of you do is to say, for example: "I am very irritable." If you say: "I am very irritable," you put the feeling of I into irritable 'I's, and, therefore, you cannot separate from them.

Now you have heard many times that you cannot *understand* this Work unless you apply your knowledge of it to your own Being and in that way see the truth of what it is. You first of all must learn the knowledge of this Work, which means you must study what it says, and then you must apply your knowledge to your own Being. This is the starting-point of living the Work. If you do this, you will have a chance of beginning to understand the Work. But if you neither get to know the Work nor apply it to your own Being through Self-Observation, you will never understand it in the Work-meaning of that difficult word, *Understanding*. When you are identified with every thought and opinion, and attitude, and feeling, and mood, and passion, you cannot, of course, observe yourself because you regard all these things as "I MYSELF". People who take all that goes on in them as 'I', cannot observe in the right way. As I indicated, they say: "*I* feel irritable," "*I* am in love," but they should really say: "Which 'I' is in love?" (No doubt your romantic 'I's) or again: "Which 'I' is irritable?" As I have said before, as long as you are in the sensual mind and therefore in sensual thinking, you cannot believe that you have many 'I's because you have only one body that you can see, and feel, and love. The method of the Work is to withdraw the feeling of I from the 'I' which for the moment is using your telephone and shouting irritably at the whole world. Let us suppose you have just returned from lunch at the delightful house of Mrs X. Before you were there you were having a domestic row and your telephone was uttering the most appalling statements. Having arrived you got into your social 'I's . You were exceedingly entertaining. You then returned home and you continued to have your row. If you are going to tell me that this is one and the same 'I' at work in you, I cannot believe you.

As you know, through the action of buffers in us, the 'I's are shut off from each other so that we do not see the inner contradictions going on. Somebody who knows Mrs X. comes in and you begin to speak about Mrs X. 'I's that love scandal have got much to say here; so then you are in different 'I's. Now all this takes place quite smoothly and you see no contradictions, and yet quite different 'I's have used your telephone—that is, your mouthpiece. Just seeing these contradictions begins to weaken buffers. Some people have such strong contradictions in them, which they are unaware of, that they can never hope to get near any unity of Being, and, not observing these contradictions, they remain without any power of Self-Observation. That is to say, they cannot alter themselves because they take everything as I. They do not draw the feeling of I little by little out of these things that the Work urgently stresses they should do, as, for example, from negative emotions. They ignore far too much *what* the Work teaches them to observe, and are afraid to look into themselves, possibly through early religious fears which hold their understanding captive and thus impede their development. They know nothing of inner separation.

In full Self-Remembering the feeling of I is taken out of the machinery of 'I's. When you are in that state you can see the working of the machinery of 'I's going on like printing presses beneath you. You wonder how you ever took it for yourself. Then you identify— and become it all again.

The final thing that I will briefly remind you of is that if your name is John Smith you have got to observe John Smith and be less and less John Smith. At present John Smith is your greatest enemy even though he is covered with medals and surrounded by the applause of the world.

*Amwell, 18.7.53*

## THE SHADOW IN ONE'S BEING

If you cannot see in yourself the tricks, manoeuvres and deceptions that another uses, you may find yourself continually at a disadvantage, being too easily taken in. You can only see through another person by seeing through yourself. In saying this, to introduce the subject of this paper, I have to emphasize again two Work-ideas—namely, that *our Being attracts our life* and that *we do not know ourselves*. This lack of self-knowledge is the rule in human existence and contributes volumes to Man's useless suffering. For the human energy expended in useless suffering, when seen in vision, is incredible and terrible. However, though useless to humanity, the energy is used elsewhere in this economical and totally unsentimental Universe, where nothing is wasted. Have you, by the way, begun to notice how much energy *you* actually waste in useless suffering? Perhaps you spent this morning being

1727

miserable, or sulking, or pitying yourself. Well, that is useless suffering. We have to sacrifice our suffering—we are often told so. But do we sacrifice it? Of course not. It does not occur to us that the Work has to be applied to oneself so we go on looking like dying ducks in thunderstorms instead of facing ourselves. But if you could touch your life objectively through self-knowledge, you would not and could not have any useless feelings of this kind.

Now to return to the two things I mentioned—namely, that our Being attracts our life and that we do not know ourselves—what prevents us from realizing that this is the case with ourselves? The answers are simple. Illusions prevent us. In the first case, nothing that happens to us is ever our fault in any serious sense. It is always somebody else's fault. That is how we see it mechanically. So we cannot see that the fault is truly in us. Therefore we do not wish to change our Being nor do we see any connection between it and what happens to us in life. In fact, I fancy we really do not grasp that we have a Being of a particular shape. In the second case, *of course* we know ourselves. What nonsense to say I do not know myself. Who should know myself better than myself? This again is sheer illusion. Now it is by such illusions that humanity is kept asleep and the pain-factory of life on this planet is kept going at full blast—needlessly now, as G. said, but owing to habit and our state of sleep. Yet there are ways out, and have always been, all through the ages. For it is *the way out* that esoteric teaching is about. This Work is the way out for this modern period—the way out that is suitable to the period—that is, if you do it—but not otherwise. But few wish to find a way out because they cannot or will not see that to get out they have to start and work hard to change in themselves *just what the Work tells them to change.* They will not face themselves. They will not observe themselves and find in themselves what the Work points to. They have their own ideas of themselves. Moreover, the immensely powerful network of simple, cunning illusions about themselves prevents them from knowing themselves. To this must be added the nebulous illusion that things are bound to get better in time—the illusion of to-morrow, of mañana, which G. said we must contend with. One does not see that since one's Being attracts one's life, things will not get better *unless* one's Being changes. I ask you again: have you noticed in yourself what the Work tells you to change? No. Well, some 'I's will have to go. You may, however, be lucky enough to be given a revelation and memorably wake up, suddenly realizing the blinding truth of the Work *as regards yourself.* I must mention here in passing that without hard work on oneself and a constant recourse to and refreshment of one's Work-Memory, as you get older you get worse, and eventually crystallize out in some bad distorted shape. So we really have to do something about it all, as the Work is ceaselessly saying, only we hear it faintly as in a deep sleep. Do you know, by the way, that you are asleep?

Now you will see that the two things mentioned—namely, that our

Being attracts our life and that we think we know ourselves—hang together. It means, in short, you *imagine* you know your Being. But you do not. If you did, your life would not be what it is and self-observation would not be necessary. You do not know your Being and so you do not know why you attract your kind of life. If you had sufficient self-knowledge you might see either that you need your kind of life or that you could make it different. Now only the Work can change your Being. By knowing it, acknowledging it, and applying it to yourself, everything that happens to you can become intelligent. Consider identifying—are you free from it? Look how identified you are at this moment. Consider Self-Remembering—do you ever practise it? Consider a life-long grievance; consider a daily making of accounts against others; consider a life-long pre-occupation with negative and unpleasant emotions; consider the Giants, Pride and Vanity, and what a mess they make and how they spoil everything; consider jealousy and hatred; consider your appalling ignorance; consider your fear of what people will think; consider your violence; consider your shifting lying—are you going to say you find nothing to work upon, nothing in this Work that applies to you? I have only mentioned a few things, but is your Being free from such things? Apparently it often is, for people ask me what they have to work on. The answer may be that they simply cannot observe themselves and they remain blind. They usually are very sensual thinkers who make reality a question of the senses. They have no internal attention. All the same, even if you are a very sensual thinker, even a little consciously directed internal attention to what is going on in you may surprise you and shew you how little you know your Being and thus begin to change your idea of yourself. For is it not crystal-clear that *your idea* of yourself *must* change before *you* can change? Eventually, you must sooner or later *see through yourself*—this invented person you keep going at such cost—this you that is not you. This is *indeed* self-knowledge. In proportion as you do, so you will see through the tricks and manoeuvres and deceptions of others. Why? Because you will see them in yourself and yourself in them. Strangely enough, this frees you from their power—for it is standing too high in yourself and feeling superior that puts you so often under the power of others. Also, you are no longer surprised and indignant with others, which is a tedious and exhausting rôle to play. We seek to let the light into our inner darkness. The light heals us. It arranges things in the right order. This means we seek to be *more conscious of ourselves*. For example, I teach you to find in yourself what you judge so critically in others. You will get to know what is in *your* Being in this way—what you never realized.

For many years before I met this Work I was Jung's pupil in Zürich. One of the useful things he taught was that we all cast a psychological *shadow* and that the beginning of the way to internal evolution lay in making the shadow gradually conscious. The shadow is the part of us that we are not conscious of, but must—with pain to both pride and vanity, which is conscious suffering—eventually make conscious. It is absolutely necessary to face this shadow if we are serious. Of course it alters our idea of ourselves very much. This shadow, which is in everyone, can make havoc in our lives, as long as we are *unconscious* of it. As a part of our Being that we do not acknowledge, it attracts much that seems incomprehensible in our Life, owing to our not accepting it. A man without a shadow would be fully conscious to himself. He would have suffered usefully.

*Amwell, 25.7.53*

## REFLECTIONS ON PSYCHO-TRANSFORMISM

When O. suggested that this Work should be known by the name of "Psycho-Transformism", some thought it was a good name and others did not agree. Personally, I do not like the word "Transformism", and at the same time "Psycho-Transformation" would not sound right. In any case, the term "Psycho-Transformism" conveys the basic teaching behind the Work—namely, that Man was created experimentally as a self-developing organism, capable of undergoing a quite definite transformation into another kind of man—a New Man—and thereby completing himself. Life and the routine living of life does not complete him. Now life consists in a series of different events and a series of different states that they produce in us. By means of a gradual transformation of our being, we no longer attract the same events but alter the states they produce in us. The whole teaching of the Work is about the methods of doing this. When we know, acknowledge and apply the Work to the events that happen to us, the process of Psycho-Transformism is set in motion. We then *receive life on the Work*, which *intervenes* between the events and our former reactions to them, so that we must transform not only ourselves, but the way we take all the daily events that happen to us. Some events are more difficult to "transform" than others. For a long time we must not expect to be more than mere children at the work of transforming our reactions to things, such as the effects of people upon us, but we must understand that this is our most important task. When we see that what we dislike in others is a projection of what is in ourselves, unknown to us, we *transform* the situation. To sink into a state of sleep is not to transform the meaning of life or one's reactions to it. For example, everyone knows the feeling of heaviness, monotony and boredom, that so easily comes with the thought of the day-after-day routine and sameness of existence. This is one feeling that must be contended with and avoided. The more conceited you are, however unconsciously, the more boredom arises. Conceit puts you too high up to see aright. Life should be at eye-level.

1730

Boredom comes also from thinking of one's life only in terms of succession in Time. Actually nothing is ever the same except if you make it so through identifying. Again, the taste of negative states is always the same. For that reason we do not take in new impressions and therefore suffer from that form of psychological "scurvy" that is due to lack of fresh impressions. We are usually identified and negative. All your life some work has to be done here to correct this wrong attitude.

Actually, our lives are outside Time and Space. We should feel rather that we are inserted into Time and Space like a boy looking through a peep-hole at a circus. Your consciousness is not in Time and Space any more than your mind is. You can think, in a flash, of countries, or of stars, far divided in Space, and you can think in the same way of the days of ancient Rome and the present day. But when Time and Space get hold of us and one sees only the days stretching out endlessly, living in the same house, the same room, we violate something deep in us, which is independent of these limitations—something that is free and should not become subservient to the senses save in so far as is necessary. Only our bodies are in Time and Space. We can, and do, get very identified with our bodies and, as I have often told you, a man who identifies with his body, and who takes it as himself, and believes that there is nothing else but his body that is *him*, very soon comes to a halt in this Work. In fact, such an extreme sensual thinker cannot take in anything about this Work, from my observation so far. He will not be able to transform anything, having no feeling that he is a small undeveloped conscious spirit locked up in an apparatus of flesh and blood. His inner state will be a function of his bodily state. By this, I mean it will depend on his bodily state. Now, your inner state should not depend on your bodily state. I once said to O. that when I felt fit physically, I observed that I was most asleep psychologically, and that when I was most alive psychologically, I often noticed that I was not well physically. He said that people did not often notice this. They worried only about their bodily health. He added that illness often opens things in people which otherwise would not be opened through their own efforts. I am quite sure that in order to transform the daily things of life, and the way one takes them, it is necessary to have a strong sense that the psychological side of oneself is not the same as the bodily side. While it is certainly true that they do interact, it is possible to separate them more and more. Of course, if one has Second Body they can then be completely separated.

Now, it seems to me each day we have to collect ourselves into ourselves and feel it is ourselves approaching whatever it is we have to do, as if from one's own will. We should go to things ourselves and not be dragged. Also, we should never let one day run into another so as to make a kind of blur in which our consciousness of ourselves is very slight. Otherwise how can we practise any psycho-transformism if we are simply carried along helplessly in mid-stream (without realizing it) by the tide of life? The act of Self-Remembering pulls us momentarily out of the current. But ordinarily we are carried along as by a mill-race and make no attempt to separate ourselves. We do not feel ourselves distinct from it with all its "one thing after another" events. When you are badly asleep in this way, you do not really exist in any conscious sense of the word, and certainly you transform nothing. If you transform nothing, you live mechanically. You are just a machine. You take nothing in a new way. It never occurs to you to do so. But you can, you know, once you see you *must* transform things, as the only solution. We have to make our feeling of existence far more conscious because the great defect humanity suffers from is lack of consciousness. This lack of consciousness brings about the unnecessarily bad disasters that happen to humanity. If people were more conscious they could not do what they do, or behave as they do, or even think and feel as they do. Nor, indeed, could they invent what they are at present inventing. In this respect, it seems that the defect in consciousness is even greater than it ever was. Transformation is not destruction.

*Amwell, 1.8.53*

## PSYCHO-TRANSFORMISM AND SELF-OBSERVATION

We spoke last time about Psycho-Transformism. As I said, this term is used as a name for this Work. It at least emphasizes that this Work is essentially psychological. Its object is to change a man's or a woman's psychology. As is so often said in these papers, people do not realize that they have a psychology. They cannot see it, and for very literal, sensual-minded people what they cannot see does not exist. But everyone has a psychology which they can get to know through observing themselves. Once you do this, you have taken a great step forward. A person who begins to practise Self-Observation is quite different from other people. We spoke of life being a series of events that produce a series of states in us. We are not aware of this. We neither observe consciously the event nor do we observe consciously the effect it has on us. For example, the waiter seems rude or does not instantly attend to your needs. You fly into a temper. This kind of event of the waiter not attending to you instantly, always produces a state of violence in you. But you do not see that this particular kind of event mechanically produces a particular kind of state in you. You may remain all your life unaware of this, although other people are painfully aware of it. You also must become painfully aware of it. But since you are unaware of it you do not see it is an unpleasant part of your psychology and so you will not attempt to transform it. Instead, you try to transform the waiter.

You have heard it said that we have to change our attitudes, and that as long as we do not change our attitudes we cannot change ourselves. You have also heard that our attitudes connect us with the events of life as by means of invisible threads. If you always tend to lose your temper with waiters, who seem rude or ignore you, then once you have begun to try to work on yourself you have got to make conscious gradually to yourself what your attitude is to waiters. Supposing you are a very conceited person, it might spring from your feeling of your self-importance which will, of course, make you touchy and violent. Then it is your attitude to yourself that is primarily wrong. At the same time, you may have an attitude of contempt towards foreigners in general, which contributes to your tendency always to quarrel with waiters. Finally, you do not see how rude you are yourself, and how you ignore others. All this has to do with becoming more conscious.

Now, if you are serious in really wishing to change your psychology, which means to change your Being, you will see that you have to do quite a lot even to change one thing. But nothing will change in you unless you can become conscious of the fact that you have a definite psychology which causes you to behave in a certain way to a certain event. If you can never see this, there will be no hope of your ever changing yourself and you will continue to believe in yourself. As I said at the beginning of this Note, a person who has begun to observe himself has already taken a big step forward in his possible evolution. He has begun to take the path to self-knowledge. Still, a great many of you still have no idea what it is that you are trying to change in yourselves, simply because you never will face yourselves and so never actually observe yourselves. To observe what events cause you to react in a negative way is a great aid to self-observation, self-knowledge and the formation of Work-Memory. For you may hear about self-observation all your life, but there is always a great gap between hearing and doing. Have you observed anything in yourself this week? Do you understand that if you do not change *any* of the habitual ways in which you always take life, you must remain the same and attract the same situations. Begin somewhere to check your way of reacting. The waiter is only an example. New life depends on new Being. Do you seek new *Being*? Then old Being must go. How? By withdrawing energy from it. The Work teaches us all what things belonging to old Being have especially to be drained of force. It specifies them. It defines them. It insists we should become aware of them by observing them without justifying and become conscious of the part they play in our daily existence.

You cannot change and also cling to the same. I assure you that it is a great relief to change something—I should say, rather, let the Neutralizing Force of the Work change it—and to feel it is no longer necessary. For so long we fail to see how bound and chained we are to our habits and how wonderful it is to be freed—as, for example, to feel freed from having to quarrel with waiters. Now think of something *you* would like to be freed from and ask the Work in your heart to do it. Let us recall that this teaching is about increase of consciousness. As people are, in a state of sleep, not conscious of themselves and ignorant of their Being, it can be said that there are no human beings, but only a world of *sub-humans*, capable of destroying each other.

*Amwell, 8.8.53*

## GROWTH OF ESSENCE

Whatever you change in Essence, through development of it, is not lost, but remains with you. You may live and die without any change taking place in Essence—that is to say, you are born with a certain kind of Essence and after a time Personality is formed round it and nothing else happens. The Essence remains the same and undergoes no development beyond early life. What is acquired in Personality is not transmitted to Essence. The Essence is not continuous with the Personality. A development of the Personality does not mean a development of the Essence. We think of our development as continuous from the earliest years but this is not the case from the Work point of view. The Essence grows a little way and stops growing. The Personality then begins to be formed and surrounds the Essence like a shell. You may ask yourself: How can I make Essence grow in me, beyond its natural point? How can I really change my Essence through development so that when my Essence recurs and attracts a body to itself, my life will be different from what it was previously. In other words, how can I produce a permanent change in myself that cannot be taken away from me? Since the Essence is the central thing, to ask this question is the same as saying: How can I produce a change in my internal nature that is real and not merely acquire what is on the surface, as is Personality? It is this question of an inner change that constitutes the problem. First there is the Essence, then there is Personality, and finally, there should be a development of the Essence through what has been acquired in the Personality. The Essence is the eternal part of us: the Personality is the temporal part of us. Life does not develop Essence beyond a certain point. It then develops Personality. First of all I learn this Work in Personality. How can I make this Work cause Essence to grow? I may know the Work and even make a point of studying the diagrams. Yes, but do I *will* the Work? If I do not will the Work, how can what is most essential in me ever change and become a permanent part of my Being? To *know* and to *be* are quite different. For my knowledge of this Work to become Being can only result from willing it, and you only will what you really value and love. So therefore if I do not feel any love, I will not will the Work, and if I do not will the Work, even although I know it, nothing will happen. I will only remember it, but will not love to live it. So I will not understand the Work.

Now the most artificial thing in us is the False Personality. That is why it is called *False* Personality. False Personality makes us all do unreal things. We strive for social pre-eminence, we strive for display, for being thought well of, for being first, and so on. How can we expect any aim arising from False Personality to influence the Essence to the extent of making it develop? Surely there is something here that we do not reflect on sufficiently. If I want to be pre-eminent in this Work, to shew off and have no genuine feeling of need for it, how can it change my Essence? How can anything that springs only from the vanity of self-love change my Essence? I may pretend to many virtues for display, but if there is nothing real and sincere in me, how can my real, untutored Essence develop? The child sees through me. You cannot suppose that Essence develops through what is unreal. If I do things to be seen of men only I am not really doing them. You can each see for yourselves how everything can be done for show and from no internal feeling for it. If you reflect on this, you will be able to see how there is *discontinuity* between Essence and Personality. You will also see how the Personality, being discontinuous with the Essence, can be made passive with the result that Essence becomes active. This would not be the case if they were continuous. Essence and Personality are two different things.

The Work moves inwards. It falls first on the outer psychology, on the Outer Man in yourself. If it is received and appreciated, its action is to penetrate inwards to the Inner Man and transform him. Then you will not abstain from stealing, say, because you fear being found out, but because you dislike stealing. We spoke of all this when considering outer, middle and inner divisions of centres. At each inward movement of the Work—at each deepening of the Work in your understanding—it is as if you had to begin again. You become aware that you had got things wrong—the Work and yourself—and mixed it up with this amazing conceit common to all of us sub-humans. The stages of the Work are as if at intervals you had to be put under another—and sterner—master, as if you had moved up from one form at school to another where things were no longer play but beginning to be real. Some definite things have got to be done apparently—such as not getting angry with waiters or bus-conductors. Is it possible, then, that you are down on this planet to learn about yourself? This is a good thought to have. Do you mean I am not all right, or at least rather exceptional? Yes, that is what is meant. You are tiresome— and stupid, like the rest. Here we get offended—an effective barrier. In the Gospels people are always getting offended. They were sure they were all right.

Now the Work goes in stages or levels—layer by layer. It certainly is difficult to take the Work more deeply into oneself without a great deal of perplexity and thought and sincerity. It is just here that people stick. They begin to see that they have been doing the Work from self-love and not from love of the Work. And unless they are capable of great honesty with themselves they may not be able to find deeper reasons and emotions for continuing to work on themselves. We may take it for granted that anything unreal, anything false, anything that is mere pretence, will not affect the development of the Essence. However, everything that you have done genuinely as far as you can will come to help you in these moments of temptation which are bound to occur when the necessity of deepening your understanding of the Work is encountered. This is where Work-memory especially comes in. 'I's that wish the Work in you together form your Work-Will, whereas 'I's that do not wish to work form your Life-will. Some 'I's are on the wrong side. Never make the mistake of thinking that only stupid 'I's can be Work-'I's. We are told to be wise as serpents and harmless as doves. You have two things, the power of thinking and the power of willing. If you never really think about this Work, of course, nothing is possible. You must remember also that what is thought about but is not in your will is not yet real in you, because it leads to no action, and therefore cannot affect Essence. It is not in your life. If you have no appreciation of the Work and its ideas, viewpoints and teaching, how do you expect Essence to be affected by it? I have often told you that there is great beauty in this Work. Do you know that beauty powerfully affects Essence? Supposing you see nothing beautiful in the formulations of this Work, do you think it will make Essence develop? Do you think that a person who constantly practises painting or the piano but feels nothing beautiful in nature or music will *remember* next time in recurrence, as so many musicians and artists appear to have? Do you think that he will begin to remember any earlier? How can he? He cannot, any more than if he thought about music or painting only and never willed to practise it. For what is in the thought and the will and terminates in action enters and remains in your life. But what you only think and do not will passes away because it has no termination in action.

In this connection I do not see how a religion that is harsh and grim and backed by fear can make Essence develop. I am convinced that many dreadful mistakes are made here. In the light of the high descent of Essence from the level of the Galaxy is it surprising that what is beautiful influences it unforgettably? Therefore let us keep the Work beautiful in heart and mind so that it reaches Essence in us.

## OBSERVATION OF ATTITUDE TO THE WORK

At what time do you start making internal accounts? It depends on your attitude. You begin to make internal accounts when you feel that you are owed. With regard to some people, you feel you are owed if you make the slightest effort on their behalf. Some people's attitude towards the Work is such that if they make any attempt to work either on themselves or in conjunction with others, or if they do anything for the Work itself, they feel that they are owed something. Unfortunately we are brought up on the principle of being rewarded: "If you are a good girl I will give you a sweet," or "If you finish your exercise I will take you to the cinema." A person who expects reward for every effort that he (or she) makes grows up into a very discontented being and never fits into life. One might say nowadays that there is a general increase in making internal accounts. People feel that they should not be doing what they are doing, or getting far more pay and so on. Ouspensky used to call attention to the fact that since the introduction of machinery people take little or no pleasure in their jobs and the former pride that craftsmen had is dying out. He said that the emotional part of Moving Centre is not satisfied by modern conditions. He saw in machines one of the greatest menaces to the human race and said that machines will make man go to war.

Now the Three Lines of Work, which are work on yourself, work in conjunction with others, and work for the Work itself, require three different attitudes. It is true that you can get something for yourself in each case, but your aim will not be only to get something for yourself in each case. If it is, you will probably get nothing. If you do not work with others, you do not see them in yourself and yourself in them. Lacking this indescribably important development of consciousness, you get a distorted view of your own value. Again, if you do nothing for the Work, it will not do anything for you. If we could work without expecting to get an immediate reward and losing any faith that we had in the Work if we do not get a reward, we would have gone a considerable way in making False Personality passive. It may strike some of you as extraordinary that a person should ever make effort unless a reward were given him. But here lies a mystery which I do not attempt to explain but which I tried to indicate in the last paper. It is possible to make effort even although one does not expect a reward. There is such a thing as love of doing a thing for its own sake. There is such a thing as being free from making internal accounts and no longer looking at life with a jealous eye, asking where one comes in oneself, or how much one will make out of it. I would say that this is one meaning of the strange Work-expression that we should not work for results. To work for the necessity of working on yourself, from the understanding of its necessity in view of your gradual dawning consciousness of what you are really like, is not to work for immediate reward but to work from understanding that this is what you have to do with yourself, and this is the scheme, and this is why you are on this planet which is so far down in the Scale of Being. In view of this attitude one should of course think that one has done absolutely nothing as yet—that one has never made any real effort or faced up to anything in oneself seriously. But there are always those who indeed, almost as soon as they connect themselves with the Work, begin to blame the Work for everything that happens to them, and they make internal accounts against it. Their sheets are torn at the laundry: it is the Work's fault. Such people have an absolutely wrong attitude to the Work. It is tiny and mean. And as often as not they seem to think that it is kind of them to come to meetings. These are very immature people and need a great deal of experience of life to correct so foolish an attitude. To make internal accounts with the Work is like bargaining with the Almighty. It is, of course, connected with an enormous self-conceit due to a state of sleep that only the recurring tragedies of life can break up. In proportion as the Work is received with the understanding, it moves inwards in centres so that its truths are seen internally as truths. So does your attitude to the Work enlarge itself and you receive more force from your attitude. A small and narrow attitude to the Work can give only a superficial relation to it. The strength behind the Work from its foundations cannot communicate itself through small and exacting 'I's. Your own state of Being holds you up. Negative 'I's stand in the way. But what especially holds many of you back is that you do not see the truth of what the Work teaches for yourself. The understanding is that which can see the truth. *It is interior sight.* It does not require confirmation from others. You merely see that a thing is so. This is *understanding*, the strongest force that one can develop.

★     ★     ★

What is the cure for this sub-human, monkey-conceit that all possess? The cure lies in increase of *consciousness*. This is the method of the Work. You cannot remain as conceited as you are if you become more conscious of what is in you. I include in the term *conceit* both pride and vanity. The Work teaches that two giants go before us and arrange everything beforehand. They are your pride and your vanity. You may be fairly certain that when this Work becomes remote and cold in you, you are up against conceit. Probably you are resenting. That is, some form of your conceit which is up against the Work. We spoke about the phrase so badly translated: "Blessed are the meek." The meaning rather should be: "Those who do not resent have inner happiness." This is quite different from outer happiness. Now people with a good opinion of themselves resent and envy easily. In all states of resentment conceit is involved. Consider the part Christ had to play in this respect. He had to play consciously the part of a failure according to prophecy.

1738

He told His companions He had to fail. Now owing to conceit our attitude to ourselves is far more powerful than any attitude to the Work. It is not a matter of pretence, of pious humility, that I mean. It is seeing with the understanding that one is very small and poor and ignorant in the Scale of Creation, and in comparison to Divine Being, and really just like a silly, vain monkey. In place of consciousness we have conceit. Work is a question of increasing one's consciousness, not imitating virtues like monkeys. It is a long, painful but wonderful journey, this journey of increasing consciousness, always at the expense of some aspect of self-conceit. In it are places where the danger is great —where a man begins to ascribe power to himself that he has not yet reached and to give himself airs and think he is a god—long before he has reached the goal, and when the Personality is still active. But seen as temptations to the conceit, they vanish. So do not be surprised if the Work gets you where your conceit feels it most, for the track the Work follows is successive *releases from conceit*. That is what it has to do. If you try to understand what the Work is about, it will, in turn, help you to see how difficult it is for it to help you and how heavily-fenced in and fortified and downright stupid your conceit makes you. It will over the years shew you what a job it is to dislodge you a single jot from your conceptions of yourself and at the same time how necessary this is for you and what inner happiness release from conceit gives you which no rewards or honours or any other of the sources of satisfaction to your conceit can give. For of what use has your life been to you if you have never caught a glimpse of the way to inner happiness and are bitter and have done little else than make internal accounts against others and understand nothing about yourself or what you had to learn?

*Amwell, 20.8.53*

## UNFINISHED PAPER

Since this Work aims at a development of the *understanding*, it cannot be done by command. In the organizations created in life, the *A* influences, obedience is necessary as well as rewards and punishments, but this cannot be exactly the same in this Work for the reason that the Neutralizing Force of Life and the Neutralizing Force of the Work are two utterly different things acting from different directions. You cannot compel people to *understand*. You can compel them to obey a discipline, keep rules, fear punishment and feel merit. But the inner spirit of a man is not awakened in this way. The problem of Esotericism then is how to awaken Man from within himself—from his own understanding, and will and consent, realizing his state of sleep. No compulsion can do this. Do I not have to see for myself that I am all wrong in myself and deeply long to awaken, and cease to go on doing what I am doing day by day? Now no rules or regulations can touch my inner spirit in this respect. I may, indeed, obey wonderfully and become a star-pupil, but I will remain asleep in myself before the eyes of Heaven. I will be nothing but an *imitation* person, however good and exemplary. This is the danger. My understanding will be unawakened. I will be empty within, not fed by internal meaning. For if I do things by imitation and example and not from a developing understanding and perception of truth, I will remain dead inside, like an empty house. This is the effect of using the wrong Neutralizing Force—that is, the Third Force of Life—in place of the Third Force of the Work. The Personality is not weakened.

Let us again speak about *imitation*—"Imitating the virtues." It was said last time that to imitate *meekness* is useless. ("Blessed are the meek.") The fact that you resent so easily is the point. Do you realize yet that you are not nearly conscious enough of yourself? You do not include in your limited consciousness of yourself what you resented so much being said to you just now. Your conceit of yourself keeps out from your consciousness that you are just what you resented being said of you by that person—of all people. You notice how you are annoyed by that person? He seems to be getting on your nerves, surely. Then how can you deal with him? He is *in yourself*—not outside. He is something you are not conscious of *in yourself*. Owing to your amazing conceit of yourself, the zone of what you are not conscious of in yourself is enormous. *Somehow* I am him and he is me. If this is so, I cannot be what my conceit pictures. I have, then, to let go something, to release myself from a conceit of myself. Look now—you detest this person— yet he is in you and somehow is you. It is the illusion of the senses— the person's body—that is the difficulty.

# APPENDIX

## NOTE ON HOW TO WORK ON ONESELF

As we were speaking at the meeting to-day on a subject that is important, I would like to write a little about it. It concerns the way in which people take this Work and how and in what spirit they work on themselves.

I will begin with myself. I was brought up, in regard to religious ideas, with the sense that only the conviction of sin was important. Everything was sin, briefly speaking. In consequence, religion was a very gloomy business and personally I loathed it. Morality was only sexual morality. Virtue was only continence, and so on, and, in general, sin and the feeling of being a sinner was the main idea of religion. I never understood anything else in regard to religion as a boy, and so was either afraid or worried or hated the whole thing. I began to stammer badly. I listened to the Scriptures, mostly drawn from the Old Testament, which always seemed indescribably horrible. God was a violent, jealous, evil, accusing person, and so on. And when I heard the New Testament I could not understand what the parables meant, and no one seemed to know or care what they meant. But once, in the Greek New Testament class on Sundays, taken by the Head Master, I dared to ask, in spite of my stammering, what some parable meant. The answer was so confused that I actually experienced my first moment of consciousness—that is, I suddenly realized that no one knew anything. This is a definite experience and was my first experience of Self-Remembering—the second being the sudden realization that no one knew what I was thinking—and from that moment I began to think for myself, or rather knew that I could. As you know, all moments of real Self-Remembering stand out for ever in one's inner life, and one's real life is not outer events, but inner states. I remember so clearly this class-room, the high windows constructed so that we could not see out of them, the desks, the platform on which the Head Master sat, his scholarly thin face, his nervous habits of twitching his mouth and jerking his hands—and suddenly this inner revelation of *knowing that he knew nothing*—nothing, that is, about anything that really mattered. This was my first inner liberation from the power of external life. From that time I knew for certain—and that always means by inner individual authentic perception which is the only source of real knowledge—that all my loathing of religion as it was taught me was right. And although one always goes to sleep again after a moment of real Self-Remembering, and often for years, yet such moments of consciousness stand always in higher parts of centres and remain and await, as it were, the further moments of realizing, more consciously, what life actually is—that is to say, they are never lost, and, although forgotten in one way, stand in the background of yourself always, and come forward at critical moments to guard you.

Now I wish to speak to you about how you work on yourselves and in what spirit you take the Work. You cannot easily work from the ordinary religious ideas and moods. You recall the saying about new wine in old bottles. This Work, this system of teaching, these ideas we are studying, are the most beautiful things you can possibly imagine—and they are new to us. No, they are far more lovely and beautiful than anything you can imagine. They accuse you only of being asleep. They hold no conviction of sin in them. They ask you quite gently to observe yourself. It is you yourself who must accuse yourself. Let us take one of the ideas of this teaching—an idea about *Essence*. This teaching tells us that the Essence of each of us comes down from the stars. You will remember the Ray of Creation. Essence comes down from the note *La* (Starry Galaxy) and passing through the note *Sol* (the Sun) and then the note *Fa* (the planetary zone) enters the earth. We are not merely born of our parents; our parents create the apparatus for the reception of this Essence that comes from the Stars. And all work, whether personal work, work with others in the Work, or work for the Work itself (and these are the three necessary lines of work for anyone who wishes to remain in this Work) is to lead us back to where we have originally come from. Now each one of us is down here, on this dark planet, so low down in the Ray of Creation, because he or she has some special thing in themselves, some special factor, or *chief feature* to observe, to become conscious of and to begin to dislike, and so to work against. It may be meanness, or cruelty, or lying, or self-pride, or fear, or ignorance and so on. And if a man or woman dies without seeing why they are here and what is the real reason of their lives, can it be called anything but a tragedy? Each one of you is here, on the earth, because from the work point of view you have something very special and very important to see in yourselves and struggle against with all your skill and ingenuity, with all your strength of mind and will and soul and heart and body. But of course if you pride yourselves on your virtues—well, what can happen save that self-righteousness, and so False Personality, will be increased every day you live: and the result will be that you will crystallize out in such narrow viewpoints and attitudes and become *dead people*. You have heard me speak of the meaning of the *dead* in the Gospels—for example, as in Christ's remark: "Let the dead bury their dead." The dead are those dead to all possibility of working on themselves and so changing themselves. Now the Work can only be done in the spirit of its own beauty and light, in the spirit of its true message and significance. Life on earth is nothing but a field for working on oneself, so that one can return whence one came. To take life as an *end* in itself is not to understand the Work, and it may cause a wrong attitude which may be the source of many negative emotions and of useless efforts made in negative states. For to work in a negative way is useless. It is only through some kind of delight, some feeling of joy or pleasure or some genuine affection or desire, that a person can work and bring about any change of being in himself. Fear, for example, will not act in this way. A man may have some knowledge of truth, but unless he *values* it, unless he feels some delight in it, it cannot affect him. It cannot act on him, for a man unites with truth only through his love, as it were, and in this way his being is changed. But if he is negative, then his love-life—that is his emotional side—is in a wrong state, and it will be the same if he is in a state of fear and feels compelled to do something against his will. To do a thing willingly from a delight in doing it, will effect a change in you. And when a person begins to take up his own "cross"—that is, the burden of some difficult thing in himself that he has at last come to observe—and does it in such a spirit, then he will get results. But if he does it heavily, out of the conviction of sin, nothing will ever come out of it, and especially if he shews others what he is trying to do, and likes to look miserable or grave or sad. And in this connection you will remember what Christ said about fasting—namely, that if you fast, you should anoint your head and wash your face "that thou be not seen of men to fast". To work on oneself from the conviction of sin puts the Work into negative parts of centres, and to work in a negative way can lead to a worse state of oneself than not to work at all. Some tend to take the Work in this heavy way. But no one can fathom the delight people take in making themselves miserable and in enjoying their negative states. You all know and have often heard me say that negative parts of centres create nothing. When I first heard Mr O. say that negative parts of centres cannot *create* anything, and that people who try to work in a heavy dreary, negative way, could only make their inner state worse than it was—then I think I experienced almost another moment of consciousness. I understood that what I had felt about religion had been right; it was suddenly formulated and explained. This Work, if you will listen to it and hear it in your hearts, is the most beautiful thing you could possibly hear. It speaks not of sin, but of being asleep, just as the Gospels do not really speak of sin, but only of *missing the mark*—the Greek word means that. Can we hear the Work? There is an old book that I have, composed by a man in the Work of his time; it depicts a man lying fast asleep flat on the earth, and a ladder stretching to heaven, and angels on it blowing trumpets almost in the man's ear. Yet he hears nothing. He is asleep in life—perhaps he is a millionaire, or some very important person, or simply a harassed clerk, or a worried mother, and so on.

This Work is beautiful when you see why it exists and what it means. It is about liberation. It is as beautiful as if, locked for years in prison, you see a stranger entering who offers you a key. But you may refuse it because you have acquired prison habits and have forgotten your origin, which is from the Stars. How, then, will you ever be able to *remember Yourself* with only prison thoughts and interests, and hand back your life whole and not twisted and soiled by negative emotion and every form of identifying? It will then be only natural for you to refuse the key that will unlock all the doors of the prison, one by one, because you prefer to remain in prison—that is, as you are in yourselves. Nay, even more you may be indignant and seek to kill the stranger and fight for your prison-life and even sacrifice your life in order to remain in prison.

*Birdlip, 18.1.43*

## COMMENTARY ON THE MEANING OF THE ARK

It is always possible to take everything that is said both in the Old Testament and in the Gospels in a literal way. There is the *literal* level of understanding sacred writings and there is also the psychological level of understanding them. The parables in the Gospels, for example, are *psychological* in their meaning, but they are given a form that is literal. The story about the Ark, related in Genesis, can of course be taken in a literal sense. There may have been a flood of water; there may have been an ark constructed by a particular man named Noah out of a particular wood called gopher-wood, and so on. But psychologically the meaning is quite different. The esoteric or inner—that is, the psychological—meaning is quite different. Esoteric teaching is always about Man's inner evolution. It is about Man's higher development and his relation to what is higher than he is. Everything said in the first five Books of the Old Testament, called the Pentateuch or Torah, has an external, literal meaning and an internal, esoteric, or psychological meaning. These Books were written not as literal histories but to convey another meaning, just as in the case of the Parables. Historical incidents were used and adapted in such a way that esoteric or inner meaning could be conveyed by what apparently happened in an historical sense. But it is quite obvious that they are not merely history. One has only to look at the details mentioned, that seem trivial.

The Flood, understood in its internal or psychological meaning, is not a flood of water, drowning the earth, but a flood of evil. The Flood refers to a period when all right understanding was dying among a particular division of humanity. Violence and evil were in the ascendant and everything to do with truth and good was being lost sight of. Humanity, left to itself, is barbarian. Only teaching given over a long period can raise mankind to the level of culture and civilization. But every teaching sown into life has its period and loses force and dies. When a teaching loses its force and dies, a flood of violence and evil and falsity arises. The story of the Ark refers to such a period, occurring amongst a part of humanity, situated, perhaps, in what we call the Middle East. All this part of humanity, all this "earth" was flooded with barbarism, and all teaching was being lost sight of. But teaching always starts again and where such a flood of evil arises it must preserve itself and wait until the time comes when a new form of the same teaching can begin. Understood psychologically, therefore, the Flood is a flood of barbarism, of evil and violence, and the story of the Ark is a story about how esoteric teaching preserved itself during that Flood. The Ark floated on the waters of the flood of evil, and it contained in it all the seeds of a new teaching, represented by Noah, his three sons, their wives and all the animals. And here we must realize that all our own civilization and culture arose from behind the form of teaching called Christianity and we must also realize that any teaching of this kind—that is, esoteric teaching—has its period, and eventually loses its force and dies. Then comes a period of violence and evil—that is, a flood—as to-day. This again is followed by a new teaching.

The Ark is a story about how the interval between two periods of teaching is bridged. It means that certain people, in this case a certain school called *Noah*, having eventually three branches, gathered together everything that was valuable and preserved it until the time came when a new teaching could be given. They constructed, as it were, the form of the new teaching and preserved it, by living in it, so that everything was not lost in the flood of evil, and so that mankind did not perish spiritually, through mutual hatred and violence. Known history, ordinary history, the history taught in schools, is a history of crime. But esoteric history, of which a glimpse is caught in the story of the Ark, is something quite different and is almost *unknown*. All that we know is that suddenly, new teachings, in the form of religions, appear, which begin new cultures. That is, we can see something of the *results* but we know little or nothing of the *causes*, the history of which is hidden from us.

Now you must rid your minds entirely of the literal meaning of the story of the Flood and the Ark. When the Ark settled on Mount Ararat, it means that the new form of teaching *that it represented* began to be taught on "earth"—that is, *Man*. The flood of evil had begun to abate. That is, it was possible to begin to teach men once more how to become civilized. The right time has to be awaited and the finding of the right time is represented by the sending out of the raven, the dove, and so on. For if a new prepared teaching is given at the wrong time then it must fail. People are not ready for it.

With this general idea of what the Flood and the Ark mean, let us try to find some psychological interpretation of the various incidents mentioned in the story which begins in the 6th chapter of Genesis. It is only possible here to take up certain points in the story. First of all, the account describes how the Sons of God mixed with the daughters of Man:

> "Then the sons of God saw the daughters of men that they were fair; and they took them wives of all that they chose. And the Lord said, My spirit shall not strive with man for ever, for that he also

is flesh: yet shall his days be an hundred and twenty years. The Nephilim were in the earth in those days, and also after that, when the sons of God came in unto the daughters of men, and they bare children to them: the same were the mighty men which were of old, the men of renown." (Genesis vi.2-4)

We must understand here that a mixing up of higher teaching and lower truth took place. Then it is said that God saw that the evil of Man was multiplied on the earth and that "all the imagination of the thoughts of his heart was only evil every day". Noah alone was good. God tells Noah that he must make an ark, for a flood is coming. In the account God says to Noah:

"The end of all flesh is come before me; for the earth is filled with violence through them; and behold, I will destroy them with the earth. Make thee an ark of gopher wood; rooms shalt thou make in the ark, and thou shalt pitch it within and without with pitch. And this is the fashion which thou shalt make it of: The length of the ark shall be three hundred cubits, the breadth of it fifty cubits, and the height of it thirty cubits. A window shalt thou make to the ark, and in a cubit shalt thou finish it above; and the door of the ark shalt thou set in the side thereof; with lower, second, and third storeys shalt thou make it. And behold, I, even I, do bring a flood of waters upon the earth, to destroy all flesh, wherein is the breath of life from under heaven; and every thing that is in the earth shall die. But with thee will I establish my covenant; and thou shalt come into the ark, thou and thy sons, and thy wife and thy sons' wives with thee. And of every living thing of all flesh, two of every sort shalt thou bring into the ark, to keep them alive with thee; they shall be male and female. Of fowls after their kind, and of cattle after their kind, of every creeping thing of the earth after his kind, two of every sort shall come unto thee to keep them alive. And take thou unto thee of all food that is eaten, and thou shalt gather it to thee; and it shall be food for thee and for them." (Genesis vi.13-22)

"Thus did Noah according to all that God commanded him, so did he."

Now you will notice that the ark had three storeys—a lower, a middle and a third storey—and a single window and one door. The single window is above: "A window shalt thou make to the ark and in a cubit shalt thou finish it *above*." This means that the window opened into the top storey. As you know, in the teaching of the Work that we are studying, Man is drawn diagrammatically as a three-storey house, having a lower, middle and upper part. In the upper part is the Intellectual Centre, in the middle part is the Emotional Centre, and in the lowest storey the Instinctive and Moving Centres. You know also that impressions are represented as coming into the top storey, that is, *above*, where the Intellectual Centre is situated. It may seem to you a far-fetched matter to draw any comparison between the Ark as having three storeys and the Work-diagram of Man as a three-storey house. But you must remember that esoteric teaching always remains the same essentially and that it is kept alive in ways that we know nothing about. As was said, we know only the history of outer life, the history of crime, not the history of esoteric teaching, save that we can notice the results of the latter, acting at different periods on the general history of crime. That is, we see religious teaching struggling with barbarism and gradually founding cultures.

Now I must explain something that you will find a little difficulty in following at first. You know that the general view of Man expressed in the beginning of the Old Testament is that Man has not *progressed* from his origin but has degenerated. Man fell. That is, the standpoint expressed in the Old Testament is the reverse of the view that Man has evolved and is progressing. It is necessary to say all this, in order to understand what this single *window* in the Ark means. According to ancient teaching, Man originally lived in a golden age, then in a silver age, then in a brass age, and finally in an iron age. It does not matter about the exact terms used. The *idea* is the important thing; and the idea means that Man has progressively degenerated and not progressively evolved. He was once in far better circumstances and in a far better inner state than he is to-day. You must realize that only a very naïve mind can believe that the passage of time means progress. One must get rid of such an idea, once and for all. Time does not mean progress. One might as well think that as one gets older one necessarily gets wiser or better; or that the newest fashion is necessarily better than the older fashions; or that to-morrow is necessarily bound to be better than to-day. Now according to ancient teaching Man was once in an inner state totally different from the state he is in to-day. When he was in this more original state he could be taught in a way in which he cannot be taught to-day. You know that according to the teaching of this Work, Man has two distinct sides—the side of knowledge and the side of being: and that in order to change or evolve a man must nowadays receive first of all *new knowledge* and then apply it to his own being through self-observation. But there was a time when the being of a man could be acted upon directly, and not, as to-day, only through the side of knowledge. As, naturally enough, we can know very little about this original state of Man—save through hints given in such writings as are found in the Old Testament and elsewhere—it will be best not to attempt to say much about it. Still, we can conceive roughly of the inner state of a man who knows without having to be taught it that, say, negative emotions are evil inner states. And from this we can even imagine a man who already knows, as it were in his heart, all that this Work teaches him so gradually through his mind. We belong to an age of humanity which this Work called the *sleep of mankind*, and our individual task is to awaken again and to cease to live this life of sleep. But we can conceive an age where Man was internally *awake* and led the life of a being who was awake. Then he was in touch with what in this system is called *Higher Centres*; and, being so, he was taught internally, or by an internal route, and not by an external route through his outer senses. Esoteric teaching was *in him*. He was then in touch internally with influences coming from higher sources than himself, and knew and felt it. Only when he began to ascribe his knowledge to himself, through vanity and self-conceit, did he begin to fall "asleep", and so became gradually more and more separated from this internal source of teaching *into which he was originally born*. Then instead of being able to distinguish directly by internal perception, or insight, between what was good and what was evil, and what was true and what was false, he gradually lost these inner faculties, until finally he had to be taught everything *from outside* as knowledge. This is the meaning of the window in the upper storey. Man reached such a state that he had only one light left him—that is, one window through which "light" could come. This was no longer an *inner* window that received inner light. That is, he reached a state in which he could only be taught through his mind or intellect and only from outside. Man's intellectual *sight* was not yet lost. And so he could still be "saved"—that is, from the flood of evil that must rise as soon as Man is cut off from any teaching. Now what is difficult to understand in all this is that the Ark represents not only a certain form of esoteric teaching being preserved, but the *form* of it *that was preserved* and so the *state* of Man *at that time*. For a new form of esoteric teaching must be adapted to the state of Man at that time. The story of the Ark is both a description of the *kind of man* that remained who was capable of being taught at that period of time and also a description of the preservation of the kind of esoteric teaching adapted to him. The description of the Ark shews us that Man had lost all other sources of "light" save *one single window* opening from without into *the upper storey of himself*. He now had to be taught *from outside*, having lost all inner sources of contact. He had to be taught from the side of knowledge and so from the side of the *mind*—that is, from impressions coming from outside into the upper storey.

We have now to think of the meaning of the single door, specially said to be in the *side* of the Ark. This represents the ear or the "hearing" Man was left with intellectual sight and the power of hearing, and although he was cut off from all else internally he could still *hear* and so understand with his mind, although not in his being and will. The school of teaching and the state of Man are both represented in the general image of the Ark. The teaching that could still survive the flood of falsity and evil existing in that part of mankind at that time was one that had to be *heard* by the ear and perceived by the mind: and the kind of man at that time who could still grow and evolve could only take in teaching through hearing it and pondering about it with his *mind*, to begin with. That is, Man's *starting-point* was no longer *inner*, but from outside.

Now if we consider the image of the Ark as referring for the moment only to a school of teaching that preserved alive traces of ancient teaching and survived a deluge of false notions and evil actions, we can catch a glimpse of the meaning that it was *pitched within and without*. God said to Noah: "Rooms shalt thou make in the ark, and shalt pitch it within and without with pitch." Pitch resists water and here water, or the flood, represents what is false. Water can represent, in the ancient language of parables, esoteric truth or falsity *according to the context*, and the Ark—that is, this school—was "hermetically sealed". That is, it was capable of resisting this flood of evil and so it floated on the waters of evil. The pitching of the Ark as well as the gopher-wood of which it was made are images that refer, first of all, to its power of resistance, and more deeply, to what was shut. The window and the door refer to what remained open. And the general image of the Ark refers to both the school of teaching and to the man suitable to it at that time, and what was shut and what was open. The Ark or school contained in it all the necessary forms of knowledge, all the material of the necessary ideas, and the necessary understanding of what was good and what was evil in regard to Man's future individual evolution in so far as it then remained possible. All these were gathered together in the school and they are represented by Noah and the animals and by the food stored in the Ark. God said to Noah: "And take thou unto thee of all *food* that is eaten, and thou shalt gather it to thee; and it shall be for food for thee, and for them." This is not literal food, but psychological food. If a man has no teaching, no ideas, no knowledge, given him, then he has no *food* in this sense. We understand the expression "food for knowledge" as meaning something different from literal food. But what we do not understand so easily is that all *knowledge* can be lost and that it must be *gathered together* and *preserved* at those periods when a "deluge" takes place. Man to-day is born *knowing nothing*. All his knowledge is acquired. Everything must be taught him to-day *from outside*—through his "ears" and his mind. A school of teaching is a storehouse of special knowledge. A book, a dictionary, is also a storehouse of ordinary knowledge. But this *food of knowledge*, of whatever kind, can be lost. In such a case, a man, born without any knowledge, will grow up knowing nothing save what appertains to his instinctive life, as hunter and killer—that is, to his life as an animal.

Now the Ark, representing both the school present at the time and the man of that school, floated on the waters, and after a time the waters of the flood began to abate.

"And God remembered Noah, and every living thing, and all the cattle that were with him in the ark: and God made a wind to pass over the earth, and the waters assuaged; the fountains also of the deep and the windows of heaven were stopped, and the rain from heaven was restrained; and the waters returned from off the earth continually: and after the end of an hundred and fifty days the waters decreased. And the ark rested in the seventh month, on the seventeenth day of the month, upon the mountains of Ararat. And the waters decreased continually until the tenth month: in the tenth month, on the first day of the month, were the tops of the mountains seen." (Genesis viii.1-5)

Here we must first understand that the evil of Man or "earth" began to lessen. *The tops of the mountains were seen.* Mountains refer to higher truth. Then Noah is represented as sending out a raven:

"And it came to pass at the end of forty days, that Noah opened the window of the ark which he had made: and he sent forth a raven, and it went forth to and fro, until the waters were dried up from off the earth."

This means that it was still impossible to teach higher truth on "earth" in a general sense, and in a partial sense it means that the man of the Ark, the man who *could* be taught by the teaching of the school that was preserved in that part of the world was not yet fit to understand it. The raven as a bird represents *thought*, but not in a good sense. Falsity or *wrong thinking* still prevailed and so the raven went "to and fro" This represents the state of a man who receives teaching but is not yet able to make anything of it. So he goes "to and fro" or "up and down", now thinking this and now that. The next stage is represented by Noah sending forth a dove. A dove refers to thought that is not false:

"And he sent forth a dove from him, to see if the waters were abated from off the face of the ground; but the dove found no rest for the sole of her foot, and she returned unto him to the ark, for the waters were on the face of the whole earth: and he put forth his hand and took her, and brought her in unto him into the ark."

The waters were still on the face of the earth—that is, Man, for "earth" represents *Man* in the ancient language of parable and allegory. The school represented by the Ark could not yet teach Man for Man was not yet ready to receive the teaching. So the dove is taken back into the Ark, being unable to find where it could rest. A further period follows represented by "seven days", which means a *period*.

"And he stayed yet other seven days; and again he sent forth the dove out of the ark; and the dove came in to him at eventide; and, lo, in her mouth an olive leaf pluckt off: so Noah knew that the waters were abated from off the earth."

The dove returned at eventide with an olive-leaf and Noah knew that the waters were abated from off the earth. Eventide means the period *preceding the dawn of a new day*. The olive-leaf represents in a general sense that something *good* could result from sending out the teaching. Finally Noah sends out the dove again:

"And he stayed yet other seven days; and sent forth the dove; and she returned not again unto him any more."

The dove does not return—that is, what it represents finds a resting-place. The teaching can now be given and so Noah is shewn as removing the covering of the Ark:

"And it came to pass, in the six hundred and first year, in the first month, from the first day of the month, the waters were dried up from off the earth: and Noah removed the covering of the ark, and looked, and, behold, the face of the ground was dried."

The soil or earth—that is, Man—is ready to receive the teaching contained in the Ark, so God tells Noah to go forth out of the Ark:

"And God spake unto Noah, saying, Go forth of the ark, thou, and thy wife, and thy sons, and thy sons' wives with thee. Bring forth with thee every living thing that is with thee of all flesh, both fowl, and cattle, and every creeping thing that creepeth upon the earth; that they may breed abundantly in the earth, and be fruitful, and multiply upon the earth."

To be fruitful and multiply has not a literal but a psychological meaning, exactly similar to that in the Parable of the Sower where those who had good soil in themselves brought forth fruit.

One of the difficulites of understanding the allegory is because the Ark refers to the school itself, to the man developing in that school, stage by stage, and to the state of Man in general, at that period.

Now we come to the meaning of the rainbow. God promised Noah that there would be no more floods to destroy the earth for perpetual generations—that is, for that generation or period of the school of teaching represented by Noah. You must realize that time in our ordinary sense does not exist in the higher language of parables. Only periods or events exist. Whatever endures for the whole period or event is called perpetual.

"And God said, This is the token of the covenant that I make between me and you and every living creature that is with you, for perpetual generations: I do set my bow in the cloud, and it shall be for a token of a covenant between me and the earth. And it shall come to pass, when I bring a cloud over the earth, that the bow shall be seen in the cloud. And I will remember my covenant, which is between me and you and every living creature of all flesh; and the waters shall no more become a flood to destroy all flesh. And the bow shall be in the cloud; and I will look upon it, that I may remember the everlasting covenant between God and every living creature of all flesh that is upon the earth. And God said unto Noah, This is the token of the covenant which I have established between me and all flesh that is upon the earth." (Genesis ix, 12-17)

The bow or rainbow represents stages of light or illumination. It is light *split into parts*. Full light, full illumination, is white light. But this is composed of different colours or stages of lower vibrations passing to higher vibrations. You must remember that at the period of the Flood Man could no longer be taught directly by an internal route. He could not receive direct information. His being could not be acted on directly. He had gone to sleep internally. He had now to be taught from outside, step by step, stage by stage, until the full light of understanding was reached. Light means inner light. The mind receives inner light, when it grasps something that it did not understand before. When you say: "A light dawned on my mind," you refer to the light of the understanding. The sight of the mind is not the sight of the outer eye which responds to the light of the sun. But the "sun", *internally*, is the light of the mind—the light of understanding. And it is strange that outer light, the light of the sun, is split by a prism or film of oil into many components, or stages, and that all of them, vibrating together, form white light. Perhaps from this brief interpretation you can catch the meaning of the rainbow, as representing the conditions of inner development belonging to the Man of the Ark, the Man of that period, when it was no longer possible for him to receive the teaching of Higher Centres directly. He was cut off from *Higher Centres*—as we are. You know that this Work tells us that although we have Higher Centres in us fully developed and always working in us, we cannot hear what they say, and that to do so we must *prepare lower centres* by long work over a long time, stage by stage, to begin to catch their influences. That is, the light of Higher Centres is no longer received directly. It is only received stage by stage and so this light is split up, as in the case of the rainbow, into different colours—or into different successive stages of understanding. So you see that both the Ark and the rainbow represent the state of Man after he lost contact with Higher Centres.

In the above outline one of the psychological meanings of the story of the Ark is given. There are many meanings within meanings in this story, which is based on ancient language which made use of the parable-form of expressing meanings. There are so many things, indeed, contained in this story that it is impossible even to attempt to give them all. All that has been said above is nothing but a mere introduction to the inner or esoteric meaning of one of the great allegories or parables of the Old Testament.

## UNKNOWING

I would like to say to you to-night that all knowledge in the Work is connected with *unknowing*. I suppose that many of you think that you know. This is our usual state. You all think you know what is right and wrong. You all probably think you know all about your particular jobs. You all think you know the right people to know and the wrong people. Actually in the Work knowing is unknowing what you thought you knew. When you begin to unknow what you were sure you knew you are undergoing a change of mental outlook, you are undergoing a change of mind, you are undergoing *metanoia* (*meta*-beyond, *nous*-mind). In this Work you have to get out of your mind, you have to get out of what you imagine you know. Try to see what you imagine you know and notice especially where you judge other people. You judge others from what you imagine you know. I would like you all really to reflect on what you think you know for certain. It is amusing sometimes to see how people broadcast their opinions about other people in this Work. This is because they think they know. The idea that work consists in unknowing is foreign to them and as a result they take the Work from what they think they know. They are sure they are right, by their acquired opinions. They never think of examining how these opinions have arisen and what mechanical influences from father and mother created them. The result is that you have a person who is always judging and condemning, or approving, from a purely mechanical level. This person thinks that he or she knows.

To imagine that one knows anything is in the nature of an illusion. Let me ask you all this question: "Are you sure that you know anything for certain?" What do you act from? You act from what you think you know. You act from what you think you know is right. Now let me ask you a further question: "All of you are always thinking, feeling, acting, from what you feel or think is right. Are you sure that your system of knowing what is right, is right?" You all think that you know. Now supposing you ask yourselves this question: "Do I know?" This is one of the most powerful questions you can ask yourselves if you do it sincerely. Notice how you continually judge others. Observe yourselves. You all have definite fixed ideas of what is right and what is wrong. All this belongs to the acquired psychology called Personality. Are you sure that you know? If you feel that you know then you cannot change: your knowing will prevent you from changing. The idea of *metanoia* (translated as repentance) is to change your knowing, to change your mind. The Gospels say that unless you repent you cannot see the Kingdom of Heaven: but the meaning is that unless you change your mind, you cannot change your level of being. If you always think in the same way, if you always judge in the same way—in short, if you always know in the same way and feel that you know, nothing can happen to you. Each of you here thinks and feels that he or she *knows*. But none of you thinks or knows from the ideas of esoteric psychology. None of you knows how to think in a new way. You must learn a new kind of knowing and in order to do this, you must *unknow* what you formerly knew. You must see that what you thought you knew is not knowing. Esoteric psychology is about a new kind of knowing. If you insist on knowing as you have always known, this Work will never touch you. This Work is new knowing, new knowledge. If you do not take this new knowledge into your knowing, it will have no effect upon you. If you are certain you know about everything and at the same time try to connect yourselves with this Work you will not understand it. This Work is to change your knowing.

Many results take place in connection with this Work. Some are good and some are bad. It is impossible to control the action of the Work on different people. One can hand new knowledge to a person and it may be taken rightly or wrongly. If the person has a good Magnetic Centre the presumption is that he or she will take the Work rightly. On the other hand, if the person has no Magnetic Centre or a wrong Magnetic Centre, which is often connected with wrong sex, then it is impossible to say what will happen. You must all understand that this Work promises nothing to anyone. You can enter this Work and make the best of it according to your level. The Work does not care for you: the point is whether you care for the Work. The Work may begin to care for you if you shew that you care for it. Many people take this Work from life-attitudes and values. They imagine that because they have attained success in life they can attain success in the Work. This is not entirely wrong. A person who is good in life may be very useful to the Work eventually, but this only happens with people who have some idea of serving and obeying. You must understand that it is very difficult to teach a system that nobody wishes to serve and obey. The chief evaluation necessarily comes in here. A person must have Magnetic Centre—i.e. an acquired sense of the difference between life and this Work. You can perhaps imagine a number of events happening to you, some of which are merely ordinary life-events, your daily tasks, your profession, and so on, and some of a quite different kind. If you find this difficult to understand, try to think what kind of events have happened to you that do not belong to your business life or your domestic life and do not have any sequence of routine events. We are sometimes visited by strange events or strange inner experiences. Now if you have no power of distinguishing between ordinary things and exceptional things you have no Magnetic Centre. To possess Magnetic Centre means to have your life divided into two categories—the category of ordinary everyday things and the category of rather unusual things. Of course, if you pay no attention to the unusual things and regard them as hysterical or absurd or ridiculous or neurotic, you can be quite certain that you have no Magnetic Centre. This means you have no power of discriminating between $A$ and $B$ influences. All your most valuable experiences, and here I mean potentially valuable, will be regarded as nonsense and all your ordinary experiences will be regarded as sane, proper, respectable and right. However, the capacity for growth in you lies in what is not usual, not ordinary, not commonplace. None of you will grow through commonplace experiences which are shared by everyone else. Your commonplace experiences belong to the service of nature. One can serve nature or not, but no one can get beyond serving nature unless he has done so. First of all we have to be Good Householders—i.e. we have to attain a certain level of ordinary efficiency and you must understand that this applies to women as well as men. Life is a pretty bad proposition for most of us and its difficulties fall on men and women in different ways. Life falls equally on man and woman but in different directions and the lash is pretty heavy. There is no escape from life until you have become in some sense equal to it. This Work really begins in its most significant way when you have equalled life in some way. If you receive this Work before you have equalled life it may help you or not. If you have good understanding it will help. If on the other hand you use this Work as a refuge from life it will not help you. For this reason it is said in the Work that some people should go into life and some should not. Eventually, for this Work to act in its full way on you, you must have done something, borne something, endured something, long enough to be equal to life. Some time ago, when I was talking about this, a question was asked as follows: "What do you mean by being equal to life?" It means being equal to your vanity. Everyone of course has a vanity that seeks its fulfilment. One person may long to be in the Life Guards, another to have a title, another to be a Member of Parliament, another to marry, another to be wealthy, another to be a millionaire, another to control some branch of finance, another to be a General, and so on. And on a smaller scale the husband wishes to control the wife and the wife wishes to control the husband, or the wife wishes to be the best-dressed person in her Villa Row and to have the best furniture, or the man wishes to have the best car or the best garden or to be the most healthy muscular man in his little environment. All these ambitions and a hundred and one others constitute the ordinary daily motive powers.

Now when a man has satisfied his phantasies, when he has equalled the ideas of his False Personality, he usually begins to die in an internal sense. Perhaps you have heard that this Work is for people who have come to the end of life. Life, of course, means your life, and your life psychologically is what you want. If your life consists in wishing to make a million pounds or being the greatest Hollywood Star, then when you have attained this you have no further life, psychologically speaking. Of course you may go on living for a long time, but, if you do, you are already dead. G. once said to O., when O. had taken him into a London Club of ancient reputation:

"Why do you bring me into the presence of cemeteries and graves and dead people?" This Club was very distinguished and a great many members were sitting round in different parts of the smoking-room. You will remember in this connection what I told you once that G. said as a rule when walking down the street you meet corpses, people who are long ago dead in themselves. These people who are dead are *people who think they know.* Now when you come to fulfil your ordinary ambitions, when you become the person you imagine you should become according to your particular phantasy, when you have made your million or become the most successful star, or got better furniture than your neighbour, you become equal to life according to your idea of it. Then you begin to die. If you always wanted a title and you get it, you have become equal to your idea of life: you have become what you wanted to be in life and so you can rest content. You have become, say, better than your neighbour, you have become the best cricketer, the best boxer, the best-dressed woman, the most witty talker in your Club, you have become a Member of Parliament, you have become a notorious figure, you have passed your examinations, you have become a qualified doctor, a social success, you have become something in life that satisfies your ambition. This is in each case equalling life. It is equalling your idea of life. Having attained this particular ambition, you feel equal to life. This is a very interesting thing to reflect on, what you wish to be and what it means for you individually to attain equality with life. If your ambition is not satisfied you will not feel you are equal to life. Amongst all the forces that act on mankind in a purely cosmic sense there are always these forces that lead a man or a woman continually on and on to reach a certain stability or equality with life.

In order to distinguish oneself from life, in order to make oneself different from life, whether the forces of life touch the villa or palace, so to speak, is a very difficult thing, and the force that is necessary to enable one to escape from these purely cosmic forces is of a quite different origin from any of the forces created by life itself. Just consider for a moment: you can all see life acting around you, you can all see what life forces are acting the whole time in people, you can all see jealousy, hatred, and so on, at work in life. Do you imagine that life can get better as long as people remain as they are? Now if you talk to people who are very much in life, you will always find they are certain that they know. They are quite sure they know what is best. Although we are living in this so-called century of progress which is characterized by the worst war that ever happened, everyone will tell you that he knows what is best and he is working for this best as it is called. One might reflect that it does not seem to be going this way. We seem to have made a great mess of things in spite of our scientific knowledge, but I do not wish to argue about this point at present. What I wish to point out is that everyone thinks he knows and that by thinking he knows he goes on inevitably in the chains of cause and effect. Let us take a person who thinks he knows all about the present age, all about the present horrors of war, the decline of inner feeling. I ask him a question: "Why is the world getting worse? Why do we kill everyone indiscriminately with bombs, etc.?" He will say that he knows, that science knows. He will say that everything leads to progress and that there is an inevitable process of evolution behind every period of history. One might dispute this idea. Let me ask this question: "Are you sure that passage of time is progress?"

Now let us come to ourselves. Suppose it is possible for ourselves to evolve, do any of you think any one of you can evolve if you know already? Many of you are perfectly convinced that you know. I would say that you don't know. The reason why you don't see yourselves is that you take what you know as fixed and final. You think you know. You are certain you know what is good and bad. It is not merely your vanity that makes you think you know, but also your ignorance. From the standpoint of Higher Man we are all ridiculous, just like monkeys.

When you come in touch with this Work, you should begin, if you feel the Work, to realize gradually that you do not know and that you need to unknow. This is a very difficult experience. Of course we all know, don't we? Then, starting from the idea that we know, we try to take in this Work. We are all convinced that we know everything fundamental; we are all convinced that our lives are perfectly all right. And it is from this attitude that we take on the Work and the new knowledge of the Work. We ourselves, of course, know everything, and when we hear that this Work is new knowledge we take it in on the basis of our former knowledge. We have always thought that we were conscious, that everything we do or say is done consciously, that everything we do is the result of our own thinking, that we have Will, that we can act as we like and so on. The real trouble lies in that we think we already know everything. I am not speaking of knowing science, knowing history, or anything like that. I am saying that we all know what is right. The only phrase I can find here is that you all know "what is what". If you could really observe yourselves uncritically, which takes a long time, and a long training, you would begin to see that something in you has always taken everything for granted, said what is right and wrong for you automatically, made your decisions, although you yourself have no idea on what these decisions are based. This meek person who works automatically is the person who always thinks that It knows. I am quite aware that some of you will say this is not right, this is not true; you will say you do not pretend to have knowledge, that you are quite aware you know nothing about science, history, politics; you may even say you have no pretence of knowing anything. Are you quite sure you see what is meant? Are you going to tell me you never do anything from the idea that you know? You find fault with people every moment, you object to things every moment. I would be very glad to meet a person who was quite convinced that he or she knew nothing. Do not all of you act from knowing—i.e. from what you think you know? If a person really felt he or she knew nothing, could he or she ever object to anything? But are not all of you continually objecting, finding fault, judging people, condemning people, and so on? Are you not liking and disliking, saying to yourselves, this person is not important and that person is important? Well, let me ask you frankly: Is not this the case in your everyday life and is this not based on the feeling that you know? Do you understand what knowing means? You all think that you know and act accordingly. The object of this Work is to unknow what you know. Of course, you cannot unknow what you know unless you feel very doubtful about what you know. Try to observe yourselves from the side of what you feel certain that you know. Each one of you has feelings of certainty. You may be interested in this Work and its new knowledge but at the same time you are quite sure that you know already. Let me ask you this question once more: "If you are convinced that you know already, how can you take in new knowing?" Have you ever thought of applying to yourself what the work teaches?

For example, let us take a shattering piece of knowledge taught by the Work: the Work teaches that not one of you here has any Real I, that not one of you has any power of doing anything, that every one of you is a mechanical figure reacting to life like a machine. But no doubt all of you know differently, don't you? You all think that you are capable of doing, that you are one integrity that remains always the same. You do not notice that at different times you are quite different, you do not notice that at different times different 'I's speak through your mouth. You act as though you were one and the same person continually in time. This is one example of how you think you know. In fact, you can be so *knowing* that you do not believe this new knowledge about yourself. To receive emotionally this new knowledge that you are not one but many contradictory 'I's requires great courage, sincerity and depth of insight.

In a conversation that I once had with G. he tried to explain to me that we all have a cheap life composed of small 'I's, 'I's that lie on the surface—i.e. in the moving parts of centres. He went on to say that no one could begin to develop if he or she had lived this small superficial life. He said in his broken language to me: "Necessary be Man." I was working with him at that time in the carpenter's shop at the Institute in France. During a few hours of work there he repeated this phrase: "Necessary be Man". The starting-point of this phrase was my irritation with some wood that I was trying to drill and which split. I began to take this as a reason for being negative—i.e. I blamed the wood. G.'s remark to me made me understand for the first time in a practical way what it means to be a man and not a piece of wood that splits. Now this was new knowledge to me. What I had known before was changed into a new knowing. My old way of knowing was to blame the wood for splitting just as all your knowing is based on blaming other people. I began to know differently. How do you know, all of you, in connection with what I am saying? You all think you know. Yes, but are you sure that your power of knowing will ever lead to anything at all? All Work knowledge is to make you know in a different way. Some of you try to keep this Work alive in the present circumstances; others make not the slightest endeavour to do so. In fact, some of you think that the Work should be fed to you without your doing anything to earn it. This Work is about a new way of knowing because it is a new knowledge and you must all pay for it by effort. To know differently, to know in a new way, means that you can take everything quite differently, have quite a different relationship to things and people. However, one has to pay for this new knowing. If you expect to be given it all once a week you are making a great mistake. You are making a great mistake if you think that once a week for a few minutes you will be given understanding of this Work.

Let me ask you: Have you applied this Work to yourself? Have you endeavoured to put the Work into practice? Have you tried to remember yourself? Have you tried not to identify, not to be negative? Have you stopped self-justifying and thinking that you are better than other people? Have you applied the shock of the Work to yourself? Now you may all think you know everything already. Good Lord, look at yourselves. I ask you to apply the knowledge of this Work to yourselves and not think you know already. How marvellous it is when a person begins to unknow a little and not always know! How marvellous it is when a man or woman changes, becomes softer, quieter. How marvellous not to have to be what you think you are, to keep up this False Personality, this pseudo self! How extraordinary it is to move towards Real I, which is only moved towards by actual separation from false things in yourself, one by one. How marvellous to release oneself from this invention of oneself that one takes oneself as, and which costs so much force. However, let me add, that everyone must become equal to life in some way before he can move towards this new goal of getting rid of himself or herself. You remember the idea in the esoteric teaching in the Gospels (which is the same as this teaching, because all Esoteric Psychology is the same) where it is said that in order to reach the higher level of being, called the Kingdom of Heaven, one must be as a little child. You remember the rich man, who was full of the idea that he could do, the idea of helping humanity; he was told to sell all that he had—separate from all he was good at. It was said, you remember, of the rich man who felt he could do, that "it is easier for a camel to pass through the eye of a needle than for a rich man to enter into the Kingdom of God". Do you all understand now from what you have all known already that this does not refer to riches actually but to each of you individually, thinking you know? You take the Work externally on the basis of what you know. Do not you all feel here at this moment that there is nothing really wrong with you, that you all know what is good, and so on? Do not most of you take this Work as something extraordinary and extra and still keep to your old standards and feel rich from your various forms of respectability and adulation? Now this is the difficulty, this is the trouble, that lies between mi and fa. Think how this rich man had to sell everything before he could follow Christ. Do you think you can follow this Work with all your present attitudes, evaluations, self-esteems, self-feelings, in which all of you are rich? Remember what riches means esoterically. It means self-esteem, self-love, feeling that you know, feeling that you are always right, admirable, virtuous, unassailable.

I would only add one thing: that you are *not*—far from it—but unless you see it for yourself through long self-observation, you will come nowhere, and this Work will fail in its purpose with regard to yourself.

What a beautiful little darling you are! What a fine person you are! Are you not? And how you have suffered, have you not? And what a comfort it is for everyone that you are on this earth!


*Birdlip, April 1945*

## THE WORK AND EXTERNAL CIRCUMSTANCES

(This was read at the Meeting at Great Amwell House
on Saturday, 25th September 1953)

We often think that by change of situation our problems will become different. This is because we think that if outer things were different we should be different. This is always a form of expectancy which is only natural. More experience makes us not expect in this way. It is quite true that a change of circumstances gives more force because for the time being it gives more impressions. But wherever we go we carry ourselves with us—that is, our level of being—and, as you know, the Work says our level of being attracts our life. It attracts our psychological life—that is, after a time we begin to make the same enmities, the same difficulties, the same kind of repetition of everything. Yet a change of circumstances may be very necessary provided we do not expect this change to make us ourselves different. Here comes in the idea of octaves ending. An octave may end both in regard to external circumstances, to conditions of life, and also in connection with other people. As regards the latter, we notice we no longer know our school-friends. We sometimes wonder whether we should not have kept these early friendships going. But this is quite wrong because the octave is over. However, in the Work there are octaves that never finish in regard to relationship. Temporary friends are one thing, but Work friends are a different thing. In this connection I must remind you of a saying in the Work that life divides, but the Work unites. We are, here and in

London, a body of people trying to unite rather than divide—to pass into increasing order rather than into increasing confusion, and no external change of circumstances must alter this feeling that the Work can give us. You must understand that we cannot get rid of one another, never "not see" someone again, if we are speaking of people in the Work. Our problems with one another remain the same in spite of external circumstances. We all feel quite rightly that some octave is finished in regard to the external circumstances of the Work itself, and that a change of circumstances is necessary. But this does not mean that our work with one another, or with ourselves, or in connection with the Work itself will change. When we get a good Work-relationship to ourselves we know this without being told. We know for a fact that nothing external can alter us in this respect, although, as I said, a change of external circumstances may give some force and enable us to view things from a different angle. When you pack your bag and go off you take yourself with you. You do not have to pack yourself, and although you may forget many things that you ought to have packed, nothing of yourself will be left behind, so after a time we will find in spite of new circumstances and new impressions we will once more come face to face with the same Work in the same three lines. I remember once that G. or O. said it would be good to have a travelling circus under the façade of which the Work was concealed. I thought how marvellous it would be to be going to new places and leaving behind all the troubles that arose in the last place just as though one could escape from oneself by the constant change of environment. But later I realized this is not possible and that even constant change of circumstances becomes mechanical like everything else. G. always taught with great emphasis that everything in time becomes mechanical. You learn to work on yourself in a certain way, for example, and after a time it becomes mechanical and no longer gives you force. A change is necessary. He taught once in London that our task was to open up new parts of centres and that we have to take things in a new way, wherever we are. For example, he said that prayer is good if it is conscious, but if it becomes mechanical it is useless, and on one occasion O. said that a man living in a prison cell—that is, in continually the same environment—could do this Work by a continual change of his attitude towards his physical confinement. But as we are, constantly being in the same environment contributes to mechanicalness and so sometimes a change of environment is a good thing. But I do not flatter myself in thinking that a change of environment is going to make everything different and more easy for me. Imagination always paints the picture that if only certain outer things were different one could, for example, concentrate more. But this is imagination. In a new environment one will find just the same difficulty. External things may be different but our relationships will tend to be the same after a time, and we will gradually reproduce our typical life—that is, our being will attract the same factors and difficulties, unless we work.

Now we are moving from here to a new place and there will be one factor of great importance that can be definitely thought of as a new factor—namely, that we shall come into contact with many more people in this Work, and through this we shall feel stronger and less divided. This will be a very good thing for us all, and this I think will be one of the most important things in the coming change in our external circumstances. We shall get more impressions from one another, I mean, Work impressions. We will once more feel more connected so that the force of our Work can be increased. We will see one another more, and more people oftener, and this is a very good thing and something we all down here can look forward to. All those temporarily left behind will find they are eventually guided to this new arrangement and will be able to take their right part in it. Remember, the Work will always find a way if you trust it and can bear temporary privation without dismay. But one thing always remains the same—that is, that we must bear one another's unpleasant manifestations wherever we are and learn we are rarely right in our judgment of people.

(This talk was given by Dr. Nicoll to those of us who were at Birdlip before we moved to Ugley.)

*Amwell, Autumn 1950*

## "IN MY FATHER'S HOUSE ARE MANY MANSIONS"*

In ancient parables Man is often compared with a house. He lives in the house of his Being. In this house are many rooms on different floors. Each man has a house where he lives with certain typical attitudes, prejudices and habits, usually corresponding to the lowest rooms in himself. He can live in better rooms, yet even when he hears something new, something strange, he will return to his own house, unless a very deep impression has been made on him, when he will be lifted into new rooms in the house of his Being, momentarily, only to fall back into his old rooms—that is, into the few rooms probably in the basement, which he usually occupies mentally and emotionally. Thus, it is said that on the last day of the Feast of Tabernacles, after the multitude had heard the words of Christ: "They went every man unto his own house" (John vii.53). They did not understand anything new.

Again, in an ancient Eastern allegory, Man is compared with a house containing many servants. This is a picture of Man from another angle. Man is not one but many. In this house are many different 'I's and there is no master in this house. However, a man *thinks* he is one and the same person all the time, and does not realize that at different moments he is a quite different person. In another Eastern

* Reprinted from HARVEST VOL. II., *Castle Press 1950*.

allegory, Man is compared with an assembly. In this assembly first one 'I' gets up and says something and sits down again. Then another 'I' gets up and says something contrary. For instance, a man says: "I am going out to-day", and then he says: "No, I don't think I will because it is too cold." He does not see that two different 'I's are speaking. Then another 'I' gets up and says: "We must go out or we might lose our job because there is always the possibility of meeting someone important." So now three 'I's have got up in the assembly. Other 'I's can get up and say different things. This is a picture of Man taken as a house containing many different 'I's. As a consequence Man is the resultant of all these different 'I's that form the assembly of himself.

From another angle Man is a psychological country. Just as in an actual visible country there are many places, many towns and cities, many desirable and also many undesirable places, like marshes, bogs, low slums, dangerous streets, so is Man internally. The Psalmist says: "Cause me to know the way wherein I should walk" (Psalms cxliii.8). That is, in *himself*. It is extraordinary how we tend to walk in unpleasant places in ourselves. Just as, in actual external life, we avoid walking in dangerous places, in slums, in treacherous bogs, so it is possible to learn to avoid walking in unpleasant places in one's internal self. Yet because Man has the illusion that he is *one and the same person* at all times, he cannot really see what is meant by teachings that clothe themselves in language and images and allegories such as the above. Man thinks he is the same when he is in a violent temper as when he is in an amiable mood. He does not see that he is altogether two different persons. Nor does he realize that he is walking in two different places in his own psychological country. However, it is very difficult to break this illusion that Man is one and the same, which is the starting point of any new self-development. All these different places in one's psychological country are represented by different places in the spiritual world. It is the psychological world of oneself in which we all really live.

What is the spiritual world? First, it is the invisible world of your own thoughts and feelings. If you say there is no invisible world, then I will disagree with you. Your thoughts are invisible, your feelings are invisible. Do you really think they are visible? This is the first aspect of the invisible or spiritual world. No one can "see" your thoughts or your feelings with the five external senses. But are they not the most real thing in you? You may be so well trained as not to show your real thoughts or feelings externally, in your face or in your gestures, but yet they are more real to you than is the external, visible world. So if you say that the invisible spiritual world is unreal, you are making a mistake of a very deep kind. You are thinking you are merely your body, visible to all. You are, in fact, upside down.

If you are in a bad place in your psychological country, you will suffer even if you are surrounded by the greatest physical comforts. Say you hate. Will dinner parties cure this? A man therefore has many

1763

places in himself, many mansions in the house of his being. Where do you walk in yourself? What place in your psychological country do you continually visit? (Shall we say: your grievances?) You complain you are unhappy and feel that if only you had more material comfort you would be happier. Up to a point that may be true, because poverty is a grinding thing. But if you are always in the habit of walking in unpleasant places in yourself, hating and envying others, material riches will not cure you of your unhappiness. It is not an outer affair. So, after having learnt how to walk about in external life with a certain amount of shrewdness, we need another education in which it is necessary to learn how to walk about in ourselves, and in what rooms, on what floors, we live in the house of ourselves, and with what 'I's we live in this house and link arms. For on each floor, on each level, there is different thinking and feeling, and we have to learn *which is better*.

If we were to talk about how a man can be master in his own house, we would have to go far afield, yet at the same time a man can begin to observe himself, and if he finds out what he has to observe in himself, he can begin to step in the direction of finding the real but absent master of his own house—that is, to attract him. People think that hearing a lecture or reading a book will change them, but after having heard the lecture or having read the book, "each man will go back to his own house", and he will remain just the same as before—otherwise, with all the modern means of transmission of knowledge, the world would have changed long ago. No, a change of being is a deeper problem. Only *you* can do that.

Yes, the problem lies deeper. A man must get to know himself before he can change. And here another illusion comes in. Everyone thinks he knows himself. He is offended if told he does not. Everyone thinks he behaves with complete knowledge of how he is behaving and what he is saying and why so. So he remains in the same place, in the same house, and in the same place in his house, in the same 'I's that he takes as himself. Man is given more than he needs, and this is one of the mysteries of life. He only uses part of his brain. He is given more than he needs for just living his natural life. He is given a far larger house than he uses, or needs to use for the purposes of ordinary life. As said, he has a brain which is bigger than is necessary for him. And that is why mechanical theories do not quite fit the case. He has, in his total given house, unused functions which sometimes, say, in moments of great fatigue and stress and illness—are momentarily opened to him. He then passes into another part of his psychological country, or into another room in the house of his being. Notice—it is there already. Then he falls back into his ordinary state and it seems to him that he has experienced something of another order unimportant for ordinary life. What has happened to him is that he has experienced things on another level, in another room. He has been for a moment or two in a room at the top of his house and seen everything quite differently, just as one does from the top of a height. He may think all this nonsense. But, even apart from such rare experiences, a man may learn that even in ordinary life he can change by training himself not to walk in the unpleasant places in which he habitually walks in his psychological country, accepted by life as normal. In fact he may begin to learn how to lead another life and cease to blame others all the time. He begins to turn round inside and blame himself for having allowed himself to walk in such dangerous places. This reversal is quite possible to experience.

In the Gospel there is the idea that Heaven has many places. Taken with another great saying that "The Kingdom of Heaven is within you" it may help us to understand the importance of knowing where we are in our psychological country. The two ideas warn us that our state of being will be our own judge in deciding to which mansion in our Father's house we shall go at death.

It is not said that the disciples were just going to "Heaven", but to a special place there. Christ said: "I go to prepare a place for you" (John xiv.2). He also said: "In my Father's house are many mansions." So there are many other places and mansions apart from the one prepared for the disciples. When I first began to conceive of an after-world in these terms I felt great relief. Heaven is many, not one. There were different places in the next, as in this world. Sitting in Church as a boy and looking round at the congregation, I used to think that I did not really want to go to Heaven with all these worthy people and that if I remained a Christian I would have to do so. This created a difficulty in my mind, one of those strange early difficulties that one is aware of perhaps all one's life but does not mention. When I understood from my own reading that Heaven was not one place but many mansions and places, this particular difficulty vanished. No one had helped me to overcome my difficulty. One could hardly state it after all.

So far as I remember, I have never thought, in my inner thinking, that there is no after-life, nor did I have inner problems with Christ himself. What Christ said seemed to me on a level beyond argument, however difficult. To take the view that this world and what happens in it is *all* and is explicable in terms of itself—then it is indeed a tale told by an idiot, full of sound and fury. Later, I understood that to try to explain this world in terms of itself was impossible. Something had to be fitted over the world, some other explanation. So I would say that the idea of another world is psychological truth. Why? Because it gives more meaning than the stark truth of the physical senses. Call this world and its life a testing ground or what you like, unless you fit over it another kind of meaning, it becomes meaningless. I am certain that the young and intelligent brave who die are not finished. I believe that a place is prepared for them—even for the violent brave. No doubt physically we have no proof of all this. But psychological truth is higher than physical truth, and the next world is invisible to the senses as is all psychological understanding. Is not your visible radio mainly the invisible? The idea that we go somewhere at death according to the quality of our inner life gives force and gives initiative. It gives new meaning and so new force. Our life behaviour is not useless. So I would say there is another order of truth—and that the proof of it lies in the power and meaning it gives us. The saints and martyrs were given, through psychological truth, force to endure what they endured. But whether we speak of saints and martyrs or of the young and the brave, who also endured so unspeakably, the glimpse of the nature of the next world given by Christ can rest our minds, because it makes us see that some will go to one mansion and others to another mansion. Seen in this light, of all Christ's merciful sayings, is not "In my Father's house are many mansions; if it were not so, I would have told you; for I go to prepare a place for you", one of the most merciful to our human understanding of another life?

Some think that in Heaven we meet relatives. There will be family reunions. They think one's neighbour is the person next door. Physical thinking like this makes rather a mess of the Gospels, which are psychological. But the crucifixion of Christ symbolizes that psychological thinking will always in time be overcome by physical, literal thinking. Now psychologically one's neighbour is the one nearest in understanding. To be in Heaven amongst people of quite another understanding would be torment—in short, Hell. Christ represents psychological meaning, for instance, of a commandment—that is, the realization that, to take one example, killing begins with psychological hating, and that if men envy and hate each other, they may or may not kill physically, but are killing all the time. The purification of the emotions—let us think of self-pity, envy, hate, malice, jealousy, and not only of sex—depends on psychological understanding. "Thou shalt not kill" is a literal physical commandment; psychologically it means: "Thou shalt not hate and kill internally", for hate, which is psychological, leads to physical killing. Just notice some of your phantasies. Do you ever kill in them? I fancy that most people have murdered some of their physical neighbours and relatives at different moments. But they thank God they have not done so physically. Why not? Because they have outer restraints. They feared the law, the police, the loss of reputation—all the consequences. Although they kill in their hearts, they may seem virtuous, full of merit. But in the next world, as many mystics and philosophers have said, you are judged by what your heart is like, apart from what the restraints of law, society, fear of reputation, have made you appear to be externally. We are judged by the internal state and are sent to the place to which we thereby belong.